The Breath and Body of INNER TORAH

The Breath and Body of INNER TORAH

Miriam Millhauser Castle

With Torah Insights by
Rabbi Dovid Castle

A TARGUM PRESS Book

First published 2009
Copyright © 2009 by Miriam Millhauser Castle
ISBN 978-1-56871-515-5

All rights reserved

No part of this publication may be translated, reproduced, stored in a retrieval system, or transmitted in any form or by any means, electronic, mechanical, photocopying, recording, or otherwise, without prior permission in writing from both the copyright holder and the publisher.

Published and distributed by:
TARGUM PRESS, INC.
22700 W. Eleven Mile Rd.
Southfield, MI 48034
E-mail: targum@targum.com
Fax: 888-298-9992
www.targum.com

Distributed by:
FELDHEIM PUBLISHERS
208 Airport Executive Park
Nanuet, NY 10954

Printed in Israel by Chish

About *Inner Torah:*
Where Consciousness and Kedushah Meet

Inner Torah: Where Consciousness and Kedushah Meet is a remarkable book. Directed mainly towards the woman reader, it teaches her how to embark on a journey which will enable her to get in touch with the mosaic of her personality and the holiness that resides at the core of her being. Ultimately the goal of the book is to teach the reader to become a happier, better, and deeper Jew who will devote herself totally to the service of Hashem.

The book is well written, deep, and practical. In addition, it has the advantage of being based on years of the author's professional experience in treating women.

Rebbetzin Lea Feldman

Miriam Millhauser has written a fascinating, personal, thoughtful book about the pursuit of holiness in human life through Torah. In a time where bogus "spirituality" abounds, it is refreshing to read such a measured, inspired work about the human soul and worthy life. This is an important book for those who seek to find inner truth and life's fulfillment.

Rabbi Berel Wein

About *Walking Mom Home:*
Sharing the Blessing of This Life's Final Journey

Rebbetzin Miriam Millhauser Castle's book, Walking Mom Home, *is an inspiring work that reflects great faith in Hashem, loving dedication to and honor of one's parent, and astute insights into life, death, mourning, and grief. The experiences she describes demonstrate the elevated levels a soul can reach during its final tikkun in this world, and the many blessings for both parent and child in this final chapter...*

This is a book with great wisdom and depth offering insight into how to make a time that otherwise might be considered sad and tragic, meaningful and rewarding.

Rabbi Chaim Pinchas Scheinberg

In loving memory of my sister

Karen Millhauser Maged, a"h
מלכה בת אליהו וגיטל

With Profound Thankfulness
to Hakadosh Baruch Hu

May I and all of *klal Yisrael* be privileged to
know who we are and what
You are asking of us.

May we have the faith and courage to
respond wholeheartedly.

Contents

Acknowledgments 15
Introduction 19
Overview 29

BREATH AND VOICE
Connecting Body and Soul

The Gift of Breath 39
   The Breath of Life 40
   More About the Natural Breath 48
   Experiences of Breath 56
   How the Body Breathes 61
   Explorations 68

The Miracle of Voice 79
   The Divine Quality of Voice 81
   The Anatomy of Voice 85
   Voice as an Instrument of Soul and Self 87
   The Healing Capacity of Voice 100
   Song of the Soul 103
   Explorations 107

THE BODY
Portal to the Heart and Mind, Home of the Soul

Softening and Opening the Heart.................. 115
    Explorations 123

Grounding — Standing Solidly on Two Feet........ 127
    Physical and Emotional Grounding 131
    Grounding and Energy Flow...................135
    The Impact of Fear on Grounding 137
    Spiritual Grounding..........................140
    Explorations 143

Centering through the Legs and Mid-Body 149
    Explorations 156

Releasing the Neck, Back, and Spine 161
    The Physical Spine...........................163
    The Emotional Spine 166
    Movement 170
    The Spiritual Spine..........................174
    Explorations 178

Connecting to the Hands 185
    Hands of Holiness 186
    The Power of Touch 192
    Explorations 199

Exploring the Face...................................203
The Face 205
Eyes and Vision 212
Nose and the Sense of Smell...................219
Explorations 224

Getting to Know the Energy Body 233
Becoming Energetically Self-Aware..............236
Energetic Boundaries and Movement.............242
Learning to Work with Energy 260
Explorations 269

Understanding Sensory Processing 275

Embodied Life — Wholeness and Holiness 283

Appendices
The Relationship of Body and Soul 291
A Torah Perspective on Body and Breath.........307
A Look at Color 319

Glossary....................................325

Acknowledgments

This book is the product of many years of studying and working with the breath and the body. As I wrote about in *Walking Mom Home: Sharing the Blessings of This Life's Final Journey,* I had to learn, in the same way that I help my clients learn, how to come fully into my body, to feel myself safely held in the container of my own being and by G-d. Fortunately, there were many outstanding resources available to help me in my efforts — books, classes, and experts in an array of fields all contributed to my development.

Some of these resources fall into the category of what Torah calls *chochmah ba'goyim*, "wisdom of the nations." While Chazal forbade the learning of Greek philosophy and the like, they recognized other types of wisdom as valuable. And so we are taught, *chochmah ba'goyim taamin*, if someone says there is wisdom in the nations, believe them — Torah *ba'goyim al taamin*, but if someone says there is Torah in the nations, don't believe them. So while I benefited greatly from all that I learned, I understood that nonetheless it was limited. Only in the context of Torah, could the full import of the teachings be sorted out. That required looking at what I learned through the lens of Torah, retaining only what was in alignment with Torah.

It is this distilled version of my many years of study of breath and body that I bring to you. I am indebted beyond measure to those whose work I explored along the way, including many of the great breath teachers, body workers, voice teachers, pioneers in the field of energy medicine, innovators in various healing modalities, and authors who took the time to commit this tremendous body of knowledge to writing. Some of the explorations included in this book, in particular, reflect the bounty of their wisdom.

Because the breath and body are gifts from G-d, they are limitless in the possibilities they afford us to grow and develop into our true selves. No book or person could ever offer exhaustive coverage of this subject; there is always more to discover and more to learn. So you can consider this book a glimpse into a vast world which, *baruch Hashem*, many people are working hard to reveal and make accessible to those of us who want to become all that Hashem created us to be.

The inclusion in this book of the Torah insights of my husband, Rabbi Dovid Castle, took it to a new level. A true *talmid chacham*, my husband brings great breadth and depth of Torah knowledge to every facet of this work. My gratitude to him knows no bounds. May Hashem bless us to continue to work together in His service for many years.

Pnina Frank graciously provided another of her incredible paintings for the cover. Beyond that, she sat with the manuscript and me, lovingly sketching just the right images to enhance the words on the page. Her contribution adds a dimension beyond words for which I am enormously grateful.

Diane Nemett reviewed, and offered insightful comments

Acknowledgments

on, the manuscript. A gifted osteopath and physical therapist, Diane shares my fascination with breath and body. With her encyclopedic knowledge of anatomy and physiology, she made my foray into these realms much easier and more enjoyable.

Abby Rosen, Miriam Plotnikoff, and Ahuvah Gray provided varied and valuable input throughout the process of writing this book. Ita Olesker did an outstanding job copyediting the manuscript (and generally helping it to see the light of day), Diane Liff brought her substantial talents to the cover design and layout of the book, and Gittel Kaplan helped in every way imaginable to bring the book into final form. Many thanks to all of you. Thank you as well to Targum Press, its CEO Aryeh Mahr, and its editor-in-chief Esther Heller, who were instrumental in the book's publication, as well as other members of Targum's staff who, as always, were enormously helpful.

My gratitude to my clients, students, and readers is ongoing. Their commitment to becoming all that Hashem created them to be is inspiring. And many of the teachings in this book were revealed in our work together. May they continue to be *matzliach* in their inner work and outer lives.

As I was finishing this book, my beloved father-in-law, Milton Castle, Michoel ben Yechezkiel, z"l, left this world. He embodied what it means to live from the entirety of one's being. Every cell of his body was invested in his words and actions. He was authentically himself, free of pretense. His passionate commitment to truth, Torah, and integrity was and continues to be an inspiration. Likewise his capacity for insightful wit and humor, even in the face of much illness and suffering. Though no longer with us in this world, his wisdom and warm heart continue to envelop us and inform our lives. May his soul be bound in the Bond of Life and may his memory be for a blessing.

Introduction

Introduction

From deep inside the body, comes a voice of longing. Sometimes barely audible, other times loud and clear, it calls out, saying:

I want to feel my own root; to feel connected to the Source of my life. I want to stand in my rightful place, in right relationship to everyone and everything around me. I want to know myself as a spark of the Divine through direct experience, not through the mirror of the opinions of others. I don't want to borrow life force from those around me. I don't want my giving to be corrupted by needing.

I want to carry within myself the validation, recognition, respect, and love that are needed to sustain me. I don't want to manipulate others to give me these essentials. And I don't want to use their authentic offerings to try to fill holes in myself that are my responsibility.

I want to remember that inside every difficulty is a gift of growth waiting to be unwrapped. I want to be who G-d created me to be – and for that to be enough.

Introduction

This desire to stand tall in the totality of our life circumstances — to know ourselves as sparks of the Divine, to embrace our life stories with all their ups and downs, to be fully who we are and to bring that fullness to our relationships with Hashem and with others — is a *ratzon*, a will, that is a powerful force in its own right.

Torah teaches us that a *tzaddik*, a holy person, is one who needs nothing but the potential and *chein* (grace) of what he is, of what Hashem created him to be. He is always — and only — himself, and therefore completely reliable. He has no desire for more than himself, for what can never really be his.

Just the longing for such integrity of self, for such wholeness, for the closeness to Hashem that the *tzaddik* embodies, can open doors and change lives. If each of us were to take responsibility in this way — if we were to work toward becoming balanced, whole, and holy adults — our relationships with each other and *Am Yisrael* would be radically altered. We could stop blaming and ferret out the truth more clearly, even in situations where we disagree. We could see the intricate design of Hashem's creation made manifest through all the different souls that He placed together on this earth at this time, hoping they would be able to recognize each other and the beautiful pattern that their combined existence has the potential to reveal.

Instead we often live in collective chaos, bleeding into each other's lives and feelings without any recognition of the boundaries we are violating and the damage we are inflicting. And all that overlap only increases our sense of loneliness. We lose the ability to achieve intimacy with ourselves and, as a result, with anyone else. We fail to recognize that we must know the self that lives within our own borders in order to truly meet others, and that such a meeting is most profound at the place where our world and theirs meet.

We don't know how to stay within our own *daled amot* (our own personal space) and connect to each other from there. We're constantly reaching too far outside of ourselves or pulling back too far inside of ourselves. We can't seem to simply stay where we are, taking in what is, without reacting by either pulling away or pushing in. We can't seem to hold our own centers, stay connected to our own roots, while interacting closely with others. We bend and twist, we collapse and inflate. We do anything but hold still and give ourselves a chance to absorb whatever is happening, realize our relationship to it, learn what the Torah asks of us in such a situation, and then decide how best to engage the person or event.

Yet Hashem gave each of us the capacity to stay in right relationship with ourselves and others. That capacity is so basic to our ability to be what He created us to be that He implanted it in the breath — the most essential component of life itself — and in the body — the soul's home in the physical world. The breath and body can help us to come into deep contact with ourselves and maintain that contact in our encounters with others.

Where the body and soul connect is where, in Judaism, the self — free will — is found. The soul either thrives or suffers from the body's actions. The self, "I," is the decider who chooses what to do. It is up to us to choose to relate to our breath and our bodies, like everything else in our lives, in ways that bring us closer to G-d, closer to our true selves.

This book, the third in the Inner Torah series, explores the terrain of breath and body in service of helping readers make just such a choice. The underlying premise is quite simple. It is that bringing awareness to the body and breath is a way to connect

Introduction

with and be enlivened by the powerful life force that is within all of us. That life force is the essence of who we are; it is the spark of Hashem that animates our beings and connects us with Him. When we are able to experience ourselves on this essential level, we are able to be more fully ourselves and interact with others more authentically, no matter what the circumstances. It is an ability that can be cultivated with attention and practice.

This book offers ways to do that – but the ways are secondary to the understanding that it is our own consciousness, our own awareness, that is the key to coming into relationship with this dimension of reality. So while I write in detail about the breath and various parts of the body, the words are meant only as guide ropes to this ability to pay attention, to bring one's awareness into the miraculous container that Hashem devised to house our souls in this world. From there, from the essential core of who we are, we can navigate the challenges of our lives with unimaginable ease and serenity.

As part of the Inner Torah series, this book elaborates and expands on ideas discussed more generally in the original book, *Inner Torah: Where Consciousness and Kedushah Meet*, and is intended to be used in conjunction with the second book, *Practical Inner Torah: A Guide to Going Within*.

Working with the breath and body alone is not enough. It needs to be coupled with the Inner Torah process, the approach to coming to know and heal oneself that *Practical Inner Torah* describes at length. Like any other activity undertaken to improve the self, the breath and body work explored in this book is meaningful only to the extent that we recognize what our true innermost self knows — that the ultimate purpose of our existence is to draw closer to G-d. Anything we do to better ourselves needs to be with the intention of manifesting our G-dly essence, of helping us to better serve G-d and His world.

The Breath and Body of Inner Torah

In this way, breath and body are additional entryways to one's Inner Torah, to taking one's rightful place in Hashem's world. And they are always available to explore since we are always in our bodies — to one degree or another — and always breathing — at least in some minimal way that keeps us alive.

Following the style of *Practical Inner Torah*, I've written this book in a way that allows readers to work with it on their own, both individually and in groups. Toward that end, I've included exercises and activities that I term "explorations." The reason for naming them as such is to remind readers that the exercises and activities are not significant in their own right. They are useful only as a means to help us develop awareness in the physical realm and spend time with ourselves in ways that feel connected and genuine.

Rote performance of these explorations cannot effect change at a core level. As with rote performance of anything, the results are only superficial; the deeper self, the spirit, will not be engaged. The explorations are really only suggestions as to possible ways to work with oneself. The focus is on experiencing what happens, not on doing something to get somewhere. And the experience changes all the time. There is no one correct experience.

What is encouraged is to develop awareness so that we can use the awesome gifts of breath and body that Hashem bestowed on us as He intended us to use them. For they are indeed miraculous creations designed to support us in our *avodat Hashem*. With just a little attention, we can better develop these resources and allow them to help us become more fully ourselves, more fully the people Hashem created us to be.

There is another reason, too, for this focus on the body. Our bodies are vessels for G-d's light. His light is intended to penetrate into every corner of our beings. Our goal ultimately is to know the highest and most mysterious truths from inside the depths of our beings — to viscerally experience and rejoice in our connection with Hashem. We see this reflected in the words of the prayer *Nishmat Kol Chai*, which we say every Shabbat at the end of *pesukei d'zimrah*:

> ...*Therefore the organs that You set within us, and the spirit and soul that You breathed into our nostrils, and the tongue that You placed in our mouth — all of them will thank and bless, praise and glorify, sing about, exult and revere, sanctify and declare the sovereignty of Your Name, our King, continuously. For every mouth shall offer thanks to You, every tongue shall vow allegiance to You, every eye shall look toward You, every knee shall bend to You, every erect spine shall prostrate itself before You, all the hearts shall fear You, and all innermost feelings and thoughts [lit. each of my internal organs and kidneys] shall sing praises to Your Name, as it is written: All my bones shall say: Hashem, who is like You... let all my innermost being [all my internal organs] bless His Holy Name.*

We see it, as well, in the words of the prophet Yirmeyahu (31:30–33):

> *Behold, days are coming, says the Lord, when I will make a new covenant with the house of Yisrael and with the house of Yehudah...I will put my Torah in their inward parts and write it in their hearts; and will be their G-d and they shall be My people, and they shall teach no more every man his neighbor and every man his brother, saying, "Know the Lord," for they shall all know Me, from the least of them to the greatest of them, says the Lord, for I will forgive their iniquity and I will remember their sins no more.*

Working with the breath and body not only brings us into more authentic and deeper connection with ourselves, but it can begin to transform our very beings into vessels of G-d's light, vehicles for Divine will. The body can start to "know" what the soul knows, to experience reality from the soul's perspective. From our flesh, as it says in *Iyov* 19, we can begin to see G-d.

Introduction

A Note of Caution

Torah emphasizes the importance of training the soul to prevail over the body. As the Ramchal (Rabbi Moshe Chayim Luzzatto) writes in his classic work, *Derech Hashem* (*The Way of G-d*), "The body inclines toward the material, while the soul leans toward the spiritual... If the soul prevails, it not only elevates itself, but elevates the body as well. . ." In that context, the soul is likened to the rider and the body to the horse. We are encouraged to strengthen ourselves in the soul realm, to try to raise our bodies to the level of our souls. For it is the work of the soul to influence and refine the body.

Yet this book is inviting the reader to focus for a time on the body itself, and the energy field within and around it; to become aware of the body's different parts and how they can be of service in the process of becoming more fully who Hashem created us to be and knowing Him through our very flesh. This endeavor of paying attention to the physical and inner body is not a simple one. We must take care not to get lost, not to lose sight that our goal in connecting more deeply with ourselves, is to connect more deeply with G-d, the Source of our existence.

There are many disciplines that focus on the body for its own sake. They elevate the wisdom of the body over that of the soul. The Torah teaches us that this is not the way for a Jew. Rabbi Schneur Zalman of Liadi, the Baal HaTanya, described a Jew as "a human being in touch with his inner essence and possessed of the ability to unveil it and bring it forth." For a Jew, the body is intended to serve the needs of the soul, of the higher intellect that Hashem gave man to allow him to come close.

The body in and of itself does not know from *kedushah* (holiness). It is up to us to think and act in holy ways, the ways of the soul, and thereby infuse our bodies with this G-dly dimension. And it is that mindset that we want to maintain when working with this book.

The body is a miraculous gift from Hashem. By becoming more familiar with it and comfortable inhabiting it, we can be all the more thankful to Hashem for it and more committed to using it appropriately in His service.

Three appendices are included at the end of this book. One looks in depth at the relationship of body and soul (Appendix 1); another gives a Torah perspective on body and breath (Appendix 2). These appendices contain more complex Torah discussions than were included in the earlier *Inner Torah* books but are worthy of the extra time and attention needed to digest their content. They offer understandings that will grow your connection to Hashem and to your body in different ways again. There is also an appendix that looks briefly at the meanings and associations of different colors, both from a Torah and healing perspective (Appendix 3).

Overview

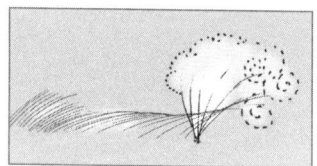

Overview

In the Inner Torah process the body helps us gauge what's happening in our inner world. We first pay attention to the breath and to physical sensations in the body, and from there we move into an exploration of feelings. In that context we are relating to the body and the messages it sends as gates through which to enter into fuller relationship with ourselves. A tight chest, churning stomach, shallow breath, and a host of other bodily sensations alert us that something is happening within that needs attention.

Having entered through these gates, we then come into relationship with the part of the self that is experiencing distress and, G-d-willing, are able to facilitate healing and growth. At that point, the body again plays a crucial role by letting us know if the intervention is truly helpful. If it is, the bodily signals of distress – the tightening, churning, etc. – should subside and, hopefully, be replaced with a sense of ease that was not there before.

Overview

In this way, someone doing Inner Torah work begins to develop somatic awareness and an ability to interpret the signals the body sends. The actual impact on the body — the shift from a state of tension to ease — is a byproduct of the healing relationship that is developed between the adult and the younger, vulnerable self. The bodily sensation itself is not worked with directly.

Yet, there are also ways to enlist the body to help us come more fully into ourselves and into relationship with Hashem. These ways involve working with the body itself to soften, open, release blocks, increase stability, become more fluid and resonant, access deeper places, dissolve masks, and generate more life force.

The two approaches work in tandem. Focusing on the relationship between our adult self and younger, vulnerable selves can result in bodily openings and releases. And focusing on the body can strengthen the adult self, help younger, vulnerable selves surface, and deepen the relationship between the two.

For some people, adding the component of breath and body work to the Inner Torah process is inviting. Others may not be so inclined. As I wrote in *Practical Inner Torah*, the Inner Torah process stands on its own and does not need to be supplemented with any physical practice. But for those who are drawn to such practice, there is much to be gained from coming into more conscious connection with your breath and body. For those who are somewhere in between, know that your nervous system also understands the language of imagery, so even just imagining yourself doing the explorations can be of some benefit.

Batya was filled with anxiety whenever she thought someone might be upset with her.[*] In a complicated family situation, with

---

[*] All of the stories in this book are based on actual situations. Names, certain identifying details, and other features have been changed to protect privacy, and some stories are composites.

a stepmother, mother, grandmother, father, and siblings, all of whom were on varying degrees of speaking terms with each other, it wasn't unusual for Batya to get caught in the middle, one way or another. On top of that, she had in-laws who spent what she felt were excessive amounts of time at her house, which created its own tension.

Just thinking about all these family dynamics and the possibility that one or another of her relatives was annoyed with her would tighten Batya's chest so she almost couldn't breathe. Instead of being able to give her full attention to her children and her household, she found herself constantly going over the details of whatever incident had provoked the latest tensions.

The whole thing was getting out of control. She knew she had to get a grip on herself and not let these situations, which seemed to arise repeatedly, get the best of her. She decided to begin by paying attention to what went on physically when she got caught in these familial tailspins. Immediately she noticed that she was disconnected from her body. She was so consumed with her thoughts that it was as though she didn't even have a body. Ah, she thought, that's a good place to begin.

She looked first at her breath, remembering that it could help guide her back into bodily connection with herself. When she saw how short it became in these moments, she focused on her exhale and invited herself to let more air out on each breath. She realized that if at the same time she brought her awareness to her feet and how they made contact with the ground, it made it easier to exhale longer. Just making this association pleased her. She felt like it was her first indication that her body was taking on a sense of reality for her. Then she added a sound that soothed her both in making it — as she sensed the vibration it created — and in listening to it. All of these things served to bring Batya's awareness back to herself and remind her of her own reality independent of the relationship machinations that swirled around her.

From that place more inside of herself, Batya once again reflected on the latest family feud. But this time, instead of flying off in her mind, trying to figure out what everyone else was thinking and feeling, she had more of a focus on herself, on her piece of the puzzle. She thought about the role she had played, how she had handled herself, what she had said, and she asked herself whether she was okay with how she had behaved. Finding that she was, Batya then asked herself whether there was anything else she wanted to do to foster *shalom*. For the first time, she didn't busy herself with trying to figure out the others involved. Also for the first time, she felt, in a very real way, that Hashem was also in this picture. She could only be responsible for her piece of the puzzle. Other family members held other pieces, and Hashem held still others.

Securely anchored in her own breath and body, Batya felt more able to let events unfold without anxiously trying to engineer an outcome to relieve herself of the excruciating pressure she felt in such circumstances. She was more able to concentrate on her children and her other responsibilities, and to trust that whatever needed to happen would happen in time. She was willing to do her share but not to do everyone else's anymore. While Batya wanted to understand more about what made her so anxious in these situations to begin with, she didn't feel ready to go down that road yet. So she was happy to have at least eased the intensity of her response with the breath and body work.

Chaya took easily to working with her breath and body. It helped her to come into the moment, to not get caught up in endlessly going over the many times in her life, beginning in early childhood, when she had been wronged. Until then it had been her habit, each time she experienced a new injustice, to remember the many others that had preceded it. And the pain would be close to unbearable. Her great despair at repeatedly reaching this place led her to Inner Torah, where she chose first to concentrate on the breath and body work.

Her life at that point was still too crisis-driven to give her the time and peace of mind to do the other aspects of Inner Torah. Realizing that was an important first step in her new resolve to take better care of herself and get out of the vicious cycle of painful feelings in which she had been caught for decades. With her husband and mother both seriously ill, she had very little time to tend to herself. What she liked about the breath and body work was that she could easily incorporate it into all the things she was being called upon to do and handle. It required awareness and consciousness that she felt sure would strengthen rather than deplete her energies.

At the moment what was happening was that in the course of trying to care for her sick and aged mother, she was running into longstanding issues with her siblings. These new experiences were triggering memories of many other such difficult times in the past. At the same time, she was facing struggles with the medical personnel who were supposed to be caring for her husband. That was bringing back memories of all the medical mishaps she had endured both in childbirth and with her own illnesses. Just thinking about all these episodes made her feel weak and defeated.

By staying present in her body as she was navigating these challenges, Chaya found it easier not to go spinning off into her mind. It was the beginning of coming into deeper and fuller relationship with herself, of taking responsibility for her life and starting to function as the adult woman who deep down she had long wanted to be.

Overview

However you decide to go about it — whether you work with the Inner Torah process alone or in concert with breath and body work, or you initially focus just on breath and body — remember that we all need to keep growing spiritually, to keep manifesting more and more of who G-d created us to be. G-d is Infinite. To emulate and connect with Him, we must also dwell in the realm of the infinite, continually plumbing the endless depths of our beings.

"Man was created to toil" (*Iyov* 5:7). Our work is to make visible Hashem's presence in this world, to serve Him with the entirety of our beings, to free G-dliness from its prison of physicality by revealing the G-dliness within us. We are commanded to "be holy, for holy am I, Hashem your G-d" (*Vayikra* 19:1). There is much at our disposal today to help us in this effort. It is up to each of us to determine how best to go about our work.

Part I of this book is devoted to breath and its natural extension, voice — vast subjects that could easily fill entire books on their own. Breath is the medium through which we are most directly connected with Hashem. The spark of G-d that animates each of us is in our breath. And He blessed every one of us with a unique breath rhythm which connects us to our authentic self.

Hashem not only breathed life into our bodies and empowered our bodies to breathe on their own, He also gave us the capacity to participate in that process, to bring consciousness to our breathing — an aspect of our lives and our selves that would otherwise operate involuntarily and unconsciously. This seems to be an invitation to join Him, to engage more fully in helping our souls manifest. For at any given moment, no matter what the circumstances, we all have the capacity to come back into relation with our own breath cycle. It is a master key to our inner homes.

Part II of this book includes different ways to begin to reclaim one's bodily home and come into relationship with whatever might be hidden there. The body knows everything that has happened to it. With patience and a willingness to listen, we can begin to hear a story that otherwise might be lost.

Our goal in cultivating body awareness — as it is with breath — is a higher level of consciousness, recognition of the G-dly dimension in every aspect of existence, and a closer connection with Hashem. The work of refining and elevating our consciousness and allowing that consciousness to penetrate the physical matter of our bodies is continual as long as we are alive. There is no end to the G-dly light we can access and manifest on this physical plane. The more we are able to open to this reality, to experience our eternal nature, the more our bodies will loosen their grip on the fear, hurt, and other emotions that keep us contracted and separated from ourselves, from others, and from G-d.

Most sections in Parts I and II include a discussion followed by explorations to facilitate actual physical practice. Even if you can't do the practice, just reading the discussion sections will increase your self-awareness. With this greater awareness, you'll be more alert to subtle cues from your breath, voice, and body, which can help you better know yourself and better live your life.

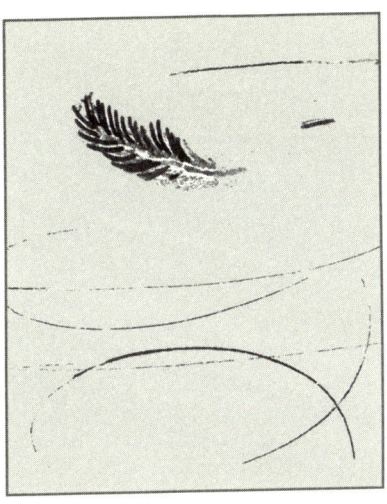

Breath and Voice

Connecting body and soul

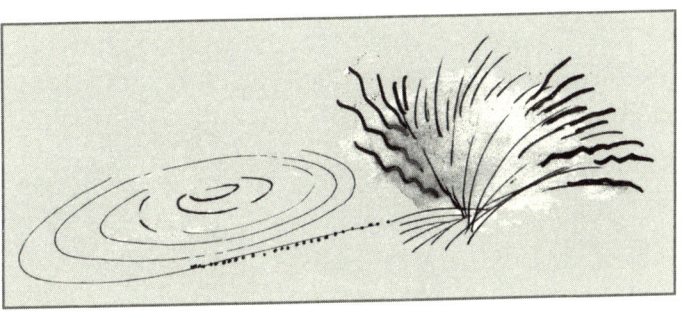

The Gift of Breath

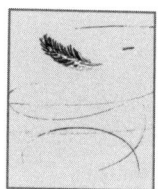

The Breath of Life

It all begins with breath. "And the Lord G-d formed man of the dust of the ground, and breathed into his nostrils the breath of life, and man became a living soul" (*Bereishit* 2:7). Through breath the soul enters the body at birth, leaves the body at death, and is tethered to the body in life. The Hebrew word for breath, *neshimah*, and the Hebrew word for soul, *neshamah*, are virtually identical, sharing the same root, נשם. Some say that the letter *yud*, which is added to the word *neshamah* (נשמה) to make it *neshimah* (נשימה) is to remind us that G-d, to Whom the letter *yud* refers, breathed into us the very breath of our lives and through it our souls are always connected to Him.

Breath is life. It is the way halachah determines whether someone is still alive, requiring that a feather be placed in front of the person's nose to see if he is breathing. Breath is also a bridge between body and soul, between conscious and unconscious parts of ourselves, and between people. If we could fully utilize this miraculous capacity that Hashem bestowed on us, we would be more enlivened, more connected to *HaKadosh Baruch Hu*, more in sync with ourselves, and more in harmony with each other.

Yet it is known that most people use only a small percentage of their respiratory capacity. This has ramifications not only in the context of our ability to be all that Hashem created us to be, but also in the realm of maintaining our basic health and well being. The exchange of gases — oxygen and carbon dioxide — that is the hallmark of breathing is essential to the production of energy in our cells.

Every function of the body requires oxygen. Breathing supplies this life-giving oxygen and removes the gaseous waste produced by all our cellular activity. We need a constant turnover of air to stay healthy. The movements of the diaphragm and other parts of our respiratory apparatus that characterize breathing are intended as well to massage our inner organs. Both body and soul long for us to breathe as fully and naturally as possible.

What constitutes full and natural breathing differs for everyone. Each person, according to her physical structure, has her own way of breathing for maximum efficiency with minimum effort at any given moment. There is no one correct way to breathe for all times. Rather, there is optimum use of our perfectly designed respiratory system according to our unique individual needs. That's why if we're able to be in our own natural breath rhythm, we are more able to be who we truly are.

The difficulty is that breath is affected by everything that happens in our inner and outer worlds. If we're having a nice experience, or even thinking of one, we breathe more expansively. Conversely, when we're in, or even thinking of, a difficult situation, breathing volume decreases and we often feel a sense of tightness. This phenomenon is reflected in the commentary on the verse, "So Moshe spoke accordingly to the children of Israel; but they did not heed Moshe, because of shortness of breath and hard work" (*Va'eira* 6:9). Rashi states that anyone who is under stress is unable to breathe deeply; and in the *Siftei Chachamim* it explains that the Israelites' shortness of breath reflected their troubled state of mind.

Every feeling and thought, every outside influence, expresses itself in our breath — as, of course, does tension, which causes muscles to tighten and air pressure to build in the lungs. Posture also affects breathing; slumping stops the breath from opening fully.

It's understandable, then, why natural breathing is easily disrupted. Before we are even old enough to have any awareness, most of us are already off of our G-d-given breath rhythm. Without attention, we continue on that distorted path and later in life find ourselves far from home, far from our own centers and our own connection to reality. Yet often we don't even know it. Our patterns — of breathing and living — become so habitual, so familiar, that we mistake them for our true way.

This happens in part because breathing is primarily regulated by the autonomic nervous system, which, for the most part, operates on its own. So the body seemingly breathes itself. That allows distortion to be incorporated into the nervous system and the musculature of the body, and restricted breathing to become the norm. In other words, we begin to automatically breathe in ways other than our natural breath, and that becomes our experience of normal. The body accommodates us with muscular and structural holdings that keep the habitual patterns in place.

As with the impulse to do Inner Torah work, it usually takes some disruption in the status quo, some sense of imbalance or dissatisfaction, to motivate a person to try to reach a place of greater authenticity in her breath and herself. Recognizing the need to change is a necessary first step. It's the impetus to begin to pay attention, to do what one can to release the various holdings that were unconsciously developed, and allow a return to a more authentic breath.

What's important to remember is that the movement off of our natural breath occurred at a deep unconscious level over a period of many years. Already as very young children, we often start to breathe less, or breath hold, in order to feel less. Then it becomes a habit. Young children are also very susceptible to tension and pressure, both of which wreak havoc on small respiratory systems. The impact can be significant, actually altering personalities and changing the course of lives. To return the breath to its rightful rhythm, we need to access it at this same deep level. And that takes time. We can't get there by force, by trying to control or manipulate the breath.

In fact, in this context, artificial means of manipulating the breath may actually be counterproductive. They can cement existing limitations into place or add layers to what is already distorted. The involuntary breathing muscles are deep inside the body. In contrast, voluntary controls involve muscles that are more external. When we exert conscious control and mechanically do breathing exercises, we destroy the breath's sensitivity to changing inner states. We lose the opportunity to know and experience ourselves on a deeper, more essential level.

That is not to say that there is never a place for controlling the breath, for working with the breath from the outside. Such work is usually directed toward a specific purpose, such as increasing oxygen intake, stimulating circulation, relieving symptoms of illness, or improving performance. Using the breath as a means to achieve these preconceived ends may, at times, be appropriate.

We also are not talking about situations where there are

actual breathing disorders that need to be addressed medically. Obviously, in such cases, controlled intervention may be called for. It's also important to realize that sometimes apparent distortions in breathing are compensating for a metabolic disorder elsewhere in the body and are actually a survival mechanism. So there needs to be an understanding of the purpose for which we are attending to our breath.

In Inner Torah work, our intentions are to let the breath guide us into deeper and truer relationship with ourselves, closer to our G-dly essence. So, for our purposes, we want to access breath in its purest, most authentic state. We are cultivating change from the inside, seeking in ourselves only that which is in alignment with our souls' truth. Benefits sought in more directed breathing work are often a byproduct of this approach; the difference is that they are achieved more slowly and without forcing.

In an Inner Torah context, our aim is to remove habitual controls and allow the involuntary, G-d-given breathing process to take over. What we want to do is to move under the distortion and uncover what is authentically ours. We want to release the holdings, tensions, and restrictions that limit the free flow of breath. To do this we need to become aware of the function of the involuntary nervous system without interfering, to observe without jumping in to control – an ability that is anyway useful to cultivate in life.

This approach lies in between unconscious, involuntary breathing, which is what we do when we are totally unaware of our breath, and conscious, voluntary breathing, which is what we do when we control the breath. We're essentially witnessing the unconscious functioning of our breathing without disturbing its course. Instead, we're inviting it to shift by virtue of our awareness and whatever stimulation we provide that allows change to happen.

Since restricting our breath is a common way to repress emotions, there is often a relationship between the muscular tension of the body and held emotions. In that case, the emotion must be freed and the tension released for the capacity for natural breathing to be restored. Inner Torah work itself contributes greatly to achieving this core level of release.

When younger, vulnerable selves that are hidden in the holdings in our bodies are uncovered and related to in healing, nurturing ways, the body releases its grip on that particular part of our structure. That's the ease that most people feel when they've genuinely reached and been able to comfort a distressed part of themselves. That ease is invariably reflected in the breath, which then flows a little freer.

One reason for this release is that for an Inner Torah intervention to be successful, it must be truthful. And nothing frees the breath more than speaking honestly. G-d's stamp is truth. Being truthful with oneself (and, when appropriate, others) generates expansion within, giving the soul space for expression. Falsehood causes contraction and tightening and forces the soul into hiding.

Then there is the release of the emotion itself, the invitation to the part of the self holding the difficult feeling to finally express herself and be listened to wholeheartedly. That, coupled with the willingness on the part of the adult self to take responsibility and commit to being sensitive to the needs and feelings expressed, alleviates the need to hold on.

Breath can be a barometer of where we are with ourselves. When we're honest with ourselves, when we relate in ways that are genuinely responsive, there is a sense of ease in the rib cage and diaphragm, and the breath flows easily. Disturbance in the breath, the slightest sense of being off-balance, is a sign that a greater level of truth, of self-awareness, is waiting to be accessed. Each time we heed that call and come more into alignment with ourselves, we are strengthened. That strength, in turn, enables us to look at ourselves and all that surrounds us more directly and forthrightly.

Breath is also a metaphor for how we live in the world. Any grasping, holding on, controlling, and pushing away we do in our lives is reflected in our breath. Breathing with real freedom requires no effort to pull the breath in or to push it out, no grasping, no holding on, no controlling. Each breath is allowed to come and go on its own.

It sounds like it should be easy. But it isn't. Affected as it is by everything that happens to us, the breath is easily thrown out of alignment. Without even realizing it, we hold our breath or breathe shallowly whenever confronted with a difficulty. That may help minimize uncomfortable feelings in the moment, but it doesn't help us to be fully ourselves and bring all that we are to the situation at hand. And that is the goal in Inner Torah work. We want to be able to access as much of our true capacity as adults as we can, to become increasingly more trustful of ourselves. Becoming aware of our breath can help.

It begins with the simple act of paying attention. First just notice the breath without trying to manipulate it in any way. Then notice the flow of breath out of the body, allowing the exhale to continue as long as the body wants. Next sense the pause that occurs at the end of the exhale and watch the next inhale arise of its own accord out of the pause. Finally, notice the very slight pause that follows the inhale. This small act of awareness, in and of itself, can bring us into contact with ourselves and help us to see a situation more clearly.

In *Inner Torah*, I noted that doing this is particularly useful for women with issues in the realm of existence because of the ease with which breath synchronizes with the breath of those around us. Breath naturally attaches to what is outside and can easily stay attached. In response, we need to be able to stand firm in ourselves, in our exhale, so that taking in and giving out are in right balance. Otherwise, without even knowing it, we can take on a breath rhythm that is not our own. This makes it harder to experience and act from an authentic place in ourselves and to separate from whoever our breath has attached to.

Another group for whom breath awareness is particularly important is those who tend to live energetically in their upper bodies, virtually vacating their lower torsos (see "Getting to Know the Energy Body"). For these people, the breath can literally serve as a guide back into the body, most notably on the exhale. The key is not to superimpose a rhythm on the body's natural rhythm. Many have a tendency to cut short the exhale or the pause and grab the next breath. That's a way to unconsciously pull out of the body. By allowing the breath without interfering in any way, one is gently led back into the body and able to function better from there.

More about the Natural Breath

Our true authentic breath that lies underneath the restrictions and holdings we've developed over a lifetime, knows exactly what we need in any given moment. Through this breath we are able to be in touch with all levels of existence, not only with the conscious and unconscious, but also with the wisdom of the soul. It connects us with the Divine at levels well beyond our conscious awareness. The place of natural breath is peaceful; it allows what is to be and empowers us to respond appropriately to whatever that is.

The sensitivity of breath to everything that happens inside and outside of us — to our thoughts and feelings, to our interactions with others, to everything we hear, see, touch, and smell — is in service of maintaining balance. Breath helps us mediate all of these internal and external influences so that we can stay in right relationship to them.

To do that, the natural breath is intended to constantly change in response to whatever is happening. It isn't supposed

More about the Natural Breath

to be fixed in any way. That really is the miracle of breath — that it has the capacity to be so perfectly attuned to what we need, what we can handle, and what the circumstances require.

When we are in our natural breath rhythm, we access emotions at the level that we are then able to experience — and we integrate them responsibly. Our nervous systems don't flood or shut down; we're not swept away or closed off by emotion. Over time, as various influences chase us out of this flexible breath, our breathing moves into more rigid patterns. We end up locked into responses that are no longer so perfectly calibrated to whatever is happening. Often, these responses are outdated. While they once may have been necessary — or at least perceived as necessary — for survival, now they limit our ability to live fully and exercise real freedom of choice.

It is these patterns that most of us relate to as our unique way of breathing. We no longer realize that they are overlaid on an even deeper, purer stream of breath that we can invite ourselves to tap into. Because the habitual patterns are usually unconscious, we often don't even become aware of them until something changes and we're able to experience ourselves breathing differently. Before that, the very notion of a more authentic breath is surprising to many people and often sparks cynicism that there even is such a thing.

Breathing is such a given, something so many people take for granted, that it's hard sometimes to accept that we are misusing, underutilizing, or even abusing this precious G-d-given gift. Through actually experiencing our breath, participating in the process, we invite integration of our conscious, unconscious, and Higher selves and come to know breath for the miracle that it is.

To begin to recognize the limits of our breathing, we need, as described earlier, to pay attention to the breath, to be aware of the exhale, the inhale, and the pauses in between. Even the uninitiated can usually notice a lot from just this small act of paying attention. One person may notice that her breath is quick and shallow, another that she is only breathing from the top of her chest; one may sense that it's easy to inhale fully but hard to exhale, while another may find it easy to exhale but hard to inhale fully, and so on.

With this awareness can come a shift to inviting the breath to come and go on its own, to not interfering with the natural breath. Such an invitation allows the inhale to become something that is received naturally at the end of the pause following the exhale — not something that is grabbed or grasped. When the breath is allowed to leave on exhale and the body to rest in the natural pause that follows, then the inhale will happen on its own. We only need to receive it.

There is actually no need to *take* a breath; the body will breathe itself in the exact measure necessary for whatever is going on. Again that sounds easier than it is for many people. To receive the breath in this way requires trust, a willingness to wait until the breath comes on its own and fills you. It is, in a sense, an expression of *emunah*.

We say in *Tehillim* (150:6), "Kol haneshamah t'hallel Kah, Hallelu-Kah." Chazal interpret this to mean, "Every breath is a conscious praise of G-d." In other words, every breath we breathe should have in it consciousness of the praise of G-d, Who gives the breath. We should realize that we couldn't breathe even one breath without His influx of Divine energy. Then the very act of our breathing reflects our acknowledgment that in the beginning of creation G-d blew the breath of life into the nostrils of man, and with every breath He is continuing to give us life. Waiting to receive the inhale, not feeling the need to superimpose our own control over this natural process that Hashem designed to connect us to Him, is one expression of that acknowledgement.

We remind ourselves of this connection between our breath and G-d every morning when we recite the prayer *Elokai Neshamah*, and say:

> *My G-d, the soul You placed within me is pure. You created it, You fashioned it, You breathed it into me, You safeguard it within me, and eventually You will take it from me, and restore it to me in Time to Come. As long as the soul is within me, I gratefully thank You, Hashem, my G-d and G-d of my forefathers, Master of all works, Lord of all souls. Blessed are You, Hashem, Who restores souls to dead bodies.*

With the inhale, we internalize that which is exterior to us. The Hebrew word for inhaling is *she'ifah*, which also means aspiration. From this we see, as Rabbi Yitzchak Ginsburg explains, that inhaling is an expression of the soul's innate desire to ascend and go beyond its conscious self into the realm of its super-conscious link to Divinity. It reflects our aspiration to reach toward the Infinite.

This process of receiving the breath requires that we surrender and allow the air to enter our bodies. The very slight pause between inhaling and exhaling, this almost imperceptible holding, gives us a chance to be empowered and strengthened by what we've taken in, by our aspiration. And then there's the release into exhale, the giving of expression to what we have inhaled, the expelling of the waste, the letting go, which also is an acknowledgment. The pause or silence that follows at the end of exhalation before the next inhalation takes us into the unknown, into a realm of trust. We don't know when the breath will come, or even if it will come.

I remember sitting with my mother, *a"h*, as she lay dying.

The Breath and Body of Inner Torah

The days of laboring to leave seemed to have ended, of traveling between this world and the next, of talking passionately with long-deceased family members, of crying out in pain, of struggling to say goodbye. Now she was on her way out. What was left was her breath. From her still body that already seemed at peace, came slow breaths. As I watched, the time between them grew longer and longer – almost unbearably long. I couldn't tell if there would even be a next breath.

Then the sound started to change and it happened. The last exhale after which she never again inhaled. The last exhale on which her *neshamah* left. I felt it go. It was palpable. The *neshamah* drifted out the open window behind her bed as though riding a wave. It melted into the spring air cleansed by an unusually powerful late afternoon thunderstorm a few hours earlier. And I was left sitting in the silence by her body no longer animated by her spirit. (This type of peaceful and serene death is referred to as "being taken with a kiss," an act of deep spiritual intimacy. It's a reference to the mouth, which is an outlet for breath.)

At that moment, the connection between the breath (*neshimah*) and the soul (*neshamah*) was more real to me than it had ever been. Once my mother stopped breathing, the woman I had known for a lifetime was no longer there. Her body was an empty shell devoid of her essence. A moment earlier, when her breath was still in her body, I still experienced her presence.

The difference was stark. Anyone who has been present at a death knows this moment. One minute the person is in this world – even if in a coma – and the next minute, with the cessation of breath, he or she is gone, no longer in existence on this plane of reality. And the body literally is left lifeless, a container that has served its purpose and, for now at least, is no longer needed.

So the pause after exhale also expresses our *emunah*, that

More about the Natural Breath

we are in ongoing connection with Hashem, the nature and duration of which only He controls. Natural breathing invites recognition of this — that we are not meant to control what is in Hashem's hands but rather to allow it, to invite it, to receive it, to be present to it, to appreciate it, and to remember its Source.

The fact that every breath cycle is unique and different also makes vivid the reality that we attest to every day in our prayers when we say that Hashem "renews daily, perpetually, the work of creation." (See the first *berachah* preceding the Shema.) It helps us to be more aware of G-d's hand in our lives and to feel in a more tangible way the opportunity He gives to constantly renew and develop ourselves.

Through continuity of the breath cycles comes breath rhythm, unique as well to each person. The rhythm shifts as needed. Through being in our own rhythm — continuous though varying — we can most easily grow and maintain our balance. That rhythm contains our innate ability to respond and adjust to whatever happens, whatever influences us from within or without. It is programmed from Hashem to do so in a healthy, balanced way.

If it becomes stuck or restricted it can't do what it was intended to do, and we end up overly reactive or otherwise out of balance. By becoming aware of our breath and of how the breath moves in the body, we're better able to spot when we fall into an old breath (and probably reactivity) pattern, or hold our breath, or otherwise disrupt this natural flow of life force from Hashem. Then we can go both to the breath to invite free movement, as well as to the conflict or trigger that created the charge (Inner Torah) to come into fuller, more adult relationship with ourselves and others.

What is asked of us is to sense the breath and consciously follow its movement without interfering, to be present and pay attention to the movement of breath without controlling it. We can — as suggested in the explorations — move, make sound, offer stimuli, and do other things that invite breath, but without demand. The breath will respond to these offers involuntarily; all we need to do is to let the response through.

That's because natural breathing is reflexive — automatic and inborn. We can't imitate a reflexive action. All we can do to restore the breath's potential is to remove restrictive tensions and provide stimulation that will provoke deeper and stronger reflex actions than are normally exercised in our habit-run daily lives. For this to be effective, we can't let our conscious minds rush in and try to make a breathing exploration something familiar or push us to bypass our experience to get to results. We have to go within and make discoveries from there.

In other words, we need to work with the body to connect to this deeper stream of breath and ultimately allow it to move and inform us. By staying with the sensation in our own bodies, we're better able to recognize feelings that belong to us and not project or transfer them on to someone else. We're better able to contain ourselves and to do what Hashem is asking of us.

To relate to breath in this way, it helps to remember that air is our most vital nutrient — and it comes exclusively from Hashem. Our most basic experience is breathing air. The Talmud says that the air of the land of Israel makes one wise (*Bava Basra* 158b). Likewise, the air or atmosphere we create in our homes affects everyone who lives there. Breathing is the root of all that we take in, all that we give out, and all that we are. It makes sense then that we would want to develop our G-d-given ability to breathe just as we develop so many other gifts that He gives us.

Rav Yitzchak Hutner, *zt"l*, explains the shofar as being an echo of the very first breath of G-d, so to speak, which infused life into the world. The shofar is sounded on Rosh Hashanah,

More about the Natural Breath

the day that marks the anniversary of the creation of man, a human speaker. The mere sound serves as the reverberation of that Divine breath, and when we hear the sound of the shofar we remember and are once again connected to the root of our existence — the Breath of Hashem (*Rosh Hashanah 25, Pachad Yitzchak*). To the extent that we can let breath animate our bodies, we can let Hashem animate our lives. Breath moves us.

Experiences of Breath

Malka wanted to work on the fear and discomfort she felt when meeting and engaging with people. A mother of five and a teacher, she was well respected and liked in her community. Yet, navigating the terrain of *simchahs*, charitable functions, family gatherings, and the like, was a formidable challenge for her that took an enormous amount of energy. She doubted that anyone was aware of her feelings since she had long ago perfected her social skills. In fact, she worked so hard to forge connections with others that she sometimes overextended and abandoned herself in the process. When that happened, she would find herself connecting with people who weren't necessarily right for her and then not knowing how to disengage from them. As she started to explore the source of her difficulty, she realized that it would be helpful to work with her breath as well.

She began by paying attention to her breath, letting it come and go on its own. As she did so, she became even more aware of the feeling of fear. "It's like I got scared out of my own skin long ago, and now it takes all my courage and concentration to stay inside of it," she said. Undeterred by the heightened sensations of fear, Malka decided to set aside time every day to work with her breath. She also tried to be conscious of what happened to her breathing when she interacted with others and took time, before starting to talk, to connect to her breath.

As she was able to stay with her breath more, to sense the potential it held to support her, Malka's experience started to change. She became more able to stay inside herself while engaging with others. She didn't feel a need to work so hard to make contact. When she spoke, it was from a more genuine place within and required less effort. Gradually she began to realize that it was safe to be herself around other people. She didn't need to leave herself to make anything happen. She also recognized that she needed time to get to know people and allow them to know her. It wasn't a process that she should rush.

In reflecting on her experience, Malka sensed that she had been forced to step out of her natural bounds as a child and had continued throughout her life to extend beyond where she was genuinely able to go. Now, as an adult, her breath was guiding her back to her rightful place.

Rivka was someone who did a lot for her family and the community but didn't feel all that connected to what she was doing. Even her creative endeavors, her art and music, remained outside of her, something she had to consciously remind herself about rather than something that felt integrated into her sense of herself. After years of living this way, Rivka tired of the feeling of emptiness that haunted her no matter how busy and involved she was. She decided to explore what was happening and began by focusing on her breath. To her surprise, she found it hard not to superimpose her will on her breathing. Feeling how she controlled her breath helped her to see how controlling she was in other aspects of her life. It took quite some time for her to relax into her natural breath, to allow her breath to begin to flow more freely without intervening.

One of the first things she noticed was that she was "inside" or relating to the breath work itself more than she had to other things she had done in her life. This felt sensation of being inside something, being connected to what she was doing from the inside, was new to her. She sensed that maybe because she had never been inside her own breath, she couldn't really be inside anything else that she did. Once she had this real and felt experience of being inside what she was doing, it became easier to relate to her other activities in the same way. Her breath opened a passageway to allow all the wonderful things she was involved in, that before were hovering outside of her, to actually enter and nourish her inner world.

Esther didn't feel real to herself. On the outside she appeared confident and well-adjusted, but inside was a different story. It was as though she couldn't experience her own existence, her own reality, no matter how much she accomplished and how successful she was. When she began to pay attention to her breath, she first noticed tightness in the back of her diaphragm and the muscles surrounding it. From there, she observed that she had a tendency to hold her breath at the end of her inhale. She realized that she stayed at the end of the inhale longer than necessary and didn't move into her exhale fully or with ease. This pattern seemed to her to be very old and deeply entrenched in her body. She wondered whether it went all the way back to her non-labor Caesarian birth when, according to what she had been told, she had experienced breathing difficulties.

The sensation she associated with her breath pattern was one of gasping and holding her breath. As she reflected on this sensation, she realized that she had repeated that gasping and breath-holding action many times in response to many traumatic and difficult life events. She started to sense how her physiology had taken on the shape and contour of that stance, with her organs, muscles, and connective tissue literally pulling up to support it.

She continued to explore the tension in her body. It seemed to extend from her diaphragm up into her neck and down into her pelvis. She could tell that her brain was also involved. She understood that the nervous system learns patterns from repeated responses, that anything done frequently creates neural pathways in the brain, and the pattern is resorted to more often. Releasing the tension in her tissues wasn't going to be enough. The neural holding, fed by her belief system – would try to maintain its grip.

That meant going back and sending her nervous system a message that what it experienced as too much or too overwhelming in the past was no longer happening. That was then and this is now, and now she had the ability to contain and process the events of her life, even those that were difficult and traumatic. She no longer needed to be at their mercy, holding her breath and holding back from coming into herself to manage them.

Esther explored ways of relaxing her body that would allow her to slip under the structural obstructions and begin to experience more ease in her exhale. At the same time, she talked to the many vulnerable parts of herself which had been confronted with traumas and reacted with gasping and breath-holding. Slowly she encouraged each one to let go of her fixation with the past and come into the present.

The result was noticeable. Little by little, Esther felt her breathing change and a new sense of connection to herself being forged. She knew it would take time to get all the way there and that she might need help from a bodywork specialist to release some of the deeper structural holdings. Still, there was no question that through working with her breath, Esther had begun to access authentic parts of herself that had been cut off by the pattern established from her gasping and breath-holding – parts that she needed to feel real and whole.

How the Body Breathes

An important step in becoming conscious of one's breath is to know how the body breathes. What parts of the body are involved? How do they work and how do they relate to each other? This is particularly important for purposes of getting to one's natural breath, which requires mostly undoing and letting go of old holdings and habits. To even sense where those holdings are and how those habits operate, it is necessary to understand what is happening anatomically.

On inhalation we receive the breath through the nose. The nose is designed for regular breathing (more than the mouth) because the nostrils are lined with small hairs that filter out dust and dirt from the incoming air. Also, it has membranes that warm and moisten the air. These membranes secrete mucous that, along with the waving motions of the hairs, collect unwelcome particles that enter the body through the nose.

The more dust, dirt, bacteria, or other tiny particles that accumulate, the more mucous is secreted to trap them. Keeping the nasal passages clear is vital to breathing. So it's important to blow the nose regularly to clear it of debris. (Sneezing also does this.) Acupressure, reflexology, homeopathy, herbs, and dietary changes can also help to alleviate nasal congestion.

The Gemara indicates that when Aharon's two sons died, two pillars of fire went into their nostrils and they were consumed. Nothing happened to their bodies. The soul was accessed directly through the nostrils. Similarly, prior to the time of Yaakov *Avinu*, people died by sneezing. (Yaakov davened to Hashem that sickness precede death, so people could put their affairs in order.)

The nose also represents man's ability to filter purity from impurity on a spiritual level. It is the part of the body that is used to smell, and the sense of smell is closely related to the soul (*Berachot* 43b). A pleasant smell encourages us to breathe deeply, opening the respiratory system more fully. A bad smell triggers shallow breathing and, if it's bad enough, can virtually block the respiratory system. The sense of smell opens the door to deep levels within us. The sense is greater at the top of the nasal cavity, as witnessed by the way we inhale the scent of a flower and try to draw it up into the nose (see "Nose and the Sense of Smell").

Air not only carries smells but also information. Anyone who has spent time on safari or otherwise in communion with nature can watch both the animals and people accustomed to living in such environments pay close attention to the air. It carries information about what is happening and who or what is nearby. From an energetic perspective, air also carries the energy of thoughts. We even use idioms of speech that link the nose and knowledge, such as "smelling a lie."

The inhale can be thought of as taking in information. It feeds. One is merged with everything outside on inhale. In contrast, exhale is standing in the self and participating from there. It gives back something particular to the person exhaling, saying, in a sense, "Here I am." This phenomenon is reflected in the words of the *Zohar*, quoted and explained in the *Tanya*, chapter 2: " 'He who exhales, exhales from within him,' that is to say, from his inwardness and his innermost, for it is something of his internal and innermost vitality that man emits through exhaling with force." Exhale activates the parasympathetic nervous system — relaxation. Inhale activates the sympathetic nervous system — tension.

From the nose, the air flows down past the pharynx — the cavity at the back of the mouth where the nose and mouth are connected — past the larynx — the voice box — and into the trachea — the windpipe — which splits into two bronchi or tubes, one passing into each lung. The trachea and bronchi are also lined with mucous-secreting cells that trap pollutants, and there are tiny hair-like lashes in the bronchi that massage debris away from the lungs and up toward the trachea.

When too many particles accumulate in the bronchi, they trigger a cough to get rid of the unwanted material. In the lungs, the bronchi divide into smaller and smaller branches, which end in bubble-like sacs called alveoli. The exchange of oxygen and carbon dioxide happens in the alveoli. Fresh oxygen enters the system on inhale, to be carried through the body by the blood. Carbon dioxide and other gaseous waste products are returned by the blood for elimination on exhale.

The process of breathing takes place mainly in the chest cavity. This cavity, called the thoracic cavity, is bounded on the top and sides by the rib cage, which extends from the base of the neck to a few inches above the navel. Its floor is the diaphragm, a big flexible dome-shaped muscle that sits in the chest like a parachute. The diaphragm attaches all around the lower border of the rib cage and ties down to the lower spine in back. It arches up into the thoracic cavity, simultaneously forming the floor of the thoracic cavity and the roof of the abdominal cavity, the part of the torso that begins at the lower border of the rib cage and fills the space down into the pelvis.

The lungs and the heart are housed in the rib cage just above the diaphragm. The lungs lie like two inverted cones with their bases toward the mid-body. They are best filled from bottom to top, though they can be filled partially from the top as well. The lungs are very elastic, able to move in any direction, except where they are attached through tubes and arteries to the heart and trachea.

This means that the back of the torso is also involved in the motion of breathing. In that sense it helps to think of the body as a cylinder which, in breathing, functions all the way around, not just in front as it often seems to. The entire circumference of the mid-region of the body needs to expand and contract with the movement of air in and out of the lungs.

The diaphragm is the muscle most responsible for respiration and is sometimes called the spiritual muscle. (See Appendix 2.) Other muscles, such as the intercostals between the ribs and the abdominal muscles in the front of the belly, assist the diaphragm. There are also secondary respiratory muscles in the front of the neck, in the upper chest, and running from the base of the skull.

Because the diaphragm is attached to the inside of the lower ribs and to the lumbar spine, it is affected by the mobility of the spine and pelvis and their associated muscles. Connective tissue reaching as far up as the neck and throat also affect the movement of the diaphragm. So it's easy to see that breathing really involves the whole body. Virtually any place in our bodies where we are restricted and holding can affect the freedom of the breath.

Other organs surrounding the diaphragm are the stomach, pancreas, gallbladder, intestines, liver, spleen, and kidneys. When the diaphragm moves with the degree of expansion that full breathing is intended to generate, all these organs are massaged and bathed in new blood, fluids, and oxygen. The organs are squeezed and released, which brings a sense of well-being to the whole body.

In the process of breathing, the diaphragm moves up and down. On inhale the diaphragm lowers and the rib muscles expand and elevate the ribs. A larger space in the chest is created causing a partial vacuum that sucks the lungs out toward the walls of the chest and down toward the diaphragm. The pressure in the atmosphere at this point exceeds the pressure in the chest, and air flows in to balance these pressures, moving the diaphragm down as it does so.

To exhale completely, the diaphragm has to relax and billow back up into the chest, compressing the air in the chest and allowing it to flow out. The rib muscles also relax. Old air is expelled through the windpipe as the lungs recede from the walls of the chest and shrink back to their original size. The abdominal region moves along with the diaphragm, moving outward as the diaphragm moves down and flattening as the diaphragm moves up. The abdominal muscles support, but are not meant to force, this motion.

Before the lungs can be refilled with a new supply of air, they have to be sufficiently emptied of their waste-containing old supply. While there will always be some air left in the lungs to prevent them from becoming deflated, we can exhale much more air than we normally do.

You can see the importance of emptying the lungs in order to breathe fully by observing what happens when someone short of breath tries to inhale deeply to get more air. It doesn't work. Such breathlessness actually indicates a need to empty the lungs so that they can be refilled – a need to exhale fully and then let the inhale happen automatically, which will naturally satisfy the body's needs for oxygen. So while we tend to focus on inhalation as the key to breathing, it's really the full, relaxed exhale that needs to be cultivated.

Long-standing restrictions and holdings in any of the body's muscles or connective tissue that impact on breathing sometimes require manual intervention to facilitate release. Osteopathy, physical therapy, massage, structural integration, cranial-sacral, and other bodywork modalities can all be helpful in cueing the body to relinquish old patterns that inhibit free breathing. Often pain or discomfort motivates us to seek this sort of help, and changes in breathing patterns are noticed as a byproduct of the effort to alleviate the pain.

But a sense that our breathing is not all that it could be can also be a reason to seek such assistance. Especially if the patterns that we're trying to release go back a long time, it can be difficult for the body to make the shift entirely on its own. At the same time, body work can only be effective to the extent that we are willing to change, to deal with whatever set up the restriction in the first place. Otherwise, after a short time, the body is likely to revert to its old ways of maintaining the status quo, including restricting the breath.

Being aware of how the body breathes makes it easier to watch what happens when we let the breath come and go on its own. We can start to feel where tightness inhibits the movement, where rigidity stops the flow, where we intervene and superimpose our will. We can also notice simple obstacles such as nose congestion or a belly that's too full with food. In one way or another, we come into more conscious connection with the body; it becomes something more real, more vital, and more recognizable as the miraculous creation that it is.

With the increased awareness of the body that attention to the breath brings, we begin to notice that we can sense breath throughout the body, well beyond the confines of our respiratory system. Though not literal, this experience of breath in all parts of the body is a real sensation that can help us feel alive and awake in new ways.

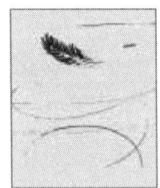

EXPLORATIONS

It takes time to become sensitive to the breath, to experience how your breath responds to the stimuli offered by these explorations. Try to be patient. Let yourself enjoy the process of developing sensory awareness and feeling changes in your breathing. Your body will give you the feedback you need.

For some, tuning into the body in this way will itself be a new experience. It involves development of a kinesthetic sense that, until now, may not have gotten much attention. Again the key is to be patient. Anything you notice, even if it's that you're not feeling anything, is a starting point in this work. Eventually this body sense will develop, adding a whole other dimension to your ability to know yourself.

Over time, the sensations you experience will change. You may become aware of a different sense of ease, of more spaciousness and less pressure. You may feel breath in more of your body. When these types of changes start to happen, try not to be afraid to let the old patterns go.

Inviting change in your breath invites change in your being. And you need to be prepared for both. Often, our

Explorations

greatest struggles come from our resistance to change. While we may want things to be different, we're not always prepared to let go of what was and let something new happen. Fear of the unknown and a reluctance to leave our comfort zone (no matter how uncomfortable it might be) often get in the way. If you recognize this phenomenon at work and address it directly, it will be easier to ease yourself into whatever change is needed.

In order to fully inhabit a part of your body, to invite breath there, you need to be able to hold, emotionally and spiritually, whatever that part contains. We can't force breath there. We can only invite it and let it find its way on its own. Our natural breath has its own intelligence about who we are in our wholeness and integrity, and it can take us there if we are willing and ready to go.

The nature of breath is to call us home to the whole of ourselves. We need to be present to hear that call and willing to not resist it. That means that genuine attention is essential for all of these explorations. If you feel yourself just going through the motions or losing concentration, stop. Better to do just a small amount with awareness than to do a lot mindlessly. There is nothing accomplished by doing these explorations without real awareness, without felt sensation of the movement of breath. It is the process, not any end result, which is of value here.

It also doesn't help to try too hard. You'll inadvertently create tension that will only restrict your breathing even more. So again, be gentle with yourself. Be patient. Go slowly. And see if you can enjoy what you're experiencing rather than focusing on results. We're aiming to let the natural breath come through, not to force it.

And remember that the explorations are meant only as suggestions, as possible ways to pay attention to and work with the breath. What is encouraged is to develop awareness so that noticing what's happening with the breath becomes second nature in everyday life. The explorations are helpful for that purpose but not essential.

1. Breath Awareness

Observe whatever you can about your breathing without trying to control it in any way. How would you describe it? Which areas of your body are involved in your breathing? To which areas do the effects of your breathing spread? Can you feel the various parts of your respiratory system working? What are the characteristics and quality of your breathing? Is it labored, easy, shallow, restricted, full, deep, slow, fast, rhythmic, jerky, strong, weak? Just note your general impressions. This will help you begin to develop breath awareness and enable you to recognize changes in your breathing as they happen.

2. Sensing Breath

Sensing the breath begins with becoming aware of the air flowing into and out of your nose. Feel whether it is warm or cool. Feel the vibration as the air passes over the tiny hairs in your nostrils. Notice whether the passageway is clear or congested. Sense the air flowing from your nose through your throat to your trachea. Be aware of the temperature and any vibration. Now follow the breath from the nose all the way down into your lungs on inhale and back out on exhale. Sense the air touching all these places in your body and let it relax them.

3. Inviting Breath through Scent

Imagine that you are inhaling and savoring the scent of a rose. Allow, but don't force, the air to move high into the nasal cavity. Feel how this invites the body to receive a fuller breath. Notice if your shoulders expand and draw back and your rib muscles expand as you do this.

4. The Natural Breath Cycle

Relax into your body, feel where it makes contact with the surface you are sitting, standing, or lying on. Take a minute to come into the experience of bodily sensation and release any unnecessary tension you feel. Keep releasing tension from the stomach area, the chest, the shoulders, and the lower belly. Then begin to pay attention to your breath cycle, the exhale, inhale, and pauses.

See if you can resist interfering with the process. Let the breath release out of you. Wait, but don't hold the muscles, until you feel the need for a new breath. Yield to the need and let the breath in — allow yourself to receive the inhale following the pause without actually taking a breath. Let your body breathe itself.

Then let the breath release again. Follow your exhale as long as it continues without forcing out the last bit of breath. Enter the pause following the exhale with a willingness to simply wait until the body is ready to receive its next inhale. As you feel the impulse of need, give in to it and allow the new breath in. Try to pay attention to your breath not with your thoughts, but with your ability to sense and feel.

a. When following your exhale, sense if you hold back or push air out. Do you hurry the exhale, press on it, let it out in spurts? Does your exhale last as long as it needs to or are you forcing it to end? Can you follow the sensation in your body when exhaling and see how deep within it goes? Notice what gets in the way of your letting the exhale come through on its own. Make sure that you're not tensing your abdomen.

b. When attending to the pause, notice what happens between exhale and inhale. Are you cutting short the exhale and pulling your inhalation through? See what you are doing that may interfere with the natural transition from exhale to inhale? Are you willfully inhaling and eliminating or shortening the pause? Are you holding on to the pause and forcing a delay in your inhale?

c. When following your inhale, sense if it comes on its own or you're actively taking in air. Are you letting all the air stream in or cutting off the flow? Notice what's getting in the way of allowing your body to receive the incoming air.

d. Notice whatever very slight pause follows your inhale. What happens in that brief instant of holding? Are you prolonging it or pushing past it?

The more specific you are able to be about the precise ways you are interfering with your natural breath, the easier it is to know what you need to do less, so that your natural breath can come through.

5. Noticing How Breath Affects and is Affected

Think about a pleasant situation in your life and then repeat the steps in exploration 4. Do the same while thinking about a difficult situation. See how focus on the situation affects your breath, and how focus on the breath affects your reaction to the situation.

6. Focus on Exhale

Allow yourself to sigh, experiencing the long, relaxed exhale and the intake of air that follows it.

Count silently as you exhale to gently invite it to continue a little longer. Then try whispering the count and eventually counting aloud. Don't try to reach any particular number in your counting. Just let the counting ride your exhale.

7. Involving the Back in Breathing

Think of the trunk of your body as a big balloon. Watch it collapse all by itself as the air flows out of your lungs, and watch it inflate as the air flows in. Allow the back of your body to be involved. You can make the balloon different colors and play with this image, noticing any differences as you do so.

8. Perceiving Breath through Your Organs

Imagine your body as a cylinder with the muscles and bones as the container and the soft organs as the inner content. You can be specific if you know the location of an organ but it's not necessary. Feel the breath through the organs. To feel the difference between initiating breath from outer versus inner layers, shift your attention to your muscles and bones as they press against the skin. Notice how your breathing and state of mind changes. Shift your awareness inside again and feel the movement of breath within and around your organs.

9. Inviting Breath through Touch

Rub your hands together until they are warm and place them one on top of the other on your belly. Sense the impact on your breath. You can also gently massage your belly in small circles. Try putting your warmed hands other places on your body and sense how your breath is affected. Be sure to be present to the feeling of your hands touching your body; don't just do it mechanically.

10. Inviting a Longer Exhale

a. On exhale, open your mouth wide and let the air flow out as freely as you can without any pushing or forcing. Keep your mouth relaxed and opened wide. (If you let your tongue rest on the bottom of your mouth and keep your throat and neck comfortably wide, you can more easily open your mouth wide.) Try not to help the air out in any way; just let it stream out on its own.

b. After a single exhale through your open mouth, go back to breathing through your nose again. Notice what happens to your breath after exhaling through your open mouth and allow all of the reactions to come through. When your breathing has evened out and there are no more strong reactions, try another exhalation through your open mouth. Take all the time needed for your breathing to become calm again. There is no advantage to restimulating your breathing before it is finished reacting to the prior stimulus. It just confuses the breath.

11. Exhaling with Sound

Hold your palm vertically, fairly close to your mouth. As you gently exhale, make a soft, barely audible, continuous haaaaa sound (ha as in "harbor"). Let your breath stream out of your mouth slowly, as gently and steadily as possible, and only as long as the air flows with ease. Try to leave your throat wide open without any pressure on it. Feel the temperature and moisture on your palm from your breath and notice how your exhalations become gradually warmer as you continue. Give yourself a chance to experience the reactions to the haaaa sound exhalation, and wait for your breath to become even again before repeating the sound.

12. Releasing Constriction

Smile on inhale, and purse your lips like an elephant trunk on exhale. The smile can release constriction, and the elephant trunk makes the exhale clearer.

13. Breath-Tongue Exploration

Gently press the tip of your tongue onto the back of the roof of the mouth. Notice how your breath moves in your body below the ribs and how your abdominal wall expands and retracts. Continue for one to three minutes.

14. Breath-Feet Exploration

Sitting on the edge of a chair, use your ankles to lift your toes towards your knees while pressing your heels gently into the floor. Notice what happens to your breath, where it is moving. Next, lift your heels and gently balance both feet on the balls of the big toes. Again notice where in your body your breath is moving. Now place your feet flat on the ground and notice where you perceive breath moving. You can do this anytime you find yourself sitting for long periods. The pressure of the different parts of the feet on the floor stimulates the breath.

15. Breath-Fingers Exploration

a. Press the pads of the two middle fingers on each hand together and wait until you feel the breath more clearly and strongly in your body. Notice where you feel it. Now do the same with the little fingers and you will sense the breath in another area of your body. Then try the index fingers, the thumbs, and the ring fingers; sense where you feel the breath each time. Try pressing the ring and little fingers together at the same time and then the thumbs and index fingers at the same time. Don't press too hard — the finger pads should not pulsate — or too gently. Try pressing all ten finger pads together and notice the increased breathing throughout your whole body. You can also press your finger pads against objects such as a table top and experience the same effects as with pressing the finger pads together.

b. This exploration tends to invite an increase in inhaled breath. For the exhale, fold your hands and apply a little pressure on the back of the hand with each finger pad. This results in increased exhalation and prolongs the rest period after the exhalation.

16. Breath-Movement Exploration

a. Stretch in any direction away from the center of your body as freely and gently as you can. You will soon be aware that the body inhales during stretching without your help and exhales when you return to your original position. Let whatever part of your body feels like stretching — arms, legs, neck, back — gain the length and width it is looking for. Ease out of the stretch gently and feel if the sense of opening stays with you. Notice whether you're breathing more easily and fully than before.

b. Try stretching from your joints and vertebrae with small gentle movements. You can also stretch internally, your internal organs, without actually moving parts of your body. Find a way to move the organs from the inside — liver, kidneys, intestines, any organ. See how the breath opens. The organs themselves affect tension in the body.

c. Notice the connection between breath and movement. See if you interfere with your breath when you move or perhaps even before you start to move. See if you hold your breath, actively inhale (instead of receiving the inhale), or otherwise disturb your natural breath. Movement will stimulate breathing if you let the breath adjust freely, and then breathing will support and carry the movement. You can work with this awareness any time as you are doing your daily activities.

d. Move in non-habitual ways, such as twisting, raising your arms above your head, doing anything that you don't typically do. Because movement affects breath and most of us move in habitual ways, we have to introduce new movements. New movements also help you to perceive blockages and can lead to discovery of how to release them. You're offering your nervous system a new experience that it can use to help create shifts. Ask your body what it needs, what movements would be helpful, and then stay aware as you do them. Try in daily life to do things non-habitually, when possible, such as with different hands.

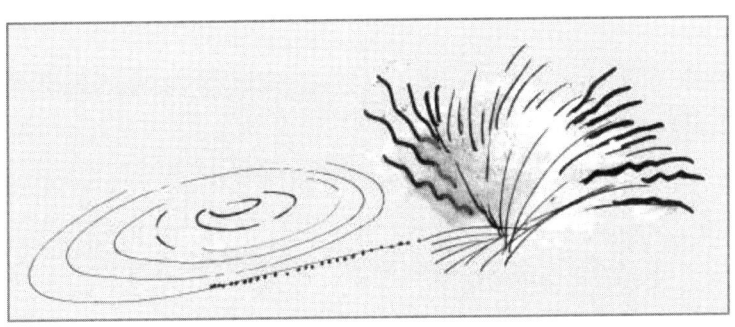

The Miracle of Voice

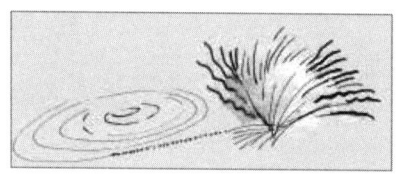

The Miracle of Voice

From Inner Torah: Many women are not speaking in their true voices. The sound and the content of what is said is affected. The voices are higher and tighter than what they should be; there is often little resonance. Substantively they are not communicating their deeper soul truths. Sometimes women find that they are literally mute when they try to speak from a deeper place in themselves.

They are so habituated to cutting off their deeper registers that they can no longer access them. The inner energy body as well as the musculature, connective tissue, and other parts of the physical body have constricted and distorted to the point that the unnatural feels natural. It then takes conscious and prolonged work to free the system physically and energetically. Once a woman is made aware of the discrepancy between her voice as she has become accustomed to hearing it and her true voice, she has an instant tool by which to gauge the depth and authenticity of her communications. It is typically a stunning revelation.

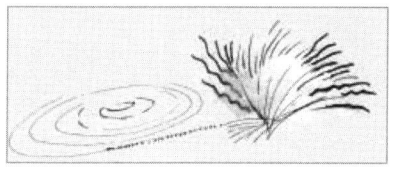

The Divine Quality of Voice

Voice is the natural extension of breath. Its sound is created by the passage of air from the lungs through the vocal cords. To work to its true potential, voice needs the energy of breath. So any work we do to come into our natural breath is reflected in our voices as well.

Many Torah sources say that it is not just the breath of life, but actually the capacity to speak that Hashem blew into the nostrils of man. According to these sources, G-d breathed into man's nostrils a "speaking soul" by virtue of which man understands and speaks. "For he who breathes into the nostrils of another person gives into him something from his own soul. . . 'And the breath of the Almighty gives them understanding' " (*Iyov* 32:8) (*Ramban Commentary on the Torah, Bereishit* 2:7).

This ability to speak sets us apart qualitatively from all other creatures. With our words, we verbalize our intent, linking our souls with our actions. This is one of the reasons that we recite blessings before performing mitzvot, and some also say words of "*lesheim Yichud.*" The words are the vehicle for spirituality.

The Jewish people as a nation are defined by voice. "The voice is the voice of Yaakov" (*Bereishit* 27:22). Voice represents intellect; it is the ability to speak which opens the way for the highest form of worship of Hashem. The prayer recited when donning tefillin notes the presence of the soul that shares space with the brain, the intellect, and asks that they be subjugated to Hashem's service. When Yitzchak *Avinu* says, "The voice is the voice of Yaakov," he is saying that the essence of Yaakov, of the Jewish people, is intellectual-spiritual strength. Voice is the medium through which that essence manifests.

Even more than being the distinguishing feature of man and the identifying feature of the Jewish people, voice is the ultimate mark of Hashem. It is written, "Through ten utterances was the world created" (*Avot* 5:1). These ten utterances include the nine times "and G-d said" is written in the account of Creation, plus the first verse of *Bereishit*, "In the beginning..."

Created in the image of G-d, man reflects his Creator in every sense. Though Hashem's essence is totally beyond our comprehension and Hashem is One, we relate to Hashem through attributes that are familiar to us. The Divine power to create through speech is mirrored in our ability to act and affect the world through speech. Torah considers the power of speech so great that there is an entire body of law governing it, the laws of *lashon hara*. Speech is also considered to be on a higher level than dreams, which themselves are a form of Divine revelation. The spoken interpretation of a dream actually governs its impact (*Zohar, Parashat Vayeishev*). "Death and life are in the power of the tongue" (*Mishlei* 18:21).

We are commanded to choose our words carefully, to use

our words for good and not evil. It is recognized that words "go down into the innermost part of the body" (*Mishlei* 17:8). One who embarrasses another in public through words, or any other way for that matter, is described by the Talmud as a murderer. At the other end of the spectrum is the power of speech to heal and sweeten reality, as reflected in the verses "Pleasant words are like a honeycomb, sweet to the soul, and health to the bones" (*Mishlei* 16:25), and "Anxiety in a man's heart depresses it, but a good word gladdens it," which is interpreted by Chazal to mean that worry in the heart can be alleviated by speaking it out (*Mishlei* 12:25).

Voice is also the medium through which Hashem makes known His Presence; it is with voice that He reaches us most directly. Only at the revelation at Sinai did the Jewish people as an entirety hear G-d's voice. It was His voice that unequivocally made G-d a reality for us. It reverberated with such force that it broke cedar trees, made mountains quake, caused hinds to give birth, and stripped the forests bare (*Tehillim* 29). Each individual perceived Hashem's voice according to his unique capacity to experience the *Shechinah*. Yet, after the first two commandments, *bnei Yisrael* were so frightened that they begged Moshe to transmit the rest of the commandments rather than hear Hashem's voice again. They were unable to bear the intensity of Hashem's voice.

The Midrash says that before these separate utterances of the commandments, Hashem first uttered all Ten Commandments simultaneously — in one breath — to demonstrate clearly that the Ten Commandments came directly from Him. No human being, demon, or angel could have performed such a miracle. Thus the ultimate Divine revelation, the revelation at Sinai, occurred through voice, and the proof that the voice was Divine was demonstrated through breath, through the uttering of all Ten Commandments in a single breath, a feat beyond human capability.

And it's not only the revelation at Sinai, but any miracle that involves G-d's "speech" is known to be of increased significance. The Written Torah describes only miracles foretold in advance by a prophet or by G-d Himself. Other equally miraculous events that were not foretold are transmitted in the Oral Torah, but not included in the Written Torah. Divine revelation is a function of the combination of the miracle and the prophecy that predicted it.

Voice and speech are inseparable from acts of holiness. In the realm of prayer, it is voice that is our vehicle for worshiping Hashem. As it says in *Tehillim* (55:18), "Evening, morning, and midday, I will speak and moan and He hears my voice." *Targum Yonatan* translates this verse as: "In the evening, in the morning, and at midday, I will pray and I will feel and He hears my voice."

Not surprisingly, voice is a key component of Inner Torah work. The vulnerable and adult selves often connect through speaking. By saying the words aloud, we learn more about how we are really feeling. The ease and quality of one's voice reveals as much as, if not more than, the words themselves about the authenticity of the communication. There are ways to pay attention and work with the voice to encourage more natural and genuine expression. Such work is helpful in contacting deeper dimensions of ourselves, coming closer to Hashem, and in interacting with others.

As always, the first step is awareness. As you start to pay attention to your own voice and the voices of the people around you, you can gain access to yet another avenue of self-knowledge. You can begin to differentiate your socially conditioned voice and your true voice that is free of self-consciousness, self-criticism, judgment, and fear. Your voice can become the mouthpiece for your true self, just as Hashem intended.

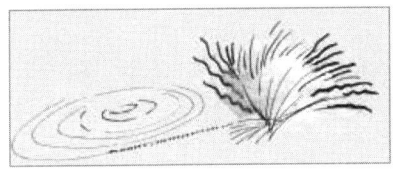

The Anatomy of Voice

The voice passage is essentially a tube that begins at the lips, opens into the mouth, and curves around at the back of the mouth to become the throat. It continues downward to form the larynx or voice box, and then becomes the windpipe that descends into the chest and splits into two tubes, one passing into each lung. The air we breathe travels along this tube in both directions.

In the voice box are the vocal cords, two folds of tissue. When we breathe, the vocal cords are relaxed and air moves through the space between them without making any sound. When we talk or make sound, the vocal cords tighten up and move closer together. Air from the lungs is forced between them, making them vibrate. The sound of the voice is produced by this vibration — the rapid opening and closing of the vocal cords many times per second. The faster the cords vibrate, the higher the sound. The slower the cords vibrate, the lower the sound. This vibration resonates in the voice tube as the air passes up and out of the mouth. It also massages the body from the inside. The tongue, lips, and teeth form the sound into words.

On exhale, the muscles of the abdomen and upper torso contract, the lungs are squeezed, and air is expelled up through the vocal tube. When we use a lot of muscle power to squeeze the lungs empty, the breath travels up the tube under high pressure, causing the vocal cords to vibrate harder and the sound to be louder. When we don't use so much muscle power, the air travels under less pressure and the vocal cords vibrate more softly, producing a quieter sound.

Internal tension in the body is often experienced as a sensation of tightening across the upper chest. This happens because when tension increases, air pressure in the lungs increases. By helping to expel air from the lungs, speech relieves the pressure and relaxes the chest muscles. So when you encourage someone to talk about something that is bothering her — or you let your younger vulnerable self talk about what is bothering her — you are literally helping her to "get it off her chest." Actually, many voice sounds are a natural response to the need to release this pressure. A sigh, a nervous laugh, continuous chatter, sobbing, whistling, humming, moaning, and groaning all lessen internal tension. In many ways, sound is a safety valve for the body.

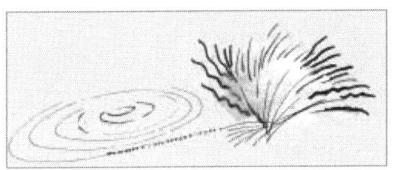

Voice as an Instrument of Soul and Self

The voice is an instrument of the soul capable of expressing the most complex and subtle emotions, moods, and thoughts. It has the power to reveal and conceal. Voice is one of the ways we represent ourselves to the world and one of the mediums through which we know ourselves.

Everyone has his own distinct voice. And everyone is recognizable by his voice. As our Sages have said, "How is a blind man permitted to live with his wife? And how are people permitted to live with their wives at nighttime? Only by vocal recognition" (*Chullin* 96a).

The objective of voice work as an aspect of Inner Torah is a voice in direct contact with emotion, shaped by intellect. As it says in the Gemara, "As my mouth, so is my heart" (*Megillah* 16b). Speech is said to be the pen of the heart. But, as with the breath, we often move away from our authentic voices over the course of life and come to know and express ourselves in distorted ways.

Our voices take on tensions built up over a lifetime, as well as defenses, inhibitions, suspicions, and various negative reactions to external and internal stimuli. Though familiar to us and those around us, our voices are no longer natural, no longer capable of the full range of expression for which they were given to us.

Most people are aware or can easily be made aware when their voices are deadened, disembodied, forced, constricted, flat, shrill, or otherwise not natural, not connected to their hearts. In that way the voice operates as a mirror, helping us to see ourselves more clearly and honestly. A natural voice is transparent — revealing emotions and thoughts directly, not by way of description. It allows the person, not just the person's voice, to be heard.

Shoshana was new to Inner Torah work. At one of her early sessions, she was drawn to spending time with herself ten years earlier when she gave birth to her third child. She had no trouble listening to the younger woman's feelings, to all the difficulties surrounding this birth. And she had no trouble validating the sense of hardship the woman was experiencing. But when her adult self today tried to step in to tell the young woman that now she would be there for her, now she would help her take care of herself in ways she couldn't then, Shoshana heard her voice as flat and hollow. She realized that she didn't mean what she was saying, that she didn't want to be there for that woman, that she didn't really know how to be there for her, and that it all seemed too hard to even begin to bother with. It was the tone and quality of her voice that alerted Shoshana to the insincerity of her words.

Recognizing where she was, Shoshana searched for words

that she could say that would resonate as real, words from her heart. She found herself able to express care for the younger woman and a willingness to start to take her needs into consideration in her life today. She also found herself able to give voice to her concerns about what that would take and whether she had the wherewithal to do it. By continually checking her voice, Shoshana was able to stay in truth with this younger, vulnerable self and not just mouth words that she didn't mean.

In the context of Inner Torah, working with voice is intended to help free one's authentic self. We are looking to contact our natural voices, not to develop a vocal technique. Our focus is on removing blocks that inhibit the voice, not on developing the voice as an instrument. Since the sound of the voice is generated by physical processes, the inner muscles of the body must be free to receive the sensitive impulses from the brain that create speech.

Physical tension obviously blocks and distorts this process, but the natural voice is also impeded by emotional, intellectual, and spiritual blocks. Physical awareness and relaxation can only take us so far without attention as well to thought and feeling. It's important to attend to all of these dimensions when working to free the voice. As obstacles are removed the voice is increasingly able to communicate genuinely.

Ultimately, working on the voice is in the interest of the truth that voice has the ability to express. As we've noted before, G-d's stamp is *emet*, truth. When we speak truth, we link our intellect, our Higher Soul self, with our actions. This is what G-d did when He created the world through speech, and this is how He sustains the world as well. We recognize this in our daily prayers when we say: "*Baruch she'amar v'hayah ha'olam,*" Blessed is He who spoke, and the world came into being – "*Baruch omer v'oseh,*" Blessed is He who speaks and does.

The Breath and Body of Inner Torah

G-d's actions are linked to His Divine plan through speech, true speech. We can emulate G-d by likewise linking our actions to the Divine soul within us through the power of true speech. The great Chassidic master, the Ba'al Shem Tov, explains: Just as Noach was instructed to "go into the ark," and the Hebrew word for ark (תבה) also means "a word," so we too must "go into" our words and invest our whole selves in every word that we utter. If we do, all the powers of the soul can shine and energize from within our words.

In contrast, if we speak falsely, we separate our *neshamah* from our actions, taking ourselves out of the spiritual realm. This has great significance for Inner Torah work. It reminds us that beyond whatever physical interventions are suggested here, clear thinking and honest expression are essential to freeing the voice and enabling it to be used as the holy instrument it was intended to be. Muddy thinking is a major obstacle to clear expression, as is trying to hedge what we say to mask the true message. When we think clearly and are genuinely committed to what we are saying, there is resonance and an enhancement of energy — the soul is engaged. Anything less causes dissonance, dissipation of energy, and sends the soul into hiding.

In this context, blocked emotions can be a major obstacle to a free voice. If we are willing to acknowledge our true feelings to ourselves, and when appropriate to others, the voice is not forced to hold unnecessary tension and can be used freely. When speech is not in alignment with the inner self, the resonance and energy is diminished. As long as we are emotionally protective or dishonest, our voices cannot be free, cannot be used in service of Hashem as intended.

In Inner Torah work, this means being careful in your adult self's speech to know what you are trying to say and to express yourself clearly. It also means listening carefully to your

Voice as an Instrument of Soul and Self

younger self, paying attention to both her voice and her words. Be on the lookout with both your adult and younger selves for exaggerations, dramatic statements, and other generalizations that in all likelihood don't accurately reflect reality. Also be alert to changes in tone, pitch, speed, inflection, and other aspects of voice that can signal another layer to what is being said or alert you to the likelihood that the speaker is not really connected to her words. Remember that words have no meaning independent of the sentiment behind them.

Chani had a challenging life. She had a big family, a lot of responsibility, and limited resources. When she talked about her situation, her voice carried an underlying tone of resentment. It would take on a sing-song cadence, something in the nature of a whine, as she went over the litany of things she had to do on any given day. More than her words, the tone of her voice seemed to be communicating volumes. When I brought it to her attention, she knew right away to what I was referring. Though not directly conscious of her inflection, she was familiar with that posture and recognized it as a stance she had taken for much of her life.

I asked her to try to engage with the part of herself that was behind that tone in her voice. Very quickly she discovered a little girl who was very angry, who felt life wasn't fair, who wanted somebody to take care of her, who felt put upon, burdened, and resentful. From talking to her, adult Chani could see that this little girl was still very much present today and, in some ways, sabotaging her life. She saw that a lot of the little girl's feelings were justified at the time and needed to be acknowledged and validated. She also saw that she had to explain to the little girl the difference between "then" and "now."

"Then" the little girl had to bear the unfair burden of doing more than her share in her parents' home and being privy to problems that were too much for a little girl. "Now" her responsibilities revolved around her own home and family and were age appropriate. Yet her nervous system was hanging on through her voice to a sense of injustice, unfairness, and resentment.

Once she made the connection and internalized the distinction, Chani felt a sense of relief. That old, outdated attitude had been wearing her down even more than the actual things she had to do. Her voice then became her barometer of whether she was really living her life in the present or had unconsciously slipped back into the past.

Emotional holding creates tension. This tension, to a greater or lesser degree, often settles in the back of the neck, tongue, jaw, and throat. As long as tension exists in such a vital part of the vocal channel, vibrations are trapped in contracted muscles. The vibrations are released by undoing the tension. In his commentary on *Va'eira* 6:9, the Kli Yakar observes that the distress of the Israelites not only shortened their breath as noted earlier, but actually prevented them from speaking out a response to Moshe Rabbeinu as they should have.

In Inner Torah work, the inability to utter a sound, to get out the words one would like to say, is its own sign of deeper issues that need to be addressed. We're not talking here about being rendered speechless by surprise or fright, which may be wholly understandable in the moment. Rather, we're talking about thoughts and feelings that one can access within but cannot physically bring forth. Often people are stunned to find that words actually get stuck in their throats. At best, they may be able to get out a faint whisper. Often even that is not possible. They are literally mute, unable to give voice to their deepest sentiments. When this happens, it is important to go slowly and allow whatever small expression of feeling is possible, without trying to force speech.

Voice as an Instrument of Soul and Self

Many people were silenced early in life, not allowed to give expression to feelings and thoughts that made others uncomfortable. Holding back expression, including to ourselves, can soon become habitual, so that by the time we are adults we don't even realize how limited our range of expression has become. Invitation and permission to express must be given to these younger aspects of the self by the adult self today in order for the earlier conditioning to be released.

Dvora felt her younger self weighing in with objections every time she had to make arrangements with her in-laws. She felt part of herself digging in her heels and not wanting to go along with whatever was being planned. But when she tried to connect with that part of herself and find out what was bothering her, the little girl would only say, "I don't wanna." At first Dvora didn't know what to do. Then she realized that she had to convince the little girl that she was finally free to speak her mind. She didn't have to protect anyone else's feelings, or worry about anyone getting mad at her, or feel like she was doing something wrong.

For the first time, it was safe for this little girl to say aloud what she was really feeling and thinking. When Dvora tried explaining all this to her younger self, the little girl didn't trust it; it had never been her experience in the past. Understanding this, Dvora told her that she realized that it would be a new experience, so maybe it would be helpful to open up just a little bit at a time so she could see for herself that it was now okay. The little girl liked that idea and slowly started to say more about what was hard for her. When she felt Dvora listening attentively and genuinely being concerned about what was bothering her, the little girl relaxed and began to trust that she really could say what she felt. Dvora now had access to a whole other part of herself.

With voice, the goal is to allow sound without forcing it.

The more deeply we can touch ourselves inside, the more deeply we can touch others with our voice and our presence. Going deeply in is what enables us to go deeply out, to bring what is in our interior space out into expression. Plumbing our depths stimulates our growth.

From deep inside ourselves we can be authentic for others. To touch another heart with our voices, we need to be able to touch our own. "As water reflects what faces it, so does the heart of one person reflect another" (*Mishlei* 27:19). From deep inside ourselves, we can also come closer to Hashem. It says in *Tehillim* (27:8), "Look for My inner dimension." By reaching the inner level of our own hearts, the deep inner truth of our own being, we are better able to address and reach the inner dimension of G-d.

The key to working with voice is interest in knowing the self and communicating with others, including Hashem. Sound itself consists of waves that have no effect until someone receives their resonance. Voice clearly is intended to be a vehicle of communication.

Liora spoke in a soft, tired-sounding voice most of the time. Regardless of the content of what she said, the strongest message that seemed to come through was one of defeat. There were many times when she didn't even bother to say anything, feeling that it would take too much energy to get the words out or that they wouldn't make a difference anyway. Yet there were occasions where, to her surprise, she would suddenly find herself invigorated and speaking quite clearly and sincerely about something.

She had never given the matter much thought until she started doing voice work in her Inner Torah sessions. As she paid more attention to herself in the realm of voice, she noticed these two distinct ways of speaking. Her feeling was that they were completely separate from each other. Now and then she would simply find herself speaking in the freer and easier voice that wasn't hampered by the tremendous inhibitions that normally limited her. With her increased awareness, she discovered that at those times she was usually most clear about what she wanted to say and cared more than usual about the subject matter. But she couldn't sense how it happened, what actually propelled her out of her habitual way of speaking into this freer mode. It seemed to occur without any conscious involvement from her; it wasn't a matter of choice.

Still, most of the time, Liora could barely bring herself to speak. In classes, at social functions, even sometimes at her own Shabbos table when there were guests, Liora would remain silent. If she did speak, it was usually in her tired, defeated voice that didn't stimulate much of a response, or at least the level of response she wanted. Slowly Liora began to understand that her inability to effectively communicate what was inside of her was keeping her trapped in a way of being that was wearing her down. She was so burdened with all that had remained unspoken throughout her life that she could hardly bear the weight any longer.

Realizing that the way out was through speaking, Liora directed her Inner Torah efforts toward finding the younger, vulnerable parts of her that long ago had been silenced. She spent time exploring the shame, the self-consciousness, the feelings of exposure, the sense of powerlessness, and the discomfort that these parts of herself associated with speaking. In the process, she discovered a barrier inside her between her normal speech pattern and the freer speech she occasionally experienced. The image she saw was of a real, physical blockade, and she began to investigate it to see just what it was.

The work took her to interesting places in her past, things she had long forgotten. It was like assembling a puzzle. Piece by piece, she started to see how her speaking habits had developed and was able to send her nervous system new messages that encouraged and supported her speech and ameliorated the shame and self-consciousness. She made clear to her younger, vulnerable selves that whatever had happened in the past, the meaningful adult in their life today — Liora in the present — wanted to hear what they had to say and would patiently wait for them to formulate their thoughts and get the words out. She would also help them to navigate the feelings of shyness and insecurity that sometimes contributed to their reluctance to speak up.

In this way, Liora was able to slowly dissolve the barrier and begin to choose when and how she wished to communicate. As her voice grew stronger, clearer, more resonant, and made a greater impact than before, she felt lighter and happier than ever.

Voice also plays an important role in the realm of conflict, stress, and challenges. Speech is often the medium we use to relate in these circumstances. We let ourselves and others know if we are agreeing, adapting, acquiescing, resisting, or defending; our stance in relation to whatever is happening is communicated, among other ways, through our words. What is desired is to maintain inner balance, to let in what is happening, and to be able to respond genuinely and appropriately.

If we adapt or acquiesce for too long, or stay too long in a blocked position, we often will end up using our voices to explode out in an attempt to be free. This not only fails to accomplish the desired freeing, but often leaves people feeling bad about themselves. Many women speak of this phenomenon in relation to their children, who they often regret exploding at, and in relation to their husbands, who they likewise would prefer to interact with in a more even-keel way.

To avoid this, one needs to adapt or acquiesce to a point — at least long enough to let in what is happening or being said, as a way of receiving information — and then find an authentic way to gently introduce her own energy. That energy will often be expressed through voice, through what she chooses to say. This doesn't mean getting defensive. Defending is hard and blocks what is coming in, instead of trusting that you can allow the other person's reality to be received and still respond with your own.

Essentially this gives you a chance to find yourself in the context of the challenge, conflict, or stress with which you are engaging. You're using the difficulty to give you mobility and awaken you to possibilities you otherwise might not have thought about.

To work in this way, it helps to remember that no matter how difficult or distressing the situation is, there is a part of you that is separate, intact, and able to handle whatever is going on. In Inner Torah terms, the part that is caught up in the challenge or conflict is the younger, vulnerable part and the freer part is the adult self who always has options, resources, and a direction in which to create movement, however small it might be.

The adult self can speak to the vulnerable self and remind her that what is happening is not the totality of her reality, that today there is a meaningful adult in her life who can be sensitive to her needs and help her deal constructively with the problem. Through dialogue between the adult and vulnerable self, this right balance between self and other can be achieved, and a sense of centeredness can be maintained. The key is to take responsibility for what you need at any moment.

Bracha had a tendency to tighten up whenever her husband started talking about things that were hard for her to hear. Sometimes it was current events, sometimes family issues, sometimes finances. She could literally feel her chest constrict, and in a sharp, hard voice she would cut him off. This would make him angry, and before they knew it they would be in a fight. Bracha decided to try working with her breath and voice in an effort to open up some space inside herself in these charged moments with her husband.

The first thing she did was to shift her attention to her own breath cycle when her husband started to talk about a topic that was difficult for her. As he talked, she noticed that she virtually stopped breathing. So she focused on her exhale and encouraged herself to allow a full breath to leave her body. Then she relaxed into the pause that followed and allowed her body to take another breath on its own.

In the time it took her to be with her breath in this way, her husband had said more than she usually let him say. She noticed that his words hadn't hit her as hard when she was breathing more naturally. She continued paying attention to her breath as he continued talking. She found herself more able to hear what he was saying, which, in and of itself, was an accomplishment. Her husband was happy to at least be able to complete his thought.

Next Bracha wanted to work on finding a way to respond. She still disagreed vehemently with his opinions and his generally negative way of viewing the world. She reminded herself that his outlook didn't have to define hers. She was still a person in her own right, entitled to her own views.

Rather than trying to use her voice to block or refute what her husband said, she decided to use it to express her perspective on the subject. She realized that these conversations could give her practice in staying with herself while interacting with her husband. They were very different from each other, and Bracha had always feared being overwhelmed by him. The threatened part of her had responded to his words by holding her breath and lashing out. By staying in her breath rhythm and encouraging herself to find her voice, Bracha increased her ability to stay with herself — which actually increased her ability to stay with her husband even in difficult conversations.

Once she had achieved greater ease conversing with her husband, Bracha used the Inner Torah process to look more closely at the root of her reactivity to her husband's views. From the more relaxed and open space inside herself that breath and voice work had carved out, Bracha was able to connect with herself as a young girl being overpowered by her parents' opinions. Not being allowed to express disagreement with them, young Bracha had learned to tense up and shut down when they said things she didn't like.

Once Bracha connected with her, this little girl actually had a lot to say on many different subjects. Bracha was amazed at how spirited and opinionated the little girl was. Before long, her conversations with her husband, that once had ended before they started, became lively and animated. They even started to appreciate each other's perspectives and learn from them.

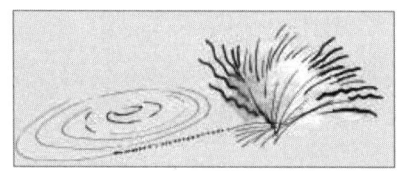

The Healing Capacity of Voice

The voice has a tremendous ability to be an instrument for healing. Every cell in our body is a sound resonator with the capacity to respond to any sound outside of it. That's one reason many people can't stand racket. A sound we don't really listen to, or don't want to listen to, can bombard our bodies and spirits. Sound is a real presence that passes through us. It can affect us in many ways, both positive and negative.

As a bio-electrical system, the human body can be altered, strengthened, and/or balanced through the use of sound. This occurs through resonance. With the voice we can stimulate sympathetic vibrations within our bodies and minds. Where there is imbalance, we can use sound resonance to restore balance. Where there is weakness, we can use sound to strengthen. Where there is a blockage, sound can help to dissolve it.

Each vowel sound and each musical tone can reach a particular part of the body. Sound is essentially audible breath. Most people are able to feel tones in specific places, but not everyone feels the same tones in the same areas. Each person's physical build is different and tones that, for example, would vibrate a thin person's belly would not necessarily vibrate a heavier person's belly because the belly's mass and density are different in each person. You can explore using different tones to see where in your body you feel the vibration.

The effect is enhanced if the sound is first related to within, so that there is literally an inner sounding before there is an outer one. This is done by silently sounding a vowel or note internally on the inhale and audibly sounding it on the exhale. The inner sounding vibrates the energy body just as sound vibrates the physical body. It's important when doing this to let the breath and sound have their own life without pushing until you are empty.

We can focus our awareness on particular places in our bodies to amplify the ability of the sound and vibration to travel there. If you feel you are forcing your voice, find more space inside yourself and make your voice smaller. The focus inside yourself, once you've sensed the forcing, can often correct it. If you allow whatever sound you make to originate from your inner self and are not concerned with what comes out, you're less likely to push your voice. This is important when tapping into the healing capacity of sound and the capacity of sound to connect you to your true self.

Meira would start to get anxious in the early afternoon before all of her children came home. She felt the pressure of the bedlam that was about to descend, of all the needs that would be addressed to her, of all the responsibilities to be discharged before the children would once again be tucked in their beds. She experienced the tension mostly around her solar plexus and sensed it would take time to get to the root of it. In the meantime, she wanted to do something to help herself be in a better place when her children came home.

Having learned a little bit about breath and voice, Meira decided to try humming into the tension. She experimented with different pitches and volumes to see what sound best penetrated her body. She noticed that when she hummed, her exhale was longer, which helped her to breathe more fully. The experiment itself was fun for her. Before long she found herself singing, not just humming, the tones. It brought back memories of when she was little and liked very much to hum and sing to herself. She even remembered her first-grade teacher punishing her for humming in class.

Meira noticed that the sound eased tension in her body. She started to feel a little more relaxed, and it no longer seemed so daunting to her to go inside and find out more about why she got so tense in the first place. She also felt like she now had a little insurance. Even if she tensed up in anticipation of her children coming home, she could "treat" herself with the sound of her own voice. It felt like a sweet way to take care of herself. She also tried humming and singing more with her children, several of whom really liked it. The atmosphere of the house in the afternoon began to lighten — and Meira relaxed even more.

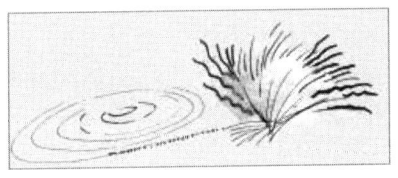

Song of the Soul

"There are chambers in heaven that can only be opened through song" (*Zohar*, part I, *Parashat Chayei Sarah*; *Tikkunei Zohar*, *tikkun* 12). If words are the pen of the heart, taught Rabbi Schneur Zalman of Liadi, the Ba'al HaTanya, then song is the pen of the soul. Melody has the power to bring forth the essence of what is within one's soul. In the Kabbalistic/Chassidic realms, melody of this type is called a *niggun* – a song, generally without words, considered to be a path to higher consciousness and transformation of being. A *niggun* is a direct expression of the innermost reaches of the soul of the one who composes it.

Like sound, song can affect people both negatively and positively. If composed and sung by holy people for holy intentions, it can raise one up to great spiritual heights. If composed and sung by unholy people, people who imbue it with selfish, unholy intentions, it can draw one down to low levels. The Ramban calls music the most refined and delicate of all physical expressions (*Torat Ha'adam, Sha'ar Hagmul*).

With its power to express the inner dimensions of the soul, one's innermost emotions, song plays a vital role in the process of coming to know one's essence and connecting to Hashem from there. Each soul is connected to and inspired by its own unique song. In the context of Inner Torah work song takes us into the level of *sod* and the category of Divinity described in *Inner Torah* (pp. 55–58 and 109–119).

Through song, we can uplift ourselves. We can elevate our actions. We can draw close to Hashem even as we are involved in our daily tasks. Many of us have observed this phenomenon when we've witnessed a deeply religious person going about a seemingly menial task with a song on her lips. The sound can even pull those around her to a higher level if it emanates from a pure and holy place within her.

This is something we are all capable of doing. It has nothing to do with the quality of one's voice. It is instead dependent on the intensity of our desire to connect with Hashem, to cleave to Him. With our yearning we can transform our voices into spiritual chariots, carrying us ever closer to Him.

Song can also bring us closer to ourselves and to other people. When truly engaged in song from a deep and real place inside, we lose much of our self-consciousness and are far more able to be present to the essence of who we really are. We get a peek at the true core of our beings. And when we sing together with others, we join and unite with them; we connect from within.

That is one of the reasons that mothers so often sing to their babies. It is an expression of a deep, eternal bond. This connection through song is valuable as well for older children. The chance to merge their voices with the voices of their parents is a chance to connect in ways that go well beyond words. Children, with their still heightened sensitivity, intuitively know this and usually can be easily engaged in a musical interlude.

Infants and children, as well as adults, are responsive to song for its soothing qualities as well. It is said that because our souls are accustomed to hearing the singing of the heavenly angels above, they are likewise responsive to the sound of song below. Song is a way to bring ourselves and those close to us to a place of deep soul relaxation. From there it is easier to elevate oneself and open one's mind to G-dly thoughts at whatever level one has access.

Song can also help crystallize thoughts that one is having difficulty putting into words. Sometimes we feel like we know something that we can't yet find the language to express. By allowing the still unformed but very real impression in the mind to be joined with song, we facilitate its descent into a form that can be more easily articulated and shared.

Through song we can shift ourselves from one state to another, from tension to ease, from sadness to joy, from frivolous to serious, from distracted to focused. It is as though we can reach inside ourselves with our voices and gently invite our beings to move. With the energy generated by such a shift, we can, if we want, use the Inner Torah process to explore what triggered our tension or sadness in the first place.

Sound and song can easily work together, unearthing the motivation and wherewithal to take the next step in one's growth. For growth and movement define life. With song — which awakens the G-dly soul within us — we can remind ourselves that whatever is happening is from Hashem. This right away puts the event in a positive perspective and allows us to engage it, even with all its difficulty, from an optimistic place.

Eventually, as King David tells us, all the world will sing a new song, and the Oneness that is G-d will permeate every corner of the world (*Tehillim* 149). In the meantime, it is our job to be holy and spiritual while living our lives in the physical world. Song can help us immensely to draw G-dliness into our earthly reality — to avoid being negatively affected by this world while doing our part to affect it positively.

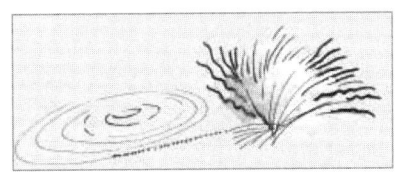

EXPLORATIONS

As you are doing these explorations, allow yourself to enjoy being present to what you are doing and to trust that you are okay as you are. You don't have to work, just to experience. Remember also that sound and speech themselves do not translate to presence, to really being with what you are doing instead of just going through the motions. Try not to get carried away by the practices but to stay focused on the quality of your presence. The explorations are intended to serve as bridges to enter inside yourself and to bring you closer to Hashem.

1. Voice Awareness

a. Observe whatever you can about your voice. How would you describe it? Notice the pitch, volume, resonance, quality, and anything else you can. Watch whether, and how, your voice changes in different circumstances and with different people. Notice whether, and when, you feel connected to your voice. Does your voice adequately convey what you are trying to express? Are there times when you find it hard, or even impossible, to speak?

b. Become aware of the voices of others. Notice what you can about them as well and see if, at times, you need to respond not only to the content of what is being said but also to the underlying message conveyed by the voice.

2. Authentic Speech

a. Try speaking aloud to yourself, paying attention to where you are speaking from inside yourself. Try to access a place that is deeper and more connected to you than you normally speak from. Slow your speech down however much you need to in order to maintain a sense of inner connection to your words. Make sure that you genuinely mean what you're saying.

b. Try to do the same thing in *hitbodedut*, when you're talking to Hashem in your own words. Notice any differences in your experience when you consciously focus on how you are speaking, not just what you are saying.

c. Try to do the same thing in conversation with another. Notice if you feel more of a sense of rapport or resonance with the person you're talking to when speaking from this more connected place within yourself. See if the feeling of the conversation goes beyond the words.

Also pay attention in conversation with another when you are defensive or feel a need to keep repeating or excessively describing what you are trying to say. Notice what happens to the resonance with yourself and with the other person when you do this. Compare this experience to one in which you stay connected to yourself while speaking.

3. Sounding Vowels

Using the vowels — a, e, i, o, u — silently sound each vowel internally on inhale and audibly on exhale. Experiment with different pitches and volume. Don't force the sound to extend beyond your natural breath.

After several minutes, stop and notice any sensations, no matter how faint, resulting from this activity. Try to avoid a habitual response and see if you can notice anything different or new. Let your lens of awareness expand. Then resume sounding.

4. Sounding Emotions through Vowels

Connect the vowel sounds with different emotions so that the sound is expressing a particular feeling. Again, work with the sound silently on the inhale and make it audible on the exhale. And again, give yourself time in between soundings to register your response.

5. Sound and Body

a. Stand back to back with a partner sounding mmm. Let your teeth be gently apart and sense your partner. With your backs touching see if it's easier to wake up your back and speak from there.

b. Combine sensing your back with making different sounds. Then put your hand on your breastbone and sound mmm. Make sound in your inner self. Don't be concerned with the outside so you don't push your voice.

6. Releasing Tension with Speech and Sound

When you start to tense and feel your chest tightening, try speaking to yourself or otherwise allowing yourself to use sound to release the tension. Notice if your chest muscles relax and the tension eases when you do this.

7. Humming

Hum the musical scale – do, re, mi, fa, sol, la, ti, do. Humming helps to extend the exhale, nurturing and calming the nervous system in the process. It also provides a natural massage for the vocal folds. You can also try singing the scale, focusing on maintaining connection with your inner world as you sing. Try not to force the sound; rather let it flow out of you and express whatever you are feeling.

8. Feeling the Vibrations of Sound

Again using vowels to makes different sounds, this time pay attention to where you feel the vibration in your body. Imagine a cave in your torso, head, and mouth as you make sound.

    A – ay (hay); a (cat); aw (saw)
    I – i (eye); ih (bit)
    E – ee (see); eh
    O – oh (note); ah (cot)
    U – oo (boot); uh (but)

Try sounding the vowels in the following order:
    Eee (as in wheel)
    Ih (as in interest)

Eh (as in whether)
A (as in absolute)
Ah (as in father)
Aw (as in awe)
Oh (as in smoke)
Ooo (as in smooth)

Then try reversing the order.

9. Healing with Sound

Focus on an area of your body that you feel needs attention. Inhale slowly, sounding a tone silently and envisioning that area of your body. Exhale slowly, audibly toning the sound, still focusing your mind on the part of your body you are trying to reach. Tone in whatever way is best for you in terms of length, volume, pitch, etc. Try to keep the inner and outer toning of equal length. Pay attention to your voice as you tone. If your voice cracks or fluctuates repeat the toning until your voice becomes smooth. That is one indication that you are coming into balance. Your voice, in essence, is giving you feedback as you use it as an instrument of healing.

10. Singing

a. Sit quietly and when a single tone comes to mind, sing it within. Go into and around the tone, playing with it inside. If and when you feel drawn to sing aloud, allow it to surface. Explore the tone by varying its timbre with different vowel sounds and by varying the volume. Gradually allow the tone to return inside. Hold it as long as feels right and then allow it to fade gently.

b. Find a pasuk in *Tehillim* that speaks to you and try singing it to your own melody. Notice how your singing affects you. Experiment with different tunes and different *pasukim*. Also experiment with singing as you go about different tasks and again be aware of how you are affected.

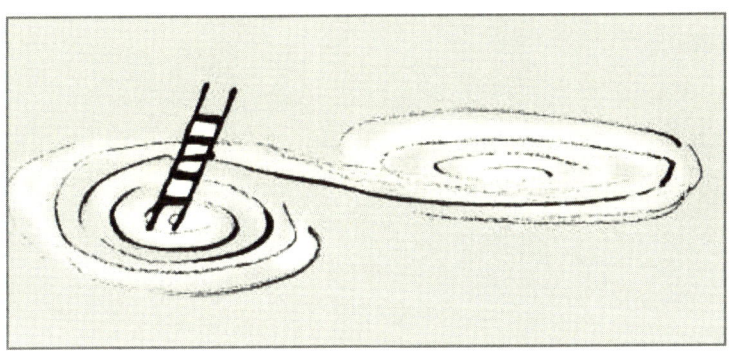

The Body

Portal to the Heart and Mind, Home of the Soul

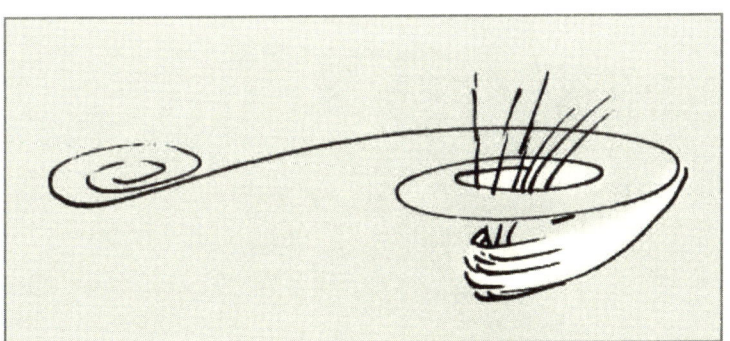

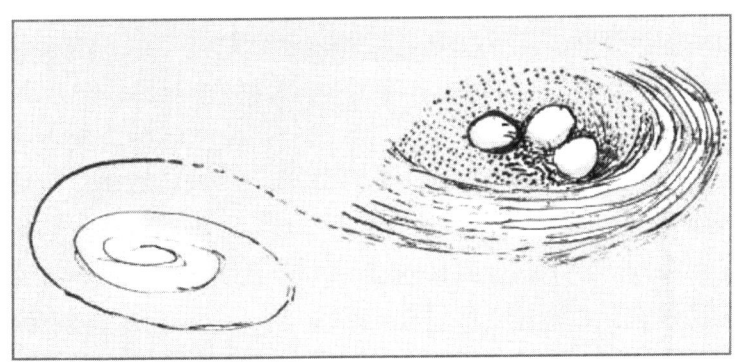

Softening and Opening the Heart

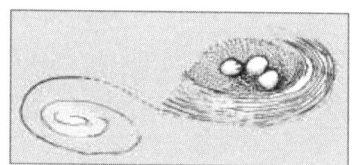

Softening and Opening the Heart

From the Preface to Practical Inner Torah: *"It's important to remember that the invitation to become more self-reflective and internal needs to be extended lovingly and without pressure. This is true for women with themselves and even more so with their husbands. Most people's more vulnerable selves need to feel that there is a loving, caring, and patient presence waiting to receive them."*

Here then is the first place we can enlist the body to help us in our inner work. The body is a good gauge of whether we are truly in a loving, caring and patient place — whether we are soft and open-hearted or hard, cold, and rigid. Key body parts to focus on in this regard are the eyes, the chest, and the belly. Armoring is easily recognizable in each of these places. If any of these areas are rigid with holding, there is likely to be fear, self-protection, and distrust — all of which get in the way of maintaining a loving, patient presence.

This hard stance is held in place by muscular tension that maintains the barriers we unconsciously erect between ourselves and others, as well as with ourselves. Often what lies beneath is a feeling, sometimes deeply hidden, that our genuine and authentic selves are unacceptable. When we are aware of it, the hardness can actually remind us to soften the body, to let go into openness. Softening the body creates more room, more space around whatever we are trying to reach in ourselves. It makes it more likely that a hidden vulnerability will make itself known to us and that our adult self will be able to hold and be responsive to whatever is revealed.

With consciousness, we can learn to relax and soften our muscles, tissue, and flesh. We can slowly loosen our grip, our clamp on our seeing and feeling. As we do, we can feel ourselves relaxing into our bodies, letting go of the need to be vigilant, to control what happens next. We can feel more comfortable going slowly, letting our vulnerable selves have the time needed to experience what is happening in the moment and to communicate those experiences to us.

For some of us, this may be new and unfamiliar. Even as babies, we may have been hurried and prodded — encouraged to do things and develop at a rate other than our own. The very sensitive process of growth that is so very individualistic may have been overridden by parental demands to perform and accomplish and progress. And we may have succumbed to the pressure, tensing and tightening before we even knew any other way. Only now, in the present, may we be able to offer ourselves a different environment, a softer, gentler space in which to be with what is and move from there.

In softness, the path between the heart and the mind is

more open. We are able to speak and reach out to ourselves (and, hopefully, others) from a different place, a place that is more accepting, more caring, more willing to be with whatever is, without needing to change it by force or will. "A heart that listens," as King Solomon called it (*Melachim* I 3:9), is an indicator of great spiritual development and maturity. It is not a momentary occurrence, some sort of altered state to be achieved by esoteric practices. Rather it is the result of years and even lifetimes of work to let go of any aspects of personality that inhibit access to the attribute of Divine love that is the soul's true essence.

A listening heart is not bogged down with its own unresolved emotional issues; it is not holding on to anger. Halachah includes a vast body of law that governs this realm of matters of the heart, in the laws of *bein adam l'chaveiro* ("between man and his friend"). It recognizes that it takes consciousness and work for us to keep our hearts clean and open.[*] Mussar teachings and Chassidut reinforce the importance of doing this type of spiritual work and offer various ways to go about it. Ultimately, the truly understanding heart is the heart that knows and desires to return to G-d. "And his heart shall understand, and he shall return and be healed" (*Yeshayahu* 6:10).

Softness helps us to move from *katnut* (small self) to this place of *gadlut* (big self) where we're able to be other-focused and G-d-focused from the vantage point of the developed self. Softness is a signal the body sends to the mind, reminding it of the vastness of the soul, which is too big to be comprehended even by the greatest intellect. Left to its own devices, the mind can easily fall into old habits of contracting in fear and distrust,

---

[*] For help understanding the laws of *bein adam l'chaveiro*, see *To Live Among Friends: Laws and Ethics of Everyday Interactions*, by Rabbi Dovid Castle (Feldheim, 2007).

of hiding and posturing, of desperately trying to "know," and of asserting inappropriate control.

With the reminder of softening though, the mind remembers that in reality it is safe, that it is okay to "not know" and to learn from whatever is happening in the moment. There is a feeling of enormous relief that in turn invites the vulnerable self to go even further into her truth. For truth lies deep within us and is often in conflict with our outer desires. By softening we help ourselves go beyond surface tensions and come closer to the truth that resides at the core of our beings.

When exploring a reaction that is too charged, softening the body can help us remember that there is no need to try to figure things out. It can signal us instead to be with the unknown, to wonder aloud as to what might be happening, and to gently probe through questions and observations. The mindset is one of exploration, of discovering together with our vulnerable self what might be at the root of a disproportionate reaction or response. There needs to be a sense of trust that there is something real underlying the feeling, something that once accessed can be released and free us from the grip of sensations too intense for the moment.

Remember that we can trust the process that is unfolding without trying to force it in a particular direction. Forcing is a sign that we are attempting to exert unnecessary control, trying to overpower ourselves or the situation in some way. Among other things, this can reflect a lack of *emunah* (faith) that all is from Hashem and that ultimately only He has control. And a lack of bitachon (trust) that everything Hashem does is for the good, that our well-being is inherent in Creation and we don't need to push to realize it.

In such cases, it helps to remind ourselves that we are born into an ever-changing reality; that our role is to do what Hashem asks of us as best we can. We need only take the next tiny step in front of us, utter the next word that feels in rightness and integrity — and trust that from there the next and the next and the next will make themselves known.

This requires an enormous willingness to be with "not knowing," to resist the impulse to put words in the mouth of a younger vulnerable self (or another), to make our adult self the expert in her inner world. That tests the adult self's patience and perhaps sense of self, which may rest on an inflated sense of importance. The counter to that is cultivating an ongoing place of curiosity, of fascination with the opportunity to view, even slightly, the workings of a younger self's (or another's) heart, mind, and soul. This inner terrain is territory that we may only know superficially or perhaps not at all.

To convey such interest in the person and trust in her process, you need to be patient, to not feel a need to rush to "results." Remind yourself as often as needed that the process is organic, something that will unfold when and how the nervous system deems appropriate. You can start from wherever you truly are and move from there. There is no right place to begin or to end, only what is real for you, what you are able to touch in yourself.

All that is necessary when interacting with your younger vulnerable self (and another) is your presence, your true nature. From there, the adult self may offer thoughts and possibilities, but only from an open-handed place that presents what could be as an offering that the younger vulnerable self (or another) is as free to reject as to accept.

Imagine your words resting gently on the palm of your hand, held out to your younger self (or another) with love and without expectation. If there is any sense of thrusting, of demanding

Softening and Opening the Heart

that the younger self (or another) take in what you say, then it doesn't serve anyone's interest. This type of forcing is often a subtle way of exerting power to avoid the discomfort of feeling powerless. Trying quietly to overpower or dis-empower in this way is usually just an attempt to help ourselves feel a little more real or secure.

It takes time to develop this level of trust within ourselves and of Hashem. It requires getting to know, on deeper and deeper levels, our fears, our feelings of helplessness and bewilderment, and the ways we are conditioned to react to endless change and all the other things in this world that truly are beyond our control. It also requires a willingness to acknowledge what's already there, to appreciate that which exists and is good in the present. Such appreciation of what is, even in the face of much that is a matter of concern, is a bridge to greater softness and satisfaction. From a soft body, it's easier to hold our fears, feelings, and self-observations lightly in our own hearts. And it's easier to be attuned and sensitive to someone else.

The body also helps us resist the temptation to exert unnecessary control by tightening up when we head in that direction. If you pay close attention at that moment, you'll probably also feel a slight closing of the heart to your younger self and, perhaps, also to your adult self or to another. That's your cue that you're overstepping your place, wading further into the domain of the younger self (or another) than you need to go to be truly helpful. It is a reminder to soften, to relax your inner grip. From this more open place it's easier to observe these impulses to control without succumbing to them. For it's not that we become totally free of these inclinations, just that we increase our capacity not to act on them with ourselves and others.

Sarah was having problems with her oldest son. Unlike with her other children, everything seemed to be an issue with him.

He reacted negatively to just about any intervention from her. Inner Torah work took her back to the boy's premature birth. It had been a fearful, confusing time for the twenty-one-year-old new mother. When now thirty-year-old Sarah went back to be with her she was instantly overwhelmed by the young woman's distress and quickly started to try to convince her that her fears were unfounded, that the boy would survive and be okay.

As she was speaking, Sarah could feel the forcing quality of her words and took a moment to notice what was happening in her body. Realizing that her adult self was tense and tight, she reminded herself to soften her body, to let go of the holding, and just let in whatever this scared new mother needed to talk about.

Sure enough, once there was space, the young woman started to open up about not feeling connected to this baby, being so afraid he might die or be brain damaged that she didn't even feel him as her son. She also expressed worry about what, if anything, she could do for him in his fragile state. It wasn't easy for adult Sarah to stay in a soft, open place and hear all this. In some ways, this young woman was saying things that, to some degree, adult Sarah still felt the residue of today. Consciously focusing on staying soft and relaxed in her body helped her make more room for the young woman's words, opening the way for healing and for forging a different level of connection with her son.

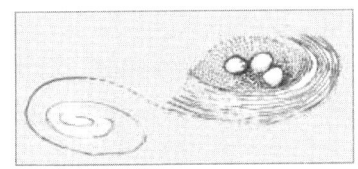

EXPLORATIONS

Working with these explorations will increase your ability to notice your body's stance and to shift it in challenging moments. The bodily shift can in turn invite a different level of response to your younger vulnerable self and to others.

As you practice these body-softening and heart-opening skills, be kind to yourself and try to be understanding of the patterns that persist until they are ready to offer up their roots to you. Practicing is itself a practice — the whole contained in each part just as the Torah teaches us.

1. Muscle Relaxation

Lie on your back on a firm surface. Tighten muscles in your hands, arms, and shoulders and notice the tension. Let half of the tension out and notice what that feels like. Then slowly relax the muscles until the tension is gone, and again allow yourself to feel. See if there are any additional muscle fibers that can be relaxed by inviting the body to let go more. Notice the contrast between the feelings of tension and relaxation.

Next do the same with your neck and face, then your chest and stomach, then your buttocks, thighs, and calves, then your feet. You can tense and relax each body part separately or work with them in groupings.

2. Softening Practice

Using the same sequence of body parts listed in exploration 1 above, and starting from the place of your normal level of holding (as opposed to tensing), imagine each area softening and melting like butter. Experience the sense of relaxation in your body and allow it to penetrate even deeper.

3. Body Scan

Scan your entire body from your head to your feet. Notice any areas where you are holding tension and bring your awareness there. Gently concentrate on that area until you feel the tension releasing. You can also place your hand on the area at the same time.

Next, recognizing that the body is made up of mostly water, bring your attention deeper into your body to the fluid system — the blood, cerebral spinal fluid, cellular fluid, synovial fluid — the liquid body. Sense the spaces between cells and the flow of fluid across membranes. Allow yourself to float in this vast sea. Notice how you feel.

Now bring your awareness to your body as a whole, feeling the relationship and connection of the parts to one another.

4. Softness Scale

Imagine a scale from 0 to 100 with 100 representing the greatest amount of rigidity and hardness and 0 the least, or greatest softness. See where on the scale you register. Concentrate on lowering the number and see how far it drops. After a moment, lower it again. Continue lowering it as far as you can.

5. Imaging Softness

Pay attention to what happens to your body in the presence of different people — when you feel ease or tension, and where. Imagine staying soft and serene in the face of someone who is a source of tension for you. Notice the feelings that arise. Breathe into the feelings, making space for them without tightening up around them. Imagine interacting with that person from a soft place, continuing to stay with and breathe into whatever sensations and feelings come up.

You can do this with any difficult situation you anticipate encountering. Under stress, your nervous system goes automatically to the patterns it has been accustomed to relying on for years. By envisioning a different possibility, you begin to scramble the code of habit and invite a new way of responding.

Grounding – Standing Solidly on Two Feet

Grounding – Standing Solidly on Two Feet

From *Inner Torah*: *To allow the energy of emotion to move and get to what lies beneath, a woman needs to prepare. She has to ground, to feel herself solidly supported on her own two feet with the energy running through her into the earth. She has to sense that the container of her body is strong enough to hold the force of powerful energies. Otherwise, her nervous system, in its infinite wisdom, will continue to protect her. Knowing she can't handle the full impact of her feelings, it won't allow them to be felt. Better to deaden than to flood her.*

. . .With an awareness of her feet in contact with the ground a woman automatically feels stronger and more connected to herself. . . She has a different experience of herself in her body that helps her access a different experience of her reality. She also has the necessary foundation to become a stronger vessel, making it less necessary for her to continue walling herself off from pain.

Grounding – Standing Solidly on Two Feet

The necessity to ground is not only an emotional imperative, but a spiritual one as well. It is written, "The heavens are My throne, and the land is the footstool for My feet" (*Yeshayahu* 66:1). We see from here that in the description of the Divine, there is a specific connection at the level of heaven and at the level of earth. Being grounded, keeping one's feet on the ground, is actually a term used allegorically to describe G-d's connection with Creation. As humans who are supposed to emulate the ways of Hashem, we must also live with our feet on the ground, and our higher level aspirations and actions connected to the heavens.

Similarly, it is written about the ladder in Jacob's dream, that it was "a ladder set earthward and its top reaches heavenward, and behold angels of G-d were ascending and descending on it" (*Bereishit* 28:12). The ladder that reaches heavenward must be set earthward. Its feet must be on the ground. If one loses that basis, the entire construct collapses. Our work is to bridge heaven and earth, to connect the transience of *olam hazeh* with the eternity of *olam haba* and bring *kedushah* into this world.

On one level, grounding is a function of the body. It comes from solid connection with the earth, especially through the legs and feet. The legs and feet support the body and enable it to move. Spiritually they represent the lower and outer reaches of a person, rooted in sensation, feeling, action, and in the solidity of the physical world. Being grounded in our legs and feet helps us to feel safe, alive, centered in ourselves, and rooted in our environment.

On another level, grounding is intimately connected with the mind and the heart. It necessitates a deep connection to the self, not only physically, but also emotionally and mentally. To be truly grounded, one must know and, at least be in the process of making peace with, one's past. What came before needs to be integrated into the whole of who one is today in order to sense oneself on solid ground. (See *Practical Inner Torah*, p. 29.)

The mitzvot that Hashem asks us to perform are their own route to grounding. The Torah teaches us that physical acts carried out by the body are essential to coming into relationship with Hashem. Consciousness is not enough. The hands and feet — the body itself — must be engaged. Davening also offers a dimension of grounding. There are certain prayers — the *Amidah* in particular — that must be said standing, which requires a different level of connection to the ground, the legs, and the feet, than sitting.

Standing also increases the body's energy and offers a person a different, more developed sense of herself. That is one reason why it is so significant when a baby first stands. She immediately has more presence and takes up space differently both from her own perspective and that of the people around her. She begins more clearly to come into her own when she stands on her own two feet. The English language reflects this phenomenon in such expressions as "to take a stand," "to put one's foot down," "to have a leg to stand on," "to stand for something," and "to have standing."

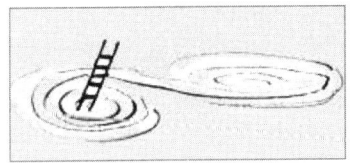

Physical and Emotional Grounding

Physical grounding connects us to our environment and helps orient us in time and space. It is one of the sources of strength Hashem made available to us. By bringing consciousness to the body, grounding also helps us to be present and focused and to experience things more directly. It enables us to better sense the validity of our own existence, of our right to be here and to have what we need in order to survive and thrive. We are more able to contain ourselves, and to move fluidly from that place of containment.

Grounding is the root of our connection to our bodies, to our experience of being alive. When we're grounded, it's easier to be conscious and aware, to avoid acting from unconscious urges or disassociating and acting in ways that are not in integrity with who we really are. To be grounded is to be connected to the biological reality of existence, which means that this is an area of crucial importance to those with issues in the realm of existence, as described in *Inner Torah* (pp. 86–92).

Without grounding, we tend to be unstable and less able to contain ourselves and all that we have. It's a lack that prevents us from building our vessels (see *Inner Torah*, pp. 74–79), from holding our power (see *Inner Torah*, pp. 103–109), from maturing, and from becoming fully who Hashem created us to be.

Without grounding, we also can't set right boundaries for ourselves. Our bodies are the solid form of our existence; they have definable boundaries. We also have emotional, intellectual, and spiritual boundaries that need to be appropriately maintained. The roots of evil lie in the breakdown of boundaries, in the destruction of the parameters of the individual. "He who breaks through the fence — a serpent will bite him" (*Kohelet* 10:8). A person who always searches for more outside of herself will never have a self, will never be herself. She will manipulate and try to expand into areas that are not hers instead of needing only the potential of what she is.

To set right boundaries, we need to know and feel that our own roots will support us. Roots need ground to grow and take hold. That means we need to have our own ground, to be recognized as entitled to our own independent existence. Yet many people growing up were not allowed to have their own ground, to grow their own roots. Instead, they had to satisfy the needs of others; they had to do and be what other people needed them to do and be.

In such circumstances, boundaries don't form and the crucial skill of boundary setting is not developed. Then, support that should rightly come from the self and from connection with Hashem, is sought from others in all kinds of ways. And because

Physical and Emotional Grounding

no adult can or should supply that core grounding for another adult, the need is never met. People are left feeling insecure and in constant need of reassurance. There is never a feeling of satisfaction of "enough" or "just this much" of anything. There is just endless pursuit and equally endless disappointment.

With a strong, rooted foundation we gain solidity, which in turn helps us to be firm and make boundaries. From there, it's easier to face the reality of our lives, stay anchored in truth, and remain calm and secure. Our legs and feet in particular have great strength and can help us in this task. Through them, we can stand firmly on the ground and decide to move with conviction in whatever direction is called for. We can live our lives on solid footing in partnership with Hashem.

To feel grounded, rooted, we also need to feel connected to our ancestors, our family, our personal past. We cannot simultaneously deny our past and maintain our roots. In order to create a solid foundation, we have to acknowledge and, if necessary, sort out the past.

Most people are unconsciously influenced by their roots. The Inner Torah process can help us bring awareness to this foundational dimension, come into relationship with the aspects of ourselves that are still captive to the past, and integrate the lessons from there into the totality of who we are today.

Our roots nourished and sustained us in our most formative stages. If in retrospect we see that the ground in which we took seed was not adequate, we need to add more fertile soil. In Inner Torah terms, this requires people to pay attention to and take responsibility for their lives in the present, to be the adult who today can provide ground that nurtures and sustains.

One aspect of childhood that can affect grounding is the amount and quality of touch and holding people received in their families of origin. It affects their ability to be sure of themselves emotionally, of the ground they stand on. Not being able to trust others to hold them, affects people's innate ability to hold themselves and to relax into themselves enough to feel grounded.

Even this deficit can be addressed by taking the time to envision and feel the type of holding and touch that would have been helpful. This will vary with the age and circumstance of the part of the self that one is coming into relationship with. For touch to be beneficial, it has to be conscious and sensitive to the needs of the person being touched, whether she is an infant, a toddler, an older child, a teenager, a young adult or an older adult. (For a more in-depth discussion of touch, see "Connecting to the Hands.")

Grounding and Energy Flow

Insufficient touch and holding also affect one's ability to ground from the standpoint of energy flow. Babies depend on their caregivers to handle any perceived dangers that arise, since they are developmentally unable to take care of themselves. If they don't feel that happening, they can easily fall into an abyss of overwhelming fear and helplessness. To avoid that horror, that sense of having no ground, of needing to rely on themselves for something they can't do, their energy moves upward. There it is less connected to the body and to whatever physical reality was experienced as threatening, so it feels safer. As a consequence, there is no longer adequate energy moving downward to allow for a sense of grounding. The downward current of energy is essentially blocked. In time, the upward movement becomes habitual, the lower body becomes depleted, and the system is thrown out of balance. In some circumstances, such as a non-labor Caesarian, even the birth process itself can be a ground-wrenching and terrifying experience.

This phenomenon can occur well beyond infancy as well. When our bodies are not safe, we often will redirect our attention away from the unpleasant experience and cut off bodily sensation. This can happen unconsciously, or it may even be a conscious choice. While it may be temporarily comforting to do this, the long-term consequences are not good. One can become physically numb, fail to notice when she needs to eat or rest, and lose contact with her emotional needs. A person with her energy always moving up in this way is hyper-vigilant to messages outside of herself. She seems to be constantly searching for ways to connect or constantly watching for danger. This heightened alertness, coupled with a deadened body, results in a mind-body split that prevents a woman from being fully herself. To compensate for lack of bodily connection, there's a tendency to overemphasize intellect, spirit, or imagination as a defense against feelings. (This phenomenon is discussed further in "Getting to Know the Energy Body.")

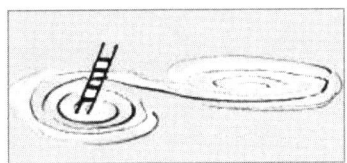

The Impact of Fear on Grounding

One's ground can also be undermined by inherited trauma. Parents who were Holocaust survivors, who experienced war trauma, who endured poverty or persecution, who lost a previous child, or had unresolved survival issues of any kind can pass their fears on to their children. The transfer of such feelings may be wholly unconscious or may be done consciously with a misguided intention to help protect the child. Whatever the intentions, the feelings become part of the child's bodily reality even though they are unrelated to her personal experience. She feels a persistent, visceral sense of low-level fear and distrust, the source of which may be a mystery to her.

An adult with damaged ground usually senses that something is wrong but doesn't know what it is. By adulthood some sort of makeshift, substitute foundation is usually in place.

So it doesn't occur to anyone that something as basic as the very ground of their existence, or their ability to ground, is missing or inadequate. Only when consciously focused on does this taken-for-granted dimension of oneself become visible. Once attention is directed there, it's usually not hard for people to see what they're lacking and what they need to do to recover their true and authentic ground.

Fear is usually the primary barrier that then needs to be worked through. It is fear that initially focused attention outward and activated the mind in an effort to ensure survival. It is fear that led to hyper-vigilance, restlessness, and anxiety. And fear that made it unsafe to relax, let down, and come into a place of ease. Fear also caused the nervous system and adrenal glands to constantly overwork and the body to be in a constant state of stress. That, in and of itself, causes one to be too aroused, too sensitive, and too reactive. A foundation riddled with fear can't be anything but shaky.

To fully ground into a solid foundation requires a willingness to engage with the fear and release it at its root. Whatever lessons are embedded in the fear need to be internalized and integrated into the whole of one's being. The Inner Torah process allows for this investigation into fear. It takes a person into the feeling and layer by layer helps her to move beyond the fear, to bring herself into the present where she has abilities and capacities that were not available to her at the time the fear took hold.

Moving beyond fear can bring one to a genuine understanding of the words of Rebbe Nachman, "Elevate fear to its Source." Ultimately, our lives are in Hashem's hands. When we truly know that in the very cells of our bodies, then all our fears can be elevated to the one place where the Torah tells us our fear should be directed, and that is to G-d.

Physically working on grounding facilitates this inner work.

Likewise, the inner work invites the body into a more grounded place. The two work in tandem to bring a person into the fullness of who she really is. From a grounded place we are better able to express ourselves appropriately and contain ourselves when necessary, two essential hallmarks of a true adult.

Spiritual Grounding

In the spiritual realm, grounding is a function of truth. When describing the difference between falsehood and truth, Chazal explain that falsehood has no "feet" to stand on (*Shabbat* 104a). They are referring to the letters of the Hebrew word for falsehood, *sheker* (שקר), which are said to stand on one leg each, as well as to the nature of falsehood, which is rootless and has no basis in reality. Attachment to reality manifests through the feet, as attested to by the Hebrew word for truth, *emet* (אמת), the letters of which each stand on two feet, on a firm base. *Sheker* is illusion; it hovers with one leg above the ground. In contrast to *sheker*, *emet*, is rooted and enduring, based in reality – it has both feet on the ground. G-d is truth, "*u'devarcha emet*, and Your word is true." Since our existence is part of His existence and we are rooted in His words, truth is our reality.

Not surprisingly, the serpent who enticed Chava to eat from the Tree of Knowledge, which has come to epitomize falsehood, was punished by losing its legs and feet. Falsehood has no base in reality; it cannot stand. In the same vein, Chazal liken the *satan* to an armed robber sitting at the crossroads who the wise man perceives as having no legs (*Bereishit Rabbah* 22:6). The fight between falsehood and truth, between man and the serpent, is described in terms that emphasize our ability to stamp out that which tempts us to stray from truth. Hashem said to the serpent, "He [man] will crush your head and you [serpent] will bite his heel [with your mouth]" (*Bereishit* 3:15).

This is a battle between staying connected to the firm root of our feet — the truth of reality that is Hashem — versus succumbing to illusion usually put forth by the mouth of those who speak falsehood. As King David said, "I contemplated my path and my feet brought me to the house of study" (*Tehillim* 119:59). He trusted his feet — and their contact with the ground of truth — to take him to the right place.

Connecting with the truth, of one's life, of one's strengths and weaknesses, of one's spiritual level, of any dimension of one's existence — and of course, to the Ultimate Truth that is Hashem — is the true key to grounding. Our bodies as well as our emotions come into alignment when we are in truth. Most people can attest to feeling grounded and centered once they let themselves know the truth about something they are struggling with. They no longer need to hold themselves up artificially with illusory thoughts or words. They can let their very beings down into the solid ground of existence that truth offers.

The path to this depth of truthful engagement with the self and others can be long and windy, passing through many emotions. Sometimes, we reach places that we would like to know as truth but that we discover are still based on illusion. They hold for a while and then give way once again to turmoil. That is the sign that we are not yet fully grounded, fully rooted in the level of truth that is Hashem's stamp.

The Breath and Body of Inner Torah

In this way, a sense of being grounded or ungrounded can help us gauge where we are in our efforts to do *teshuvah*, to return to Hashem. Knowing His ground is truth, we can check our own ground to see if we are standing and walking in His footsteps or have somehow strayed to ground of our own making.

Coming into our feet is particularly important at this time. The Ari writes that every soul in every generation is rooted in the soul of Adam, the first man. The souls of the earlier generations were rooted in Adam's upper extremities, and the souls of the last generations, in which we are included, stem from Adam's heels and feet. We who live in this time preceding Mashiach's coming, known as *Ikveta d'Meshicha* ("Footsteps of the Messiah"), will benefit from learning to solidly inhabit our own heels and feet.

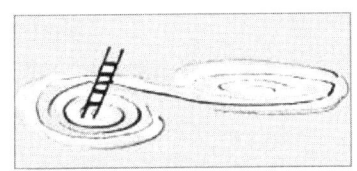

EXPLORATIONS

Learning to develop the downward current of the body literally builds ground just as one would build a foundation. It takes conscious work to bring energy flow to the legs and feet.

1. Opening the Feet, Ankles, and Legs

From *Inner Torah*: *A woman . . . can do a variety of exercises to ground, to bring energy down through her legs and feet. She can work with her breath, her body, or energy itself. One example is a short series of exercises drawn from several disciplines. The sequence is as follows:*

a. Stand and roll one foot and then the other on a foot roller or a small, hard rubber ball, putting as much weight on the rolling foot as possible to open energy centers on the bottom of the feet.

b. Kneel on both knees, with heels up and bottoms of the toes against the floor, and sit back on the heels to stretch the toes and soles of the feet.

c. Still kneeling, turn tops of toes to floor and sit on heels. Shift weight forward. Bring left foot parallel to and several inches behind the right knee with toes on floor and heel up. Let body weight of torso rest on left thigh. Lower left heel toward the ground to stretch out the ankle. (Repeat on the other side.)

d. Stand with feet parallel and hip-width apart. Slowly inhale, bend forward, and place both hands on the floor with knees bent. Slowly exhale, push the feet into the floor, lift the hips, and straighten the legs as much as possible with hands still on the floor. Repeat this squat/straighten motion multiple times until there is a strong sense of the legs.

These simple exercises can help a woman feel more connected to her lower torso and feet, which, in turn, gives her a greater sense of solidity and balance.

2. Bringing Awareness to the Feet

From Inner Torah: *Sometimes just bringing awareness to the feet and feeling them in contact with the floor can help pull a woman back into her body. This is easy to do anywhere. She just brings her attention to the bottoms of her feet and senses where they make contact with the ground. She allows herself to be supported by the firm surface under her so that she feels the floor come up to meet her, helping her to hold herself upright in either a sitting or standing position. When she feels herself supported in this way, it's easier to relax into her body instead of pulling up out of it.*

Explorations

3. Standing Solidly on Your Feet

We connect to the ground through our feet. Working on the feet includes working directly with the feet themselves and can also include doing Inner Torah work while standing, with conscious attention paid to the feet and to how one is standing.

The foot can be thought of as a tripod-based dome. The three supporting points are the ball of the big toe, the ball of the little toe, and the center of the heel bone. Imagine that the weight of your body supported by the foot is equally divided between the three points. If there is not enough weight on your heel, rock your pelvis backward slightly so that your sitting bones are poised behind your heels. If there is not enough weight on the ball of your foot, rock your pelvis slightly forward. If there is not enough weight on the inside or outside of your foot, on the ball of the big or little toe, you can visualize all three points moving apart — the toes forward and apart and the heel backward away from them. As you imagine the three points moving apart, think of a space opening up between them.

4. Foot Massage

Sitting in a chair, feel behind your right knee. Take hold of the tendons on each side and gently massage them. Place the right foot sideways on the left knee. Gently wring the foot with your hands moving in opposite directions.

Hold your ankle with one hand, your toes with the other hand, and slowly rotate the foot. Let your leg muscles relax, doing the work with the hands. Tap with your fingertips around the ankle and up the shin, and feel how this brings circulation into the foot.

Take the big toe of the right foot in one hand while holding the foot with the other hand. Pull gently on the big toe while turning it slightly, as though to unscrew it. Then turn it back to where it was. Do the same thing with the rest of the toes, one at a time. Pull and turn from the spot where the toe begins.

Gently separate each toe from the one next to it. Place the palm of your left hand against the sole of your right foot and cross the fingers of your hand with the toes of your foot. In other words, lace your fingers between your toes. Push gently down to the spot where the toe begins. Now bend the front of the foot toward the ball of your foot.

Massage the arches of your feet with your thumbs, gently at first, then with gradually increasing pressure. Massage along your instep with long strokes of the thumbs, from the toes toward the heel. By massaging the instep, you relax the leg muscles from your knees almost to your toes. Continue to massage every part of the foot.

Stand and compare your feet while standing and then walking. Do they feel different? How is your balance? How does it feel to walk on each foot? What does the rest of your leg feel like? How hard does the floor feel to each foot? Are the balls of your big and little toes sharing equal weight? By relaxing your foot, you make it more stable.

Repeat with the left foot.

5. Bringing Breath to the Feet and Legs

Take a full breath as though you were breathing through the bottom of your left foot. Bring the breath up your left leg and across the back of your hips as you inhale. As you exhale, push the breath down the right leg and out the foot deeply into the ground. Repeat this several times until the circuit is established.

Imagine that you have noses at the bottom of your two feet. Inhale energy through your feet up to your abdomen; exhale the energy back down your legs and out your feet. Take normal rather than exaggerated breaths and focus your attention on how your legs feel as the energy flows up and down. Continue until you feel you have established a circuit.

6. Connecting Heaven and Earth

Stand with your feet parallel, weight over the center of your feet, knees relaxed and slightly bent, pelvis relaxed and free, belly relaxed, shoulders relaxed and in balance, jaw relaxed, eyes relaxed. With your eyes closed, bring your awareness to your feet. Now lift your hands and reach up and back gently. Keeping your head upright arch your back slightly. Visualize yourself as a wire – the energetic connection – between heaven and earth. Feel for a sense of energy flowing through your whole body.

7. Coming into Truth

Notice whether or not you feel grounded. If you sense that you are not fully grounded, contemplate where in your life you may not be in truth with yourself. Invite yourself to allow in whatever the truth is that you are blocking. Let yourself know what you might in the past have been afraid to know, trusting that the truth will strengthen your connection to reality and make firmer the foundation on which you stand.

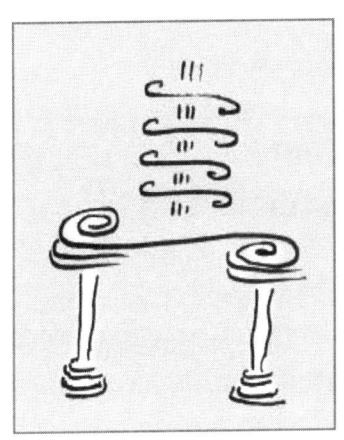

Centering through the Legs and Mid-Body

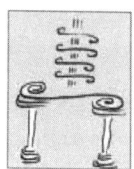

Centering through the Legs and Mid-Body

From *Inner Torah*: *The pelvis and reproductive organs are related but also independent common areas of holding. Often I find that women are virtually numb in this part of their body, cut off from a vital source of their own life force. Not only are they deprived of the potent energy intended to flow through this area, but they are using energy to keep it blocked. Again, awakening begins with awareness. It is easy to become habituated to an energetic or bodily state and lose any realization that it could be otherwise, particularly in an area that is deadened. A woman needs to be reminded of her capacity for sensation and how far she has drifted away from it. Sometimes there is accumulated trauma from childbirth, other times from childhood. Some intimate relationships also take their toll. There is often a need for great gentleness when approaching this part of the body. She needs to enter slowly. But she needs to enter. This is her life-giving center. She needs to be connected to it to give life to herself as well as others.*

Centering through the Legs and Mid-Body

The mid-body, or pelvis, is home to the body's center of gravity and balancing point, located approximately one and a half inches below the navel and one and half inches inward toward the spine. The pelvis rests on top of the femurs (thigh bones). The joints between the pelvis and the femurs are ball and socket joints enabling free movement of the legs in all directions. The legs, extending downward from the torso, are the main pillars which support the body and our principal means of movement.

The Talmud teaches that "man's legs are his guarantors; wherever he must go, they will take him" (*Sukkah* 53a). Our bodies are structured so that all the joints of the leg from the pelvis to the feet can be directly in the line of gravity, perpendicular to the ground. This ensures that we have to do a minimum of work to hold our bones up against the pull of gravity, that we are easily supported.

Moving in the other direction, the pelvis connects with the brain by means of the spine. The pelvis, which can easily maneuver every part of the body from any posture, is a reservoir of power and energy. It executes decisions arrived at by the brain. Movement initiated from the pelvis is fluid and invites participation by the rest of the body in a way that allows each part to do its job. For example, a slight gesture in the pelvis signals the spine to move the head in a way that lets the back do most of the work and frees the neck to do the more delicate movement for which it was intended. A sedentary lifestyle makes the pelvis lazy and less able to do its job. You can see this sometimes in the increasing difficulty people who sit for long periods have in rising from their chairs.

Movement is the medium of life. It is essential to growth and development on every plane. In the spiritual realm it is well known that we are either ascending or descending the ladder of spiritual growth. No one remains in the same place; there is always movement in one direction or the other. In the emotional realm, movement is the key to maintaining balance and being able to handle whatever circumstances we find ourselves in.

In the emotional realm it is possible to get stuck, but it's not desirable, at least not for long. Ultimately we need to be able to move with whatever is happening. To do that, we have to recognize when we stop moving and ask ourselves: How can I move in this situation in a constructive way? How can I move even with what I don't like, with what is hard for me? (For more on movement, see "Releasing the Neck, Back, and Spine.")

In this sense, movement is a reflection of vitality. Without movement, there is stagnation and creative life forces are stymied. The movement of the legs and pelvis that we are exploring in this chapter is not just an outer movement, but an inner movement as well. Actual physical movement of the pelvis and legs is one way to stimulate that inner sensation. But even without that, we can move within ourselves just by virtue of bringing awareness to these parts of our bodies and inhabiting them with our consciousness. From this internal motion we can experience the fluidity that is the hallmark of the body and of life itself.

The goal is to move with ourselves, to be engaged in a living process that, while it encompasses stillness, does not stagnate. This juxtaposition of movement and stillness offers a powerful sense of aliveness coupled with a deep sense of stability. It is the place from which we can serve Hashem with the best of ourselves.

A rigid, frozen pelvis not only makes it more difficult to move with ease but also to maintain a sense of being centered. Sensory connection with the body's actual center of gravity – its balancing point – supports an inner sense of centeredness and balance. Likewise, sensory connection with the storehouse of energy the pelvis contains can contribute to a sense of solidity that can be extended to other areas of the body. Tapping into the power of the pelvis can potentially strengthen one's whole system.

Not only is the pelvis deadened by inactivity, but also, as the excerpt quoted above from *Inner Torah* describes, it can close down from trauma and emotional stress. The Inner Torah process helps one connect with the part of oneself that experienced difficulty in this area of the body. Through coming into relationship with the younger self who went through the experience, a woman invites her body to take down the barriers to feeling it may have erected to protect her.

By working directly with the body, a woman approaches herself from the other direction. Without focusing on any particular incident or event, without relating to any younger self, she simple brings her attention to her pelvis and legs. She notices the level of sensation accessible and begins to explore the possibility of awakening greater levels. In the process, she may encounter feelings, images, memories, or thoughts to which she can then give attention.

It's helpful in this context to focus on the legs first and establish a strong base of support before venturing into potentially more sensitive areas. The legs correspond to the *sefirot* of *netzach* (the right leg) and *hod* (the left leg), while the pelvis and reproductive organs correspond to the *sefirah* of *yesod*. *Netzach*, meaning eternity, is an extension of *chesed*, the attribute of giving. *Hod*, meaning splendor, is a manifestation of *gevurah*, the characteristic of restraint. Both are necessary for balance and equilibrium in life – something that we experience in the physical act of walking.

With our legs we are able to move forward when appropriate

and hold back when necessary. We speak of "walking in the ways of Hashem" (*Shoftim* 2:22). The Hebrew word for walking, *halichah*, and the Hebrew word for Hashem's laws, *halachah*, are similar. We "walk" in Hashem's ways by following His laws, which themselves instruct us on when and how to act and when and how to refrain from acting. From that comes the solid foundation of *yesod*, of life, goodness, and blessing. As it says in *Mishlei* (10:9), "He who walks sincerely will walk confidently."

Naomi was anticipating giving birth for the fourth time. Her last two births were very difficult, leaving her feeling frightened at the prospect of going through the experience again. She could feel herself contract and tighten at the thought of it. She wanted to do something to try to relax her body, to help herself go into this next birth from a place of ease and faith instead of tension and fear. She was doing Inner Torah work and developing a relationship with the younger selves who had gone through her three previous births. She was getting to know them well.

In the process Naomi realized that she needed to learn to relax and more fully inhabit her body. At the same time she was looking at what had gotten in the way of doing that in the past, she started to work with her body itself. She started by exploring movement in her feet and legs, to give herself more of a solid base of support. Then she put her hands on her hip bones and lower abdomen.

When she brought her attention to where her hands made contact with her body, she immediately felt fear. But instead of tightening, she invited her body to continue to stay relaxed and used her breath to contain the feeling. As she did so, tears welled up in her eyes. She didn't try to figure out what the tears were about but simply stayed with the sensations in her body and with her breath. Within a short time, she felt like something gave way inside of her. She described it as "a taut rope that seemed to slacken." Her breath also felt freer.

Naomi was excited to have had such a real experience of letting go. She sensed that it was just the beginning and was a little nervous that she wouldn't be able to experience it again, let alone move deeper into it. But she didn't have to worry. The experience was hers. The bodily memory of it didn't leave her. It motivated her to set aside time to be with her body in a gentle, patient way that allowed her to continue to open and relax. By the time she was ready to give birth, she was no longer overwhelmed by fear. She actually was optimistic that this time could be different. And it was.

Bringing awareness and presence to the pelvis and the legs not only supports grounding and centering, but also breath and voice. Much of the strength of the voice comes from the legs and pelvis. You can see this with infants and toddlers who kick when they scream. As the legs get stronger, so does the cry.

As you go about your day, you can use the body's center of gravity as a focus point to help keep you inside yourself and to regain your connection to yourself if you lose it. Just bringing your awareness there will help to orient you in your own reality. You can put your hand there as well to enhance the cue to your nervous system that you want to return and stay within.

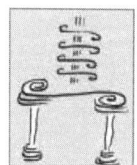

EXPLORATIONS

In the leg and mid-body areas, as in the rest of the body, our intention is to develop an inner connection and inner experience. The explorations are designed to help you get information about what goes on inside yourself without manipulating or forcing. The key is to increase your awareness from the inside.

1. Coming into the Legs

To get the benefit of the support that Hashem designed into the skeletal structure, the legs need to be relatively straight. As you're standing you can imagine the centers of the feet, ankles, knees, and femoral joints as open gateways for supporting energy to flow through. The bones through the center of the leg can be thought of as strong and the muscles and flesh around the periphery as melting so the energy can move up and down freely. There is a feeling of ease and security that is accessible when the body is functioning the way Hashem intended. The legs become a place to relax into and feel supported by.

Explorations

2. Bringing Movement to the Legs

Bring your awareness to your legs. Allow the sensation in your legs to initiate movement in any way that feels appropriate to you. Try this while sitting, standing, and lying down. Notice how the movement differs in these three positions. Invite the movement in your legs up into your pelvis. Notice if the movement is blocked in any way in the area where the pelvis meets the legs. If it is, breathe into the blockage and feel it softening and, when ready, dissolving. Don't try to force anything in particular to happen. Just be with whatever is happening with full awareness. Notice the sensation of movement between the legs and the pelvis once the blockage is gone.

3. Hip Rotations

a. Stand with your feet hip-width apart and your weight distributed equally on both feet. Visualize your torso perfectly balanced on your legs and very light. Soften and relax your knees. Now rotate your entire lower body from the waist down, moving your hips in a circle. Your weight will shift naturally from one foot to the other as your pelvis circles. Don't tighten your abdomen or your buttocks as you move, and try not to let the upper body get involved in this motion, but concentrate on your pelvis, making a smooth, even circle with the hips. Rotate both clockwise and counterclockwise.

b. Move your feet a few inches further apart and rotate the pelvis again, this time concentrating the motion on one hip at a time. Visualize the center of that hip's joint, and move the hip around that center. Your other hip will have to move as you do this, but it will be following a motion, rather than initiating one. Rotate the hip a number of times in each direction, and then switch to the other hip and do the same.

4. Coming into the Lower Abdomen

a. Locate the area one and a half inches below the navel and one and a half inches inward toward the spine — the body's center of gravity. Bring your awareness there, using your hands if desired for an added dimension of presence. Breathe naturally and notice how you feel with your awareness centered on the balancing point of your body. Try moving and speaking from there as well.

b. Imagine a small ball of light in this area. Then imagine it beginning to expand into the size of a big ball. Notice if you feel a release of tension in the back and stomach.

c. Stand with both hands on your lower abdomen and sound different vowels — a, e, i, o ,u. Feel your support coming from your feet and your pelvis.

5. Coming into the Sacrum

a. While standing, think of your sacrum (the center back of your pelvis that is also the lower end of your spine) as very heavily sinking down toward your heels, but do not contract your buttocks or abdominal muscles to do this; let gravity do all the work while you simply observe in your mind's eye.

Explorations

b. While sitting, place one hand on your belly and the other on your sacrum. As you inhale curve your back and drop down, letting your mouth open. On exhale, arch your back and sit up, making a "sh" sound as you come up.

c. Still sitting, put your fingers on your tail bone at the top of the coccyx. Again, as in (b) above, drop back on inhale and come forward on exhale. Feel a triangle (tripod) supporting you that includes your two sit bones and the point at the top of your coccyx on the tail bone. Inhale back and allow the exhale to pull you up through the triangle. Make sound, including mmm and ooo.

6. Coming into Your Pelvis

a. Stand with feet shoulder width apart. Use your hands to outline the bone structure of your pelvis, noticing that it is the only bowl-shape in the body. Visualize it as your reserve cup of energy.

b. Bending your knees a bit more, let your pelvis begin to move with your breath. As you breathe in, the top of your pelvis tips forward. The bend is at the lumbo-sacral joint, not in your middle back. Be gentle, not forcing. As you exhale, the top of your pelvis moves back. Let the movement follow the breath. Bring your awareness to the movement in your pelvis so that you're not on automatic pilot doing this exploration. You can do the same exploration lying down with your knees bent and your feet on the ground. You can also explore reversing the movement of your pelvis in relation to your breath.

7. Walking

Try walking with awareness. Put the heel down first straight in front of you. Then expand the sole of the foot, allowing it to receive the weight of the body, moving toward the toes. While the other leg moves forward, continue to keep the back foot on the ground so that the back of the knee remains extended and open before lifting the foot for the next step. Keep the external part of the heel that is bearing the weight of the body down as long as possible while extending the sole toward the toes. This helps to form the arch of the foot, which is essential to standing and walking in the way the body was designed to operate.

8. Looking for Movement

When you find yourself in a difficult situation, especially one where you feel trapped or stuck, look for possibilities for movement, internally or externally. See what you need to do or change for that movement to happen in a constructive, productive way.

9. Balancing Movement and Stillness

If you're always moving, take time to allow yourself to experience stillness. If you're too still, look for opportunities to move more. Explore the right balance between movement and stillness for you. See if you need to make any changes in your life to achieve that balance. This is a realm in which everyone is different. You need to discover what works best for you.

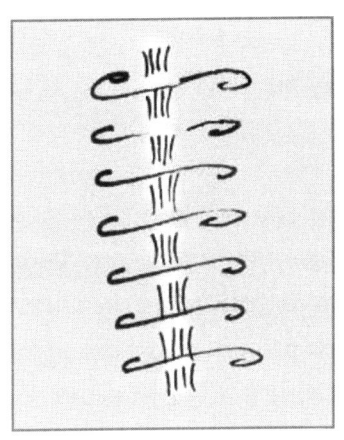

Releasing the Neck, Back, and Spine

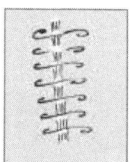

Releasing the Neck, Back, and Spine

From Inner Torah: The neck is the bridge between the head and the body. Ideally energy flows freely between the two realms, allowing a woman to draw upon the entirety of her being in all that she does. But a woman who is not at home in her body, who is unconsciously using her body to store unfinished business in her life, will want to disconnect from it. She can do that very easily by tightening in the neck area, by blocking her bodily awareness and staying up in her head. She essentially closes the bridge, and that closing is reflected in her neck on the skeletal, muscular, fascial (connective tissue), and energetic levels.

In some women holding in the neck has gone on so long that there is almost no mobility or an actual physical disfigurement. Other women are habituated to constant discomfort and an ongoing sense of strain. As odd as it sounds, many women have simply forgotten what it feels like to have a genuine sense of ease in their necks and an experience of their heads as integral to and inseparable from their bodies.

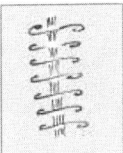

The Physical Spine

The skeletal spine consists of thirty-three bones called vertebrae, each separated from its neighbor by a flat, round cushion called a disc. The discs cushion the vertebral bones and create space between them, enabling the spine to withstand pressure and absorb shock.

The uppermost seven vertebrae support the neck and are called cervical vertebrae. The next twelve support the middle and upper back and are attached to the twelve pairs of ribs; these are called the thoracic vertebrae. Next come the five lumbar vertebrae, at the lower back; then the five sacral vertebrae, which are fused into a single solid structure called the sacrum. The sacrum attaches to the pelvic bones on the sides. Last are the four small cocygeal vertebrae which comprise the coccyx.

Each vertebra consists of a cylinder-shaped part, known as the vertebral body, and several projections which stand out from the back and sides of it. Two of these projections meet behind the vertebral body, creating an opening, or foramen, between them. The foramina of the adjacent vertebrae create a tunnel, the vertebral canal, which serves the very important function of supporting and protecting the delicate spinal cord, a rope of nerves which, together with the brain, forms the central nervous system.

Virtually all of the information about sensation and movement which passes between the body and the brain is carried through the spinal cord. From this central cord, nerve roots exit between the vertebral processes, branching again and again to reach nearly all parts of the body. Nerves are like wires connecting the brain to every part of the body and carrying information between them. They transmit messages from the brain designed to cause muscles to activate and move body parts. They also transmit messages in the opposite direction, bringing information to the brain about what is going on in the body. Everything in the body (movement, function, sensation) is controlled by the brain, and all information between the brain and the body is transmitted by nerves. There is not a nerve in our body that is not, somehow, dependent on the integral functioning of the spinal cord and consequently on the vertebral column.

The back and the neck are home to most of that vertebral column. Each part of the back supports the part above it. When the legs are strong and the hips flexible and balanced, the back will have good support. When the lower back is flexible and strong, the middle and upper back will be supported well. When the middle and upper back are strong and loose, the neck and head will not need to tense.

So it is very important to learn to elongate the spine, to release tension and create space in this important passageway. One way to do that is to focus on the place at the back of the waist where the spine moves simultaneously in two opposite directions — from the waist down toward the legs and feet, which are pulled by gravity, and from the waist upwards through the top of the head, lifting us freely.

The pull of gravity under our feet makes it possible for us to extend the upper part of the spine, and this extension allows us also to release tension between the vertebrae. Gravity is like a magnet attracting us to the earth but this attraction is not limited to pulling us down, it also allows us to stretch in the opposite direction. Centering your attention on this place where the spine moves in two opposite directions allows you to avoid effort and strain when moving.

The spine is also a conductor of energy. It acts like a lightening rod or antenna conducting energy, which moves vertically through the top of the head, down the spine, into the pelvis, down the legs, and out through the feet. For that energy to flow freely it's important to maintain good body alignment, which is helped tremendously by a strong, flexible spine and back.

Yet most of us give little consideration to our backs, usually living in the front part of our bodies. This happens for a variety of reasons. There are relatively few nerve endings in the back, there is less brain area in charge of the back, vision draws our attention in front of us, most of our sensory organs are situated in the front part of our bodies, and we move forward much more than backward. Still, the backs of our bodies are important and need our attention. Learning to sense the back brings more circulation and movement as well as a greater sense of wholeness and solidity.

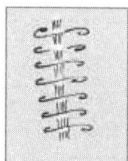

The Emotional Spine

For many people, the back, spine, and neck are storehouses for unprocessed emotions. Back and neck pain are common complaints, and many even in the medical field attribute a significant amount of that pain to emotional stress. Developing a sensory connection with the back can open doors to unknown parts of the self, to feelings and experiences about which one might not be consciously aware.

Unconscious feelings can lodge anyplace in the back and neck (as they can anywhere else in the body) causing tension, pain, and discomfort. By bringing awareness to these tense, painful, uncomfortable physical sensations, it is possible to start to know these feelings and attend to them.

Basically what happens is that emotions set in motion activity within the central nervous system, specifically the autonomic system, resulting in local vasoconstriction and mild oxygen deprivation of certain muscles, nerves, tendons, and ligaments. This oxygen lack is responsible for the pain that often manifests as back pain and as sensory abnormalities such as numbness and pins and needles, as well as motor deficits such as weakness. Anger and anxiety are two emotions that are known to generate pain and other physical symptoms when not acknowledged.

Awareness that feelings can generate pain can be the first step to healing. It sends the brain a message that the pain may not be of physical origin and is not needed to divert attention from underlying, previously unconscious, feelings. It opens the door to discovering the hidden feelings which then no longer need to be manifested somatically. Then it's possible to take the next step and come into relationship with the part of the self that is experiencing the difficult feelings and help her move beyond them.

Malki had severe pain in her shoulder and middle back. A CT scan showed significant disc involvement in her neck, with both degeneration and bulging. A course of intensive physical therapy was prescribed. This wasn't the first time that Malki had encountered this type of difficulty. The same thing had happened several years earlier and had resolved itself with physical therapy. But this time was much more severe.

In the interim between the two bouts, Malki started to do Inner Torah work. So she recognized that while some of the problem might indeed be coming from her neck and her compromised discs, it was likely that there were also strong emotions underlying her current symptoms. The degeneration in her discs had not created symptoms for several years, and this new onslaught of pain had come on rather suddenly.

She decided to do her own internal investigation. Lying down, she brought her attention to the painful area in her shoulder and mid-back. As she let herself go deeper into the sensations, she sensed enormous anger of which she hadn't even been aware.

The Breath and Body of Inner Torah

Asking herself what she was angry about, she immediately focused on an upcoming speaking engagement that she had recently accepted and about which she had misgivings.

Going deeper to find out why that angered her so, she discovered a well of pressure inside her that drove her to constantly perform. She traced the source to her childhood home where her parents demanded a steady stream of accomplishments from her and her siblings. Nothing was ever enough. No sooner was one thing done, than the focus shifted to what was next.

Malki realized that her sense of herself depended almost exclusively on her accomplishments. And she understood that her agreement to speak was coming from this driven place. It wasn't something she genuinely wanted to do for pure and good motives. It was more something she felt pushed to do as a matter of survival.

All of that had generated an undercurrent of anger about which she was not conscious. Instead, all she knew was that shortly after she agreed to speak, her back and shoulder started to hurt so badly she couldn't even use the computer to work on her speech as she normally would have. As she recognized the intense feelings of anger and identified the source, Malki felt the tightness in her shoulder and back release somewhat. She found herself progressing much more quickly through physical therapy than even the therapist anticipated.

The combination of emotional awareness, connection with previously repressed feelings, and physical exercises alleviated the pain. Malki also took the opportunity to revisit the question of whether to accept the speaking engagement. Having unhooked the unhealthy drive that had motivated her to say yes initially, she surprised herself by finding within a genuine desire to give the speech. She then went forward with preparations for it from a place of ease and interest.

The Emotional Spine

This is a good example of how paying attention to the body can bring us in contact with ourselves. In Malki's case, there was actual pain that stopped her from doing what she needed to do. But we don't have to wait for the body to broadcast distress so loudly. Any sense of holding or tension can be an invitation to focus on that part of ourselves and to listen to what the body is calling us to attend to.

Even without any discomfort, it is possible to come within and explore our deeper selves using the body as a jump-off point. All it takes is bringing awareness to a place in the body and being interested in what, if anything, is stored there. Awareness allows the conscious mind to meet the deeper, unintentional workings of the nervous system in a way that nothing else can.

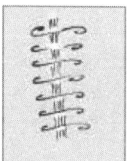

Movement

Movement is the key to a healthy spine and back. Twisting, stretching, and moving around are what the body wants and needs. It increases circulation, helping the blood carry nutrients to the cells and toxic waste materials away from the cells. It increases the body's supply of oxygen, which further speeds circulation and refreshes the brain. It improves muscle elasticity, the ability of muscles to constantly change from contraction to relaxation, and prevents the buildup of hard connective tissue which can inhibit movement. It may also increase the body's production of endorphins, chemicals produced in the brain which relieve pain and produce a feeling of well-being. It's important, though, to move with awareness and sensitivity, in a way that works with, and not against, the body. And also, of course, to breathe.

Movement is a way of extending boundaries, of breaking through limitations. Like everything else, over time most of us begin to move in habitual ways, working the same parts of our bodies repeatedly. Remembering to vary your movements, to do things in non-habitual ways, is a tonic for the body. It also invigorates the brain, which can easily inhabit well-worn grooves to the exclusion of anything new that would keep it more active and alert. Sometimes something as little as changing the placement of the clock or the wastebasket in a room can wake you up to more conscious and varied action and begin to shake you out of your neural rut.

Interestingly, awareness itself often leads to movement. When you bring your attention to a place in your back or neck and really inhabit that place, you'll be moved to move in some slight way. Often such a movement is undulating or spiraling, as though the body is resituating itself into a more natural stance. G-d created our bodies with supreme sensitivity. Only our unconscious ways and failure to take notice have led to the sense of deadness that many people experience.

Movement devoid of attention doesn't accomplish nearly as much as movement on which we focus and concentrate. The movement we are looking for in Inner Torah work originates from inside the body; it's not imposed from the outside. Giving attention is a way of supplying energy. The combination of physical action and your aware presence results in an enlivened feeling that is different than what can be felt by virtue of one or the other alone.

We also have the ability to move internally in a way that is not reflected on the outside. Even in a limb or body part that is unable to move, we can experience a feeling of movement within. All that is required is to mentally go inside that part of the body, pay attention to the sensation there, and allow tiny movements to arise spontaneously. Just staying with this sensation of movement inside can wake up the nervous system and bring life to the body.

Even relaxation has a dynamic, moving dimension. In Inner Torah work, to relax doesn't mean to collapse, but rather to release tension. Tension is accumulated in the body and in the mind by years of forcing, of trying to control what cannot be controlled, of doing in a mechanical way without attention or presence, of blocking what feels too hard to bear. These habits usually give way only in an environment of self-acceptance. This is what gives permission to the nervous system to cease forcing and blocking. This is what allows us to be with what is, concentrating on what needs to happen in the moment, and doing what we can with awareness and presence. Then tension releases.

Another aspect of relaxation is found in quieting the mind, which in turn relaxes the brain. A simple moment of silence with attention within can do a lot to rejuvenate and allow us to access a deeper level of intelligence that emerges from the place where the mind and body are unified.

Elana felt tension in her back and neck as soon as she went into her children's bedroom to get them up. While she was managing the morning schedule okay, she felt stiff in her interactions with the children, forcing herself to be cheerful and feigning attention to what they were saying and doing. Before looking into the emotional issues involved, Elana decided to do some work with her breath and body.

She began by giving herself time to focus on her back and neck, to invite them to soften and relax, before she entered the children's bedroom in the morning. She noticed her breath and reminded herself to exhale fully and allow the next inhale to come on its own. She essentially slowed down and paid attention to what was happening in her body. In doing so, she felt something relax inside of her and a little more ease in her system.

Instead of bracing herself to go in and calling out a forced good morning, she stayed inside her breath and body and spoke from a more real place within her. She was surprised to hear her voice. It was deeper and softer than she had ever known it to be.

After speaking to the children from this more relaxed place, she waited to receive whatever they had to say rather than pushing past them to chatter on in her usual forced cheery tone.

What surprised her even more was her pace. Instead of her usual intense and somewhat frantic movements, she found herself moving much more slowly and gently. While she liked the sensation and felt more connected to her children from there, she was concerned that she couldn't afford to move so slowly. There was too much to do in too short a time to give herself that luxury.

Not sure how to maintain a speed that worked for her without sacrificing the softer, gentler presence she had begun to cultivate, Elana started to get anxious. Her mind ran ahead to everything that had to be done in the next hour and she found herself once again tense and tight. She had to consciously call her mind back to the present and bring her focus to what she was doing at that moment with that child.

Being with what was happening in the moment allowed her body and mind to relax once again. From there, she reminded herself that she would just keep putting one foot in front of the other, doing whatever needed to be done one step at a time. What she saw was that with practice, she could quicken her pace without losing the more real sense of connection with the children she was developing.

Her back and her neck were good barometers of how she was doing. When she felt tension there, usually accompanied by breath holding or more shallow breathing, she could, with awareness, once again soften the tense area, breathe more fully, and return her attention to her children literally in seconds. She was becoming the rider, able to give her body clear directions that helped her to be the mother she wanted to be. She could dissipate her anxiety before it overtook her by working with her body and breath.

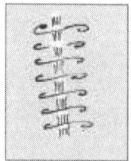

The Spiritual Spine

The spine enables us to bend our bodies as well as to stand straight. Those abilities have an important place in our relationship with Hashem. We need to be able to bow when appropriate and submit ourselves to Hashem, and we need to be able to straighten when appropriate and take on the responsibilities that Hashem gives us. This is reflected in the *Amidah*, the standing prayer, known as *Shemoneh Esrei*.

Chazal said that the eighteen *berachot* of *Shemoneh Esrei* were composed in correlation to eighteen of the spinal vertebrae (*Berachot* 28b). *Shemoneh Esrei* means eighteen, and there were originally eighteen *berachot* in *Shemoneh Esrei*. The nineteenth *berachah* against the heretics and evil was added later.

The Maharal writes that the twelve *berachot* of requests in *Shemoneh Esrei* correlate with the twelve vertebrae from which the ribs extend (the thoracic vertebrae) (*Netiv Avodah*, ch. 8). The first and last three *berachot* are blessings of praise and thanks respectively, and correlate with vertebrae from which

The Spiritual Spine

ribs do not extend, probably six of the seven cervical vertebrae. The nineteenth *berachah* against the heretics corresponds to the seventh and highest cervical vertebra which Chazal call the *luz* bone. The bottom vertebrae — the lumbar, sacral, and cocygeal vertebrae — were not represented in *Shemoneh Esrei* because they are found in the bottom section of the body, which relates, among other things, to functions of elimination.

On a *ta'anit tzibur*, a public day of fasting declared when severe troubles face the community, extra *berachot* are added to *Shemoneh Esrei*, bringing the total number to twenty-four. These *berachot* would then include the lumbar vertebrae. In a time when a severe decree looms over the heads of the people, it is important to include all parts of us in the structure of the *tefillah*.

We are required to bow down four times during *Shemoneh Esrei*, which represents the servitude of our physical being to Hashem. And, in bowing, halachah requires that we bend all eighteen vertebrae, which correspond to the original eighteen *berachot*. The Gemara (*Bava Kama* 16a) says that if one does not bow when saying the *berachah* of *Modim*, his spine will eventually turn into a snake. A snake represents falsehood, heresy, and rebellion against Hashem, as witnessed first and foremost by the snake that caused man to sin.

Modim is the *berachah* of thanks, and it is the first of the last three *berachot* of *Shemoneh Esrei* that represent thanks. One must bow down both at the beginning and at the end of the *berachah* of *Modim*. In the blessings of Bilam to the Jewish people, the Torah writes, "For there is no *nachash* in Yaakov [the Jewish people]" (*Bamidbar* 23:23). *Nachash* means "snake," and as explained above, represents the doctrine of heresy that denies the total, absolute oneness of Hashem and acknowledges other forces. When a person fails to recognize that everything she has,

175

without exception, is a gift from Hashem, and that she herself has no powers and abilities to do anything, she is embracing the doctrine of the snake.

The *luz* bone, which corresponds to the nineteenth *berachah* of *Shemoneh Esrei*, is the only part of the body of Adam HaRishon that did not accept nourishment from the *eitz hada'at* (Tree of Knowledge). That is why it is the bone that is indestructible and contains the source for *techiyat ha'meitim* (resurrection of the dead). Since it was not nourished from the sin of the *eitz hada'at* and is indestructible, it cannot turn into a snake.

Yet, when the influence of heresy became strong, Chazal saw reason to affix a special *berachah* directed against the forces of corrupted intellect. These forces permeate even the level of the *luz* bone, which, at the base of the skull, is the highest level of vertebrae and represents intellect, where the physical body is most directly connected to the spiritual realm.

The *Shemoneh Esrei* was composed to address the upper level of the body, which represents the spiritual level. However, *tefillah* (prayer) is supposed to come from and envelop the entire body, as King David said, "All my bones shall say, 'Hashem who is like You?'" (*Tehillim* 35:10). He also wrote, "And I am prayer," meaning that his whole being was so totally immersed in prayer that he himself became "a prayer."

While full connection to Hashem requires full participation of the body, *tefillah* is actually called *avodah shebalev*, "service [to Hashem] in the heart." The inner core of prayer is in the heart. From a heart that is rightly aligned with Hashem, we can infuse holiness and a connection to the spiritual realm throughout the physical body.

Likewise, being in right relationship with Hashem is essential for right alignment of our spines on a spiritual level. A key component of that right relationship is recognizing that everything we have is from Hashem. It is to Him that we must direct all our requests, and it is Him to whom we must give thanks.

Tension, pain, and other types of holding in the spine, back, and neck can be a reminder to take stock in this realm as well, to scrutinize our relationship with Hashem, to see if we have strayed into thinking that we are the source of our powers and abilities, to see if we have forgotten to be thankful for all that we have and all that we are. Just as one can bring awareness to these areas of the body and explore emotional holdings, so too can one explore spiritual blocks and barriers to the free flow of life force and proper working of the body, mind, and spirit.

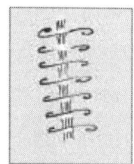

EXPLORATIONS

1. Spine and Back – Extending and Opening

Stand with your feet hip-width apart and your weight distributed evenly on both feet, knees slightly bent and arms hanging loosely at your sides. Holding your head straight, visualize your spine — including the neck — as being very long. Visualize your back as being very wide, your head going up to the sky, and each shoulder going far out in the distance.

Breathe fully and imagine that your back is soft and that each breath is expanding the different areas of your spine. Let your breath fill you so that your shoulders separate, your chest and diaphragm expand, and your spine straightens. Feel your head connected to your spinal column. Stand first with your palms turned inward and then outward.

Notice what you feel when you stand this way.

Explorations

2. Elongating the Spine

Focus on the place at the back of the waist from which the spine moves in two directions, releasing downward and extending upward at the same time. Let gravity pull your lower spine down while simultaneously allowing you to extend and lift the upper part of the spine, releasing tension between the vertebrae.

3. Reversing Attention to the Back of the Body

a. Follow the channel that runs from the eyes to the back of the skull and look out from the back of your head.

b. Relax the cerebellum (the lower part of your brain in the base of your skull), feeling how it extends from one ear to the other.

c. Notice the back of the neck in line with the spine as it follows the shape of the shoulders.

d. Feel the ribs and the lungs from the back and notice how far the breath travels down.

e. Bring awareness to the hips at the base of the back, letting the weight of the body sink down. At the same time let the body from the waist upwards elongate, increasing the opening and expansion of the lungs.

f. Sense the back of the legs, especially the back of the knees, and feel the small spaces behind the knees open, allowing energy to flow more easily in the legs.

4. Spinal Roll

Stand with your feet hip-width apart and your weight distributed evenly on both feet, your knees bent very slightly, and your arms hanging loosely at your side.

First image your spine in your mind, then begin to very slowly bend forward, moving one vertebra at a time. First bend your head until your chin touches your chest. You are letting the weight of the head drop forward until the head and neck hang off the top of the torso. Relax your jaw by opening your mouth, and take a few breaths through the mouth. After a few breaths, you may begin to feel the pulse of the breath slightly lifting the head and neck up and down in a nodding motion.

Once you feel this, gradually roll down through each segment of your spine. Curl the shoulders forward, next the upper back, and so on as far down the spine as you can bend. You are gradually giving in to the weight of the head so that the spine undoes itself, giving in to gravity vertebra by vertebra, from the top down. Try to picture the vertebrae one by one. Keep your knees relaxed and bent so that your weight remains over the middle of your feet.

Check that your weight does not rock back on your heels or forward on your toes, and that your knees don't lock. Bend only as far as you are comfortable. When you start to feel a pull in the hamstring muscles in the backs of your thighs, bend more slowly, continuing to sense the movement in your back. As you bend, visualize the spaces between the vertebrae and imagine them widening. When the weight is too much to support through balance, release your spine and hang upside down over your bent knees.

Explorations

Let your body hang loosely from the hips, making sure not to hold any part of your body rigidly. Imagine your torso hanging from your tailbone, giving in to the force of gravity. Breathe easily and let the muscles of your torso, shoulders, neck, arms, and head relax. Check that you are not holding any unnecessary tension in your neck around the base of the skull.

Now focus your attention on your tailbone and, from there, begin to build the spine up again. Let your knees gradually straighten as the balance shifts. Very slowly uncurl your spine and straighten up, bringing your head up last. To do this, press down through your feet and using this downward pressure through your legs (rather than making your back muscles lift you), begin to curl back to standing. As your spine effortlessly lifts itself, imagine your vertebrae stacking one on top of the other. Don't lift the head and neck as you rise. When you keep the head and neck relaxed, their weight will give your entire spine a stretch.

Before bringing your head up, focus on the top seven vertebrae that make up the neck and gradually build them up on top of the rest of the spine. Your head will float up as a result of building the neck like this; you won't be lifting it up. When you are standing upright, move your head in a rotating motion, stretch your arms up over your head and bend backward a little.

As you bend and straighten your spine, notice where your rigid areas are. Stop at that level and bring your breath and awareness there, at the same time feeling into what may be the source of the holding.

You can do the same spinal roll bending sideways toward each foot instead of forward. These sideways spinal rolls can be done more quickly.

5. Breathing into Your Back

Lie on your back and breathe into your abdomen, chest, and diaphragm in turn. As you concentrate on the front of your body, feel the corresponding part of your back — the chest with the shoulders and upper back, the diaphragm with the middle back, and the abdomen with the lower back — and let that part of the back also relax and expand as you breathe. Feel where your back relaxes easily and where movement is restricted.

6. Releasing the Neck — Three Options

a. Sit on the edge of a chair. Slowly turn your head toward the left shoulder, then toward the right, and try each time to look behind you. Then grasp the skin and muscles of the back of your neck with your whole hand, holding yourself like you would a kitten. Make sure your jaws aren't clenched and your tongue is relaxed. Make very small nods like you were signaling "yes" several times, keeping your head relaxed. Then make little "no" movements. Then draw tiny circles with the tip of your nose. Remember to breathe throughout. Now let go of your neck and once again, look behind you to the right and then to the left. Feel your new range of movement.

b. Tilting your head to the side, feel the muscle that runs from behind your ear down along the side of the neck and into the shoulder. Gently massage all along the length of this muscle, following the path of tension. After finishing one side, turn your head from side to side and notice the difference in your freedom of movement. Then massage the other side.

c. Relax any tension in your neck muscles. Touch your top vertebrae where the skull and the neck join and let this point be the center of a circle your head makes as you slowly rotate it in small circles. Change direction every ten or fifteen circles.

7. Releasing the Shoulders

Sit on the edge of a chair with both feet flat on the ground. Place your right hand on your left shoulder in the middle between the tip and where your neck begins. Grasp the shoulder muscle (the trapezius) in your whole hand. Letting the left arm hang down, shrug the left shoulder a few times lightly. Then rotate the shoulder very slowly from front to back. Imagine that you are sketching circles with the round tip of the shoulder. Firmly hold the trapezius muscle as you do this so it plays as slight a role as possible in the movement. Try not to let the left elbow follow the movement, so the arm really hangs loose. Now let the shoulder go and rotate both shoulders, noticing the difference. Repeat on the other side.

8. Feeling into the Back and Neck

Either sitting or lying down, notice where you feel tightness and restriction in your back and neck. Bring your awareness to the area and let yourself rest there, allowing your breath to touch the place of holding. As you do, notice if any feelings arise. Let yourself be with the feelings without trying to figure them out. Just breathe into and through them, allowing the tightness to release even more. If tears come, just let them flow. If you feel compelled to make sound, do so. Invite whatever is stored in the area to express itself however best it can. Then see what, if any, movement arises and follow that, allowing your body to unwind as it needs to.

9. Spine and Back Awareness

As you go about your day, periodically bring your attention to your spine, elongating from the waist up, and to your back, softening and expanding it. Notice how you feel, how you breathe, and how you move.

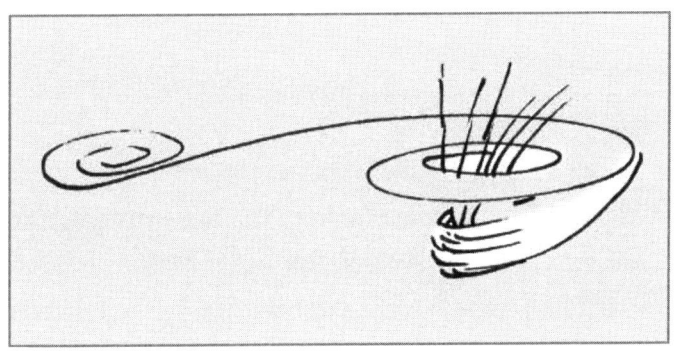

Connecting to the Hands

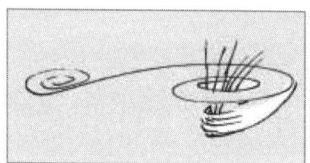

Hands of Holiness

Hands connect us to the world at the level of *ma'aseh*, action or doing. Hashem's actions are often referred to with the term *yad*, hand, in various forms. There is *Yad HaGedolah* (the Great Hand), *Yad HaChazakah* (the Strong Hand), and *Yad Ramah* (the High [Exalted] Hand). These "three hands" are said to correspond to *chesed*, *gevurah*, and *tiferet* respectively. In daily life, we speak often of *Yad Hashem*, "the Hand of G-d," when things happen that seem particularly providential.

Obviously a reference to a body part when speaking of Hashem is not literal. What we are referring to is Hashem's capacity to act, to "touch" us through His actions. As it is written "You open Your Hands and satisfy the desire of every living thing" (*Tehillim* 145:16).

Virtually every mitzvah that involves an action involves the hands. Previously we looked at the feet as the main connection between man and the ground he stands on, responsible, among other things, for movement from one place to another. (See "Grounding – Standing Solidly on Two Feet.") Both the hands and the feet have special significance as reflected in the requirement that before a *kohen* may do the *avodah* (service) in the *Beit HaMikdash*, he must wash his hands and feet. If he fails to do this, his *avodah* is invalid. The reason for this is that the points of connection between the person and his environment are susceptible to various forms of spiritual impurities, and they must be sanctified in the proper way before performing the *avodah*. For the same reason, the Sages instituted that we should wash our hands before prayer (Ramban on *Parashat Ki Tisa*).

As the primary point of connection to *ma'aseh*, action, the hands are in a category of their own when it comes to susceptibility to impurity. They are susceptible to *ruach ra* (evil spirit) and to the special impurity *tumat yadaim* (impurity of the hands), which affects only one's hands and no other part of the body. This is one of the reasons why first thing in the morning we ritually wash the hands (pouring water over each hand three times, alternating hands). It is as though the hands are an entity separate from the body in that they have the potential to contract impurities that remain confined to them and are not conducted through the rest of the body. This is because, in a way, the hands are also connected to the outside world and do not belong solely and exclusively to the body.

Further, it is the blessing for washing the hands that begins the succession of the hundred *berachot* to be recited every day. "Blessed are You, Hashem our G-d, King of the universe, Who has sanctified us with His commandments and has commanded us regarding the washing of the hands." Rabbi Elie Munk explains:

> *This rite was the first act performed by the priests as they began their sacred services in the Temple each morning. It has accordingly been set at the commencement of our daily service as well. Although the actual washing of hands should follow immediately upon waking, the brachah is held over to the beginning of the morning service to connect it to the two succeeding berachot. In the morning men's strength of body and soul is refreshed. He is like a being emerging newly born from the Creator's hand. Before he does anything else, he first renders thanks to his Creator for the rejuvenation of his physical powers, in the אשר יצר [see Appendix 2] and his spiritual powers in אלקי נשמה [see "The Gift of Breath"]. Even before this, however, he dedicates his entire being to the service of G-d by reciting the blessing over the sanctifying ablution of his hands, נטילת ידים (נטל, Aramaic for נשא, to raise, really means to lift, raise the hands from their merely physical nature to their higher, moral destiny – מגן אברהם.) Thus the washing of the hands is a symbolic preparation for the ensuing service. It is in accord with the spirit of the prophetic announcement הכון לקראת אלקיך ישראל, "Prepare thyself, Israel, to face thy G-d" (Amos 4: 12)."*
>
> (Rabbi Munk, The World of Prayer, vol. I, page 19)

Hands are used to connect more deeply to a particular manifestation of holiness. For example, men touch their *tefillin* when mentioning them while reciting *Kriyat Shema*, we touch the *mezuzah* when passing through a doorway, many men touch the *sefer Torah* when it is brought out in synagogue, and many women and men point with one or more fingers when the *sefer Torah* is raised for the congregation to see its words.

Hands are also used in the process of bringing blessing into the world. "Aharon raised his hands toward the people and blessed them" (*Vayikra* 9:22). When the *kohanim* bless the congregation with the priestly blessings, they raise their arms and extend their hands. This ritual of the priestly blessings is called *netiat kapayim* — "uplifting of the palms [hands]." (They also wash their hands before giving these blessings.) When a father blesses his children he places his hands on their heads as Yaakov did when he blessed Efraim and Menashe. It is through the hands that one acts as a conduit for blessings and makes these spiritual transfers to another. This is also seen in a number of healing modalities that rely on the hands of the practitioner to work on subtle levels with another's body and energy field.

We connect ourselves with Hashem's blessing through the hands. When reciting the blessing of *Hamotzi* on bread, we are supposed to hold the bread with our ten fingers. It is written in the verse in *Tehillim*, *Poseach es Yadecha* . . ., "You open Your Hands and satisfy . . ." The word *Yadecha* means "Your Hands," but the word *yad*, hand, is also like the word *yud*, the letter with the numerical value of ten. "*Yadecha*" is like "*yudecha*" — "Your ten" — which alludes to the ten fingers of the hands. Bread, the staff of life, represents all sustenance and signifies G-d's satisfying the desire of every living thing. Therefore, when we recite the blessing over bread, we hold it with our ten fingers, to receive G-d's gifts. (We also wash our hands with a *berachah* before eating bread.)

Created in the image of G-d, we too are able to act, to create, and to give with our hands. There is nothing in creation that is as versatile and capable as the hand. It has nineteen bones, fourteen joints, some of the strongest and most flexible muscles in the body, and many, many nerves. Its structure allows us to do an incredible variety of things. And the quality of what we do with our hands depends on the quality of their connection to our hearts and souls.

The hands can only give expression to what is inside of us. If we do something mindlessly with our hands, we can't expect the thing we make or touch to be imbued with our essence. In contrast, if we are mindful, aware of what we're doing and connected to the action from within ourselves, our hands can transfer this state of presence, this life energy. Not only is the result different, but the task itself becomes much easier and more enjoyable.

Zippora, an aesthetician, experienced this distinction first-hand in her work. After years of giving women facials that included a light neck and upper back massage, she found her fingers very stiff and tired. She thought that perhaps she had to stop seeing clients and resign herself to teaching. Before taking such a drastic step, she decided to see if there was anything she could do to make things better. I advised her to bring her awareness to her hands and fingers as she worked, to allow her presence and attention to flow through them to her clients as she did the movements that by then were second-nature to her.

To Zippora's surprise she found that her fingers no longer stiffened and got tired as she worked. They felt much softer and more malleable. The energy flowing through her seemed to move her hands and fingers rather than her having to exert a lot of muscular effort. She also felt much more connected to her clients. She was now genuinely touching them rather than mechanically executing the massage techniques she had learned. She felt more real to herself and her clients felt more real to her as well.

What had happened was that over the years, without realizing it, Zippora had disconnected from what she was doing. While well practiced at her craft, she was no longer engaged with all of her being. That disconnect had cut her hands and fingers off from their life source and left them to do the physical labor of massage on their own steam, which, not surprisingly, was running out.

The physical exertion without any spiritual or emotional influx had led to the stiffening and discomfort Zippora felt on a regular basis. When she reactivated the connection and brought her fingers back into relationship with her heart and soul, they relaxed and were able to do their work with ease. Her clients felt the difference right away; Zippora's touch was more pleasant to receive and they were able to relax more than they had before.

Delighted with the results of her experiment, Zippora thought that maybe she could help her daughter, who was experiencing a lot of stiffness and pain in her hand and fingers when she wrote. Observing her, Zippora saw that she was gripping her pen very hard and figured she probably also had no awareness of her hand and fingers or how to bring her attention there.

So Zippora explained to her how to be more present to what she was doing. At first, the little girl didn't understand. Zippora practiced with her without the pen in hand and then, when she got it, had her try writing again. They were both pleased to see that this small shift in awareness had allowed her hand to relax and made it much easier to write.

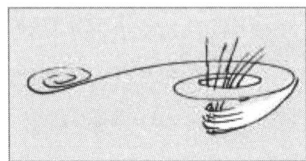

The Power of Touch

In addition to being a primary medium for action, our hands are an important medium of communication, both giving and receiving. The tremendous power of touch is reflected in the Torah's commandment to the Jewish people not to touch Har Sinai during the giving of the Torah. "Whoever touches the mountain shall surely die. A hand shall not touch it..." (*Shemot* 19:12–13).

So much can be conveyed and so much information received from the touch of a hand. Touch – tactile contact with another – is of major importance in the realm of familial relationships. Between parents and children, among siblings, and between husband and wife, touch is another language being spoken in the house. Yet, usually, little attention is given to becoming literate in this very important and sensitive language. That's really remarkable when you think about it, given that from birth onward one's experience of touch contributes significantly to shaping one's experience of the world. (See "Grounding – Standing Solidly on Two Feet.")

The Power of Touch

Touch has the power to convey security, to confirm one's existence, to instill confidence, to express love, to heal, soothe, and comfort, to contribute to a sense of wholeness. It also has the power to do the opposite. Yet, like so many other things, one's capacity to touch, to hold, to communicate through physical contact, is taken for granted. Typically it is shaped by one's own early experiences. Little or no attention is given to learning how to be attentive, respectful, caring, relational, clear, giving, sensitive, and expressive in this context.

People forget that when physical contact is made with another, it is not the body which is touched but the person who is encountered. The quality of this encounter is just as important as the quality of any other type of encounter. And the effects are often long term. Good touch that is friendly, kind, and giving activates a relaxation response. Touch that is not good activates a stress response. There is an actual chemical release in the body resulting from touch.

The English language reflects the significance of touch in such expressions as "getting in touch," "being touchy," "being out of touch," "rubbing someone the wrong way," "touchstone," "the personal touch," "putting one's finger on something," and "being touched by something."

The organ of the body through which we experience touch is the skin. Our skin both separates and connects our inner and outer worlds. Its many nerve endings make it very responsive to touch, very sensitive. Even just bringing your consciousness to the surface of your skin reduces inter-muscular tension.

Although the entire body is covered with skin that has a sense of touch, the most developed and dominant sense of touch is in the hands. Touch often begins with the fingertips exploring, then the hands making more firm and fuller contact, and then the arms as an extension of the body. Each stage reflects an increasing level of intimacy and commitment.

The normal birthing process itself brings us into relationship with touch. During labor, contractions of the uterus stimulate the fetal skin, preparing it to function in the postnatal world as an important receptor of signals and information. Really all systems of the body are activated or toned up by these contractions.

This puts non-labor cesarean-delivered babies at a disadvantage, making the amount and quality of the touch they receive after birth even more important. These babies missed out on the first "caress" that Hashem programmed into the process of birth. Interestingly too, tactile stimulation plays an important role in the development of postnatal breathing. The very breath of life is intimately connected with touch.

After birth, it is body contact with her caretaker through which an infant makes her first contact with the world, through which she first experiences the reality of the other. Bodily contact is the source of comfort, security, warmth, safety, and a growing capacity for learning. Being handled, carried, caressed, and cuddled are all essential needs for an infant. The manner in which these activities are done communicates volumes.

Infants, with their acute kinesthetic sense, are highly sensitive to nonverbal messages. Just as adults draw inferences about a person from the quality of his handshake or hug, infants draw conclusions about the feelings of their caregivers, their inward state, from the quality of their touch. The baby assures herself that all is well largely through the messages she receives from touch, from the signals she receives through her skin.

Sensitivity of touch can be developed. Blind people who are dependent on their sense of touch and use it far more than sighted people are known to be far more tactilely sensitive. As one person who became blind later in life described it, "it is tuning in and allowing the current (of whatever is being touched) to connect with one's own." In this way, they seek and receive information and relationship through touch.

Because touch involves the presence of one's own body and that of another, it is our first experience of an objective reality, something outside that is not us. At the same time we feel this objective something beyond the bounds of our own body, we also experience ourselves. Touch therefore is the first medium through which we feel self and other simultaneously. It is the first place we can learn about healthy boundaries, about how to stay inside ourselves and be in meaningful contact with another at the same time.

Yet often, that's not what happens. Instead we learn that we must leave ourselves to be in contact with another, or that contact with another is not safe or secure and we must retreat inside ourselves. Just as touch has the power to do so much good, to confirm so much that is good about life, it also has the power to do harm, to convey a sense of danger and isolation. Touch can invite one to emerge into the world from within her own skin or it can discourage such emerging and imprison a person inside herself. Touch can feel like a confirmation of one's integrity or an assault on it.

In the early months of life, touch is the primary vehicle for communicating involvement, concern, responsibility, tenderness, and awareness of the needs, sensibilities, and vulnerabilities of the other. In other words, it is the primary vehicle for communicating love and through which the infant learns to love. Body security and comfort in the early days of life is a strong foundation for a future sense of well being.

Yet these things are not givens in many people's lives. And many people don't even realize that they are missing them. So, once again, the first step is awareness. Awareness of the importance of touch in the early days of one's life, awareness of the quality of the touch that we received or likely received, and awareness of what we can do as adults to go back and provide for ourselves what a parent or caregiver may have been unable to provide.

Rachel was a child of Holocaust survivors. Her mother was nervous and somewhat depressed when she was born. She was also overwhelmed with a house full of children and limited resources. Rachel remembers virtually no physical contact with her mother. She was bottle fed and as soon as was physically possible, her mother would prop her up in such a way so that she could hold the bottle herself. Much of the time, she remembered being in a playpen in the room where her mother was, but her mother not paying much attention to her. When she did pick her up or hold her, Rachel sensed that her mother must have been distracted or otherwise preoccupied. For as long as she could remember, Rachel, now in her forties, felt like she had to hold herself up. There was no safe place to rest into.

When she began doing Inner Torah work, this was one of the first sensations Rachel encountered. Tracing it back to the very beginning of her life, Rachel wondered what she could possibly do to help herself now. The image that was most vivid for her was of herself in the playpen. So that's where she started. She pictured her adult self today going into the room where the playpen was. First she just stood a few feet away and looked at herself as a baby. Tears filled her eyes. She felt so sorry for her baby self looking so lonely and forlorn in the playpen. Yet, she was a little scared to actually make contact. The neediness of this baby felt overwhelming to the adult.

Recognizing her feelings of hesitation, Rachel nonetheless ventured over to the playpen and sat down beside it. To her surprise, the baby didn't react. Rachel put her hand out hoping to get her attention. Nothing happened. Then she started to say her name in a sweet, gentle, sing song way. That got a little response. So Rachel edged her hand closer.

She touched the baby's fingers with her own and just let them rest there, giving both of them a chance to digest the contact. It was actually a powerful moment. Rachel felt the sensation in her own body and the baby's simultaneously. It was such a slight gesture but so genuine, so connected, so different from anything the baby had experienced in real time. She could feel the hurt and distrust that already filled the baby's heart. It filled her own heart with a longing to provide the attentive care and security that had been lacking.

The neediness didn't seem so scary now that it was attached to the reality of experiencing this baby with her own hand. From finger contact, Rachel moved to take the baby's hand and wrist in hers. She did it with a firmness and feeling of confidence that she hoped would convey to the baby that she was really there, that she was really someone who could be relied on.

Rachel liked the solidity of the connection she was forming, and she liked giving the baby time to take in these new sensations. It amazed her how easy it was to feel into the baby's reality and experience what this very different type of touch was giving her. She waited patiently for a response. The baby was no longer indifferent. Her eyes were fixed on Rachel and she came a little closer to her. All the while, Rachel kept making sweet sounds as she repeatedly said the baby's name. In time, Rachel moved to stroking her arms and legs, running her fingers through her hair, tracing the outline of her cheeks and forehead.

It was as if she was helping to draw the baby out to the boundary of her own skin, of her own body. From there, Rachel would introduce her to the feeling of connection, of being held and carried in a way that felt safe and reassuring. Step by step over a number of sessions, Rachel forged her relationship with her baby self, ultimately holding her close and rocking her in her arms. She felt a depth of relaxation and ease in her body she had never known before. She described it as a sense that "parts of her that had been disconnected were getting knitted together bit by bit."

Rachel's work with herself spilled over to her relationship with her family and friends. As she learned to navigate the world of touch with her young self she found herself more able to give to, and receive from, others in that realm. A whole new world opened to her.

It is never too late to experience the healing power of touch, whether through one's own inner work or from another. I witnessed this first-hand when caring for my mother at the end of her life. Having held herself up for almost nine decades it was hard for her to let go, to receive and fully relax into loving touch. Only by going very slowly and honoring her defenses, could I help her experience the remarkable power of touch to open buried and beautiful dimensions within — an experience that I had worked hard to acquire myself. (See *Walking Mom Home: Sharing the Blessings of This Life's Final Journey*, pp. 111–112.) Often times, touch that is truly caring and undemanding is the greatest gift we can give to loved ones in their last days in this world. To be able to do that when the time comes, however, requires attending to this sacred capacity Hashem gave us to reach so deeply inside the heart and soul of another.

Our hands are an incredible gift from G-d. Through them we can do and say so much that can't be done or said any other way. From an Inner Torah perspective, the desire is to become conscious, to become aware of our hands, to connect to the power they hold, and to use them as the medium for expression and creation that G-d intended them to be.

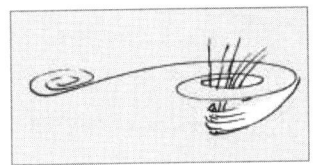

EXPLORATIONS

1. Hand Awareness

As you use your hands in everyday life, start to pay attention to how they feel. Are they tense, stiff, loose, flexible, soft, relaxed? Are you tensing other parts of your body — forearms, upper arms, shoulders, chest, upper back, face, abdomen, or neck — when you use your hands? If so, let go of the tension in these other areas. Notice anything you can about your hands. Also notice how paying attention to your hands affects them.

2. Awakening Your Fingers

Rest your hands loosely in your lap with your forearm supported by your thigh. Relaxing your wrist, rotate each finger separately. Allow the fingers to be soft as you do this. Feel the motion begin at the tip of the finger, with the base of the finger following. Try it with palms turned down and then with palms turned up. Notice any differences.

3. Hand Massage

a. Rub your hands together to increase circulation and to warm and sensitize them. Massage one hand with the other using the thumb or fingertips to move in a circular motion around the base of the hand and then up to the knuckles and along both sides of each finger. Massage each finger between the thumb and fingers of the other hand. Massaging your own hands and fingers keeps the many nerve receptors in them alive and alert.

b. Interlace the fingers of one of your hands with the other hand and stretch your fingers as far back as they will go comfortably. With your free thumb, massage the muscles of your stretched palm.

4. Working with Aware Hands

Pick one task that you do with your hands and consciously bring your awareness into your hands as you do it. Notice any feelings that arise as well as whether your hands themselves feel different. Gradually do the same with other tasks.

5. Touch Awareness

Pick one situation involving touch, with a child, a spouse, or a friend, and pay attention to the contact you are making. Slow it down enough to allow yourself to be genuinely present to the messages you are sending and receiving and to the encounter with this other person. Notice any feelings that come up inside you as you do this. If you feel discomfort or any other difficult sensation, use the Inner Torah process to explore and work through the experience.

Explorations

6. Living in Contact with Your Hands

As you go through your day, whatever you are doing, periodically bring your awareness to your hands. Notice how this affects you.

Exploring the Face

Exploring the Face

From Inner Torah: It's often a surprise to feel how much we are holding in our faces. Only when there is a letting go do we realize the extent to which our faces have become masks. Forced smiles, blocked eyes, tight jaws all exact their price. The face slowly takes on a form that is armored to protect the woman's inner world and defend her from penetration from without. This distortion is most clearly reflected in the faces of the elderly. Years of holding a face in an unnatural pose take their toll. The face looks forced and sometimes slightly unreal. In contrast, anyone who has seen an older woman who is in alignment with her true self immediately recognizes the ease and openness in her face. Usually her eyes also communicate warmth and caring.

The Face

The face, more than any other part of the body, reveals the inner self. The word for face in *Lashon Hakodesh*, the holy language of creation, is *panim*, which also means "inside" or "inner." And since in *Lashon Hakodesh* things are named for their essence, we know that it is this inner dimension that is the essence of one's face. This is seen as well in the words of *Tehillim* 27:8 where the word "face" refers to the inner essence, the inner dimension of G-d: "To You my heart has said, search for My Face. Your Face, G-d, I will search for."

That the face reflects the inner dimension of the heart comes as no surprise. Most people can see their moods on their faces when they look in a mirror and are also able to read the moods of others on their faces. Yet it's not only one's emotional state that is written on the face. Our spiritual and intellectual levels are also revealed there, for those who are able to see.

"A man's wisdom makes his face shine and the boldness of his face is changed" (*Kohelet* 8:1). When Moshe Rabbeinu descended from Mount Sinai with the second *luchot* (tablets), glorious rays of light shone from his face, reflecting his inner spiritual glory. In our own lives, many of us have had the experience of seeing a great Torah personality and feeling awe in response to something Divine or spiritual emanating from his face. We also may have had the pleasure of seeing changes in the face of someone coming to Torah for the first time or moving deeper into a Torah life. As one of my clients who was a *madrichah* (counselor) for *ba'alos teshuvah* said, "You can see their faces begin to glow and a different sort of beauty come through."

In Judaism, reading faces is not just a matter of intuitive ability; there are actually guidelines set out in the *Zohar* and *Zohar Chadash* (*Parashat Yitro*). The great sixteenth-century kabbalist, the Ari, was said to be able to read faces, and some people were ashamed when they saw him, fearing he would see past their masks and know who they really were.

In the context of Inner Torah work, the face is another doorway through which to get to know ourselves and come closer to our true essence. Ideally, we want our faces to reflect what is inside of us, to reveal our inner core of holiness. For, as we've seen, the face is meant to reflect the soul, the innermost part of our being. Yet, many women try to use their faces to hide what is inside. They plaster on a persona that may have little relationship to their inner world. It not only takes considerable energy to maintain such a façade, but there is always the fear of being seen through, being exposed for who one truly is. Worse yet, one can become fooled by her own disguise and begin to believe she is someone she is not, losing track of her real self in the process.

Some women sit in constant judgment of their faces, always wishing they looked different somehow. They forget that the features of their faces are G-d-given, perfectly suited to their unique souls and the unique purposes they are meant to fulfill. Rather than cultivating their inner beauty and allowing it to radiate from their faces, these women remain fixated on their outer appearance and suffer the agony of discontent with their lot.

It is heartbreaking to see how many women are unable to trust and believe in their authentic selves and to live life from there; to simply be who they are without pretensions. Instead, they virtually torture themselves trying to fit into this or that image of who they think they should be or who they think someone else wants them to be. Often they grow weary as time goes on, but by then they have built a whole life around a false self and have no idea how to extricate themselves.

Sometimes the work can begin just by asking a woman to see an image of her face in her mind's eye. For many this is very difficult. While they can conjure up at least a vague approximation of their bodies, what they're wearing and other aspects of their physical selves, the face often proves illusive. That in itself can be surprising and telling for a woman to discover. Asked to see her face in her mind, she's shocked to find that she can't. This simple exercise can sometimes be the strongest indication that she is cut off somehow from her inner essence, that inner dimension of herself that her face reflects.

For these women, working with a mirror can be very helpful. Taking the time to actually see and relate to the woman in the reflection, brings them home to themselves in an important way. They cease to be abstractions to themselves and become as real, and as worthy of attention, as other people in their lives who they usually have no problem visualizing.

Photographs can also be useful for this, but the mirror offers a far more dynamic presence that usually imprints itself inside a woman more than a photo. Also, photos are not as nuanced and subtle in what they report. The advantage they offer is that they afford one an opportunity to carefully study herself without the constant shifting of expression that occurs when there is simultaneous seeing and relating as there is in the mirror.

The cursory glance that most women give themselves in the mirror when dressing, putting on make up, or checking their appearance doesn't foster the type of real relationship that using a mirror in Inner Torah work is seeking to develop. It's the difference between looking and seeing. A woman looks in the mirror to take care of her outer self, focusing on the surface of her being and how it appears.

For purposes of Inner Torah work, our intentions are quite different. We genuinely want to *see*, to understand, to know, to relate to, and hopefully, ultimately, to embrace the reflection of our innermost self. That takes time and a willingness to see not only with the eyes, but with the heart and soul.

That too is often a big change for women. Used to scrutinizing themselves critically in the mirror, if they look at all, it's not always easy to slow down and turn a loving eye on themselves, one that truly wants to connect. Often the eyes no longer even know how to do that. Set into tight muscular patterns that interfere with softening and relaxing the focus, the eye immediately goes into hunting mode, scanning the face and body to figure out, fix, and otherwise exert control. There's little, if any, opportunity for vulnerability to emerge and authentic contact to develop.

Like the rest of the body, the face contains muscles. These muscles are strong and mobile, allowing one to express a wide range of feelings and perform numerous functions. And, like other muscles, they hold tension. The jaw, around the mouth, the eyes, the forehead, the nose, the cheeks, are all storage places for the residue of difficult feelings and experiences. A woman wanting to explore and come into deeper connection with herself can open some of these storage places by releasing the tension in the muscles that hold them in place.

When she brought her attention to her face, Dinah became aware of a slight tingling sensation around her nose. It was very subtle and not noticeable at all in her everyday life. Yet, as part of her Inner Torah work, she became curious about what was underlying that particular place of holding in her body. Skeptical about her ability to get inside the sensation, Dinah brought her awareness to the area surrounding her nose. She noticed the tension there and invited it to let go.

As she did, the first image that came to her was from seventh grade when another child in her class made fun of her nose, telling her she looked like porky pig, a cartoon character with a very flat, pug nose. Dinah remembered that seventh grade marked the beginning of a time of heightened self-consciousness about her appearance, and that the remark had hurt her.

The next image that came was of her older sister who had not been happy with her own nose as a child, feeling it was too big and had too much of a hook at the end. She remembered her sister often standing in front of the mirror, pushing up the end of her nose. Seeing her sister suffering this way made Dinah feel guilty about having a nose that turned up at the end all by itself. That memory was much earlier than the one from seventh grade. Juxtaposing the two, Dinah saw the confusion that her younger self was harboring about whether her turned up nose was a good thing or a bad thing, a cute feature or an ugly one.

Yet from both vantage points, her sister's and her classmate's, she couldn't comfortably accept and relax into her G-d-given nose. Dinah took the opportunity to go back and talk to her young self about her looks in general and her nose in particular. As she got into the conversation, she was surprised to find the girl troubled by her appearance in ways that Dinah was never conscious of before.

As an adult, Dinah was sufficiently satisfied with how she looked not to give it too much thought. But she saw that her younger self had been anything but satisfied. "Because my sister wasn't okay with her looks, I didn't want to be okay with mine. I didn't want her to feel bad or feel like I got something better than she did," young Dinah explained to the adult. "Also, my parents were very weight conscious, and they were always trying to make sure that I didn't get fat. So they would often criticize me and tell me I looked like I was gaining weight. But then sometimes," she went on, "my father would say something like 'looking nice doesn't mean anything if you don't act nice.'"

As she listened to her young self talk, Dinah started to understand why this was a realm she essentially avoided in her adult life. She knew that she didn't pay much attention to how she looked, but she had always assumed that was because she was generally comfortable with her appearance. Now though, she started to realize that there was a part of her that wasn't comfortable and that was avoiding the issue by ignoring her appearance.

Letting herself continue to get to know this part of herself led to an even more startling realization — that she would like to take more care with her appearance, to devote more attention to how she put herself together. She realized that a part of her femininity had been held hostage all these years by the confusing family scenario surrounding appearances.

While she knew her husband liked it when she took the time to look more put together, she also was secure in his love for her however she looked. For his part, he had simply accepted her as she was and had never complained. His forbearance, along with her own seeming apathy in this realm, had led her to essentially ignore this aspect of life and womanhood.

Now, though, she knew that there was more going on inside her than she appreciated before, and she wanted to start to attend to herself in this way. She sensed some long-buried part of her waking up and was excited at the prospect of having this new dimension in her life.

She also enjoyed thinking about the pleasure it would undoubtedly bring her husband after all these years and liked the idea of giving him this unexpected surprise. Amazed that all of this had come to light through focusing on her nose, she couldn't deny the truth of it. Already it was a little easier to hold an image of her face in her mind, which previously she had been unable to see.

Eyes and Vision

The eyes are positioned higher on the face than the ears, nose, and mouth because vision is the most spiritual sense (*Zohar, Parashat Pinchas*; *Leshem, Likut* no. 2 in *Sefer Drashot Olam HaTohu*). It uses only the medium of light, the most spiritual creation in the physical world. The eyes not only receive light and energy and send it the brain, they also transmit energy. So we can feel when someone looks or stares at us even though we might have been unaware of the onlooker's presence. Chazal tell us that the ostrich actually employs its power of "looking" to help hatch its eggs (*Eitz Chayim* 8:1).

On the physical level, the eyes are a very special part of the body, composed partially of tissue identical to brain tissue and very closely linked to the brain in many functions. Essentially, the eye converts the light it receives into energy and transmits that energy, in the form of electrical signals, along the optic nerve and other nerve pathways to the brain. It has been said that ninety percent of what we call vision occurs in the brain,

Eyes and Vision

which translates the signals it receives into images. Vision is really a process combining sight and perception.

The eyes are also connected with the rest of the body through blood vessels, nerves, and muscles. They affect the rest of the body and are affected by it. Muscle tension, for example, can be the cause or the effect of vision problems. Likewise, the eyes are affected by nutrition, what we focus on, how we focus, and a host of other things that we feel and do, including how we breathe.

For our eyes to relax and function as intended, we need to be willing to truly see whatever we are looking at. "Let your eyes look right on and let your eyelids look straight before you" (*Mishlei* 4:25). The Torah recognizes the power of seeing when it uses the word "see" in the opening sentence of *Parashat Re'eh*: "See, I give you today blessing and curse" (*Devarim* 11:26). We acknowledge this power as well in the common expression "seeing is believing." And halachah recognizes this phenomenon by prohibiting a witness from being a judge, because having seen an act committed, he couldn't be sufficiently open to the other side of the case to render a just opinion (*Rosh Hashanah* 27a).

The words of the prophets also reflect this reality, reminding us that in messianic times "Your eyes will *see* your Master" (*Yeshayahu* 30:20), and "All flesh will together *see* that the mouth of G-d has spoken" (*Yeshayahu* 40:5). That is the time when our knowledge of G-d will be perfected and we will truly see, freed from the veil of illusion that clouds our sight today.

In the context of Inner Torah, we want to come into our eyes in the same way we want to fully inhabit the rest of our bodies. Kabbalah teaches that the eye is a miniature mirror that reflects the entire person as created in the image of G-d. And so we say, "The eyes are the mirror of the soul." To allow ourselves to be fully inside our eyes is to allow ourselves to live fully from our souls. Yet in this realm too, we find that blockages and holdings take over, slowly pushing us out of our real inner homes into fabricated dwellings that are nowhere near as magnificent or comfortable to inhabit.

As explained in *Inner Torah*, *"The eyes are used more than we realize to protect and defend. If a woman is not comfortable in her inner world, she is unlikely to let anyone else enter. Since the eyes are a natural entry point, she consciously or unconsciously erects a barrier to prevent others from seeing in and her true feelings from going out. Unfortunately, this barrier also serves to block her from the connection she would otherwise experience between what she sees and the deeper world that lives inside of her. She is rendered numb and neutral by it. She is also left grasping outside of herself with eyes that have forgotten how to turn inward. It is almost as though she is trying to hold on with her eyes to an external anchor, having blocked her connection to her more secure internal one.*

As work is done to help bring down the wall behind the eyes, a woman almost always finds her relationship to herself and the world around her changing. She is better able to see what is outside of her with clarity and without projection. And she is better able to connect to the true depth and resonance of what lies within."

Without a barrier in our eyes, we have access as well to our inner eyes that allow us to look beyond surface reality. These are the eyes of the heart and soul, from which we can see from a place of inner knowing, inner understanding, and a deeper connection to G-d.

The Torah describes an example of seeing with inner eyes — with deeper soul-connected vision — in the story of the *Akeidah*. Avraham and Yitzchak were traveling toward the place where Hashem commanded Avraham to bring Yitzchak as an offering. It says, "On the third day, Avraham raised his eyes and perceived the place from afar" (*Bereishit* 22:4). Chazal, in *Pirkei*

Eyes and Vision

D'Rabbi Eliezer, teach that Avraham saw a cloud hovering over the mountain. (This midrash is also cited in *Rashi*.)

Pirkei D'Rabbi Eliezer continues to relate that Avraham recognized this cloud as signifying G-d's Presence. He said, "Yitzchak, my son, do you see what I see?" "Yes," replied Yitzchak, and Avraham realized that Yitzchak had attained the level of spiritual insight that made him worthy of becoming an offering. Avraham then asked the two attendants, "Do you see what I see?" They did not. With that, Avraham told them to stay where they were, with the donkey. "The donkey sees nothing and you see nothing, therefore, stay here with the donkey."

The eyes are a doorway to our vast inner world, to the richly textured outer world, and to the eternal world beyond. To enter, we need to be willing to soften our focus, widen our gaze, open our hearts, and be with our G-d-given capacity to know reality on many levels, many different planes of existence. Seeing rightly asks us to be receptive and to look without preconceived notions. For that to happen, we need to be willing to be with whatever is, to not try to make it something that it isn't.

Yet that is often hard to do. It requires openness to experience, willingness to change, and genuine connection with the newness of every moment. And, perhaps most importantly, it asks us to accept our vulnerability, to let go of the need to pretend to be what we're not. Only then can the eyes really soften, can the muscular holdings that keep our blockades in place finally release. Only then can we truly see and be seen and take our rightful places in this world.

Through the eyes we also have access to color, which can be its own medium for healing and for coming into deeper levels of awareness. Color is light broken down into different frequencies. Every color, every frequency of light, has its own characteristics and can affect different energies in the body and energy field. While there are many thousands of hues of colors on the visible spectrum that are discernible to the human eye, they are included within the seven basic rainbow sequence of colors — red, orange, yellow, green, blue, indigo, and violet.

Because color vibrations reach us on all levels — physical, emotional, mental, and spiritual — we can call upon them in our daily lives to help us heal and achieve balance. Much like with sound, we can work with color in our efforts to get to know and take good care of ourselves and others. For those who are interested, Appendix 3 offers a discussion of some of the meanings and associations of the colors of the rainbow, as well as white.

Ora was drawn to the idea of working with her eyes and with color as a way to begin to establish more of a connection with herself. She could feel the wall she had erected behind her eyes. And she knew that she sometimes looked at others, especially her husband and children, in a cold, hard way that actually frightened them. It was the last thing she wanted to do, remembering how her mother had done the same thing to her. One look from her mother when she was a child had been enough to stop her in her tracks and instill terror. Her mother didn't need to say a word. It was all there in the look. She couldn't believe that she was now doing the same thing herself.

To start the work, Ora lay down, closed her eyes, and, using an eye pillow, invited the muscles around her eyes to relax. As she did so, she allowed her eyeballs to drop back in her head like pebbles into a stream. She sensed what it felt like to let the area around her eyes be soft and to release the intensity of her gaze. It felt like a great weight lifted off of her. And she became aware of the heightened state of vigilance that marked her way of being in the world. As she let herself relax, a few tears rolled down

Eyes and Vision

her cheeks. Without trying to figure anything out, she allowed herself to cry briefly — something she almost never did.

In her mind's eye, she envisioned the color blue and filled her face from the inside with it. It took a little time. At first the color was very muddy, more brown than blue. I encouraged her to stay with the brown, as it is a grounding, stabilizing color and obviously what her body needed first. From there, she let the bluish brown color spread to her entire body, experiencing it as waves that gently rocked her from the inside. In time, the blue came through more and she continued to allow the waves to soothe her.

After staying with the blue for a few minutes, she noticed it changing to a peach-like color and rested into it as well. She was surprised that something that she was only imagining could have such a strong effect on her. The colors, combined with relaxing the muscles around her eyes and releasing the grip on her eyeballs, were definitely enabling her to experience a profound state of well-being.

From this place of greater ease, Ora imagined interacting with her husband and children. Immediately she was aware of a feeling of fear. She sensed how the hard, cold look in her eye was her way of steeling herself to deal with relationships that otherwise would trigger extreme feelings of vulnerability. She knew that the next step was to allow herself to be with the fear and to see, from the inside, what it was about. Only then would she be able to help her vulnerable self who was hiding behind her hard look. She thought, too, about her mother, for the first time sensing that she also probably felt scared and vulnerable when Ora was a child, and had covered her feelings with a certain toughness that was not her true essence.

In place of the judgment she had carried for years, Ora started to feel compassion for both her mother and herself. With her newfound understanding that the hardness and coldness she manifested at times was but a way of protecting a much softer, gentler part of herself, Ora felt ready to start paying attention to when she adopted this tougher stance and what was really going on inside of her when she did. Her eyes had led her to a way of reaching a part of herself that had been hiding for a long time. She didn't expect to drop her old habits overnight. She realized it would take time for her to feel safe enough from the inside to stop using her eyes to shield herself from difficult feelings. At least now she had a way to start working with it all and that felt encouraging.

With our eyes, we have the potential to be witness to many things — about ourselves, our world, and our Creator. Whatever we do to more fully inhabit our bodies, to truly relax inside the whole of ourselves, contributes to freeing the eyes. We can also work with the eyes directly, inviting the holdings that keep them tensed and blocked to release.

And we can remind our minds that valiantly tried to protect us as we developed in sometimes difficult circumstances, that today, as adults, we are equipped to see, to take in, whatever Hashem presents to us. That we now have resources and capacities to deal with whatever happens, which we didn't have when we were younger. And if we don't have the resources ourselves, we at least have the opportunity to get help from those who do. We no longer need to barricade ourselves behind our eyes to feel safe.

Nose and the Sense of Smell

We took a brief look at the nose and the sense of smell in the chapter "How the Body Breathes." That's because it is through the breathing process, particularly breathing through the nose, that the brain registers odors. At the top of the nostrils is an olfactory mucous membrane with millions of receptor neurons. At the tips of these neurons are numerous tiny hair-like threads which catch odor molecules as we inhale. The neurons then transmit information from these molecules to the olfactory bulbs at the back of the nose.

These neurons are actually part of the brain. This makes the olfactory membrane the only place in the body where the central nervous system is exposed and in direct contact with the environment. Amazingly, there are a thousand different kinds of these neurons, which individually and in various combinations, recognize and respond to about ten thousand different odors. Odor molecules fit, like a puzzle, exactly into a specific neuron or neurons.

Once the odor is registered, information is transmitted to the amygdala in the limbic system, a very primal part of the brain where memory also resides. From there it goes to the olfactory cortex, where a more sophisticated processing part of the brain decides how to react. There too the response is odor-specific, with each odor triggering a different part of the olfactory cortex.

This is all quite miraculous. Even before we know we are in contact with an aroma, some essential part of our being receives it and is affected by it. That's how fragrances can so powerfully touch our hearts and souls. Smells go directly to the innermost control centers in the brain, releasing neurotransmitters, including endorphins, which reduce pain and create a feeling of well being; serotonin, which helps relax and calm; and noradrenaline, which acts as a stimulant.

The special place afforded the capacity to smell and the power of fragrance is clear in the Torah. Smell is the only sense that was not employed in, and blemished by, the sin of the *Eitz HaDa'at* (Tree of Knowledge). All the other senses are mentioned in the Torah as having been employed in that sin. The Talmud teaches that fragrance gives pleasure to the soul, not the body (*Berachot* 43b). And the Torah speaks of ריח ניחח (*rei'ach nicho'ach*) — the "pleasing aroma" of the sacrifices. Sacrifices are intended to raise the level of Creation and bring it closer to G-d. The pleasing aroma represents transformation and elevation into something that is unblemished and pure.

When the Torah writes about the ריח ניחח, the pleasing aroma, it is referring to offerings other than those brought by Noach when he left the ark. With regard to Noach's offerings, the Torah adds the letter ה and writes: "Hashem smelled ריח הניחח." Although in English there is no difference in the translation, there is a definite difference in the language of the

Torah. Chazal teach (*Zohar Chadash* 22b) that three smells went up from Noach's offerings: that of his offering, that of his prayer, and that of his deeds. They add that there was never an aroma as pleasing before G-d as the aroma of Noach's offerings. The Torah commands: "My satisfying aroma, shall you be scrupulous to offer to Me in its appointed time" (*Bamidbar* 28:2). The *Zohar* says that this means you should be scrupulous to offer to Me the aroma of Noach's offerings. Noach's offerings are the root of the aroma of all the offerings ever to be offered from his time onward.

It was in response to the aroma of Noach's offerings that G-d made the covenant never again to destroy the world through a flood. Noach had been awakened to the awareness that he must not just protect his spiritual level, but must strive to heighten his awareness of Hashem's presence and undertake to raise the world to a more heightened awareness. In *Sefer Yetzirah* it is written that the sense of smell is associated with the month of Cheshvan. This is obviously the reason why the flood both began and ended in the month of Cheshvan, and Noah brought the offerings with the most pleasant aroma at that time.

It is also written in *Sefer Yetzirah* that the fear of G-d is connected to the Hebrew letter נ (*nun*), which is the dominant letter of the month of Cheshvan. Without going into the meaning behind the letter נ, it is clear that the month of Cheshvan pertains especially to fear of G-d. It is written regarding Mashiach, והריחו ביראת אלקים — "Hashem will give him the power of smell of the fear of G-d" (*Yeshayahu* 11:3). Thus Mashiach, who is called "the spirit of our nostrils" (*Eichah* 4:20), will be able to know who someone is just by the normally imperceptible spiritual aroma that emanates from each person. This all relates to the month during which the Great Flood began and ended. The sense of smell, not having been blemished by the sin of Adam HaRishon, represents the fear of G-d, which is the antithesis of sin.

As for the healing power of smell, the *Zohar* states: "When the Jews went out from Egypt they experienced the taste of death [resulting from the body-breaking and spiritually crushing slave labor they had suffered there] and G-d healed them... From the roads [on which He led them] went up odors of healing that entered their bodies, and they became healed" (*Zohar, Parashat BeShalach* 45a).

On a somewhat more mundane level, we too can enlist our powerful and pure G-d-given sense of smell in our efforts to heal, become whole, and come closer to Hashem. Using the scent of fresh flowers, fresh baking, spices, scented candles, perfumes, essential oils and the science of aromatherapy, or any other medium for generating aromas, we can intentionally bring pleasing and strengthening smells into our lives. Smells also have the power to instantly transport us to another time and place when the same smell once made a strong impression on us. Because memories, as well as smell, are stored in the limbic system, we each have our own personal connection to every smell, depending on the memories it triggers.

As with our breath, which we don't use to maximum capacity, we use only a very small portion of our fragrance-detecting capabilities as well. Fortunately, our sense of smell, one of our earliest senses, learns very fast when we work with it. But it shuts off after about fifteen to twenty minutes and needs a break. When exploring in this realm, it's best to experiment with one fragrance at a time in the beginning and watch the effects. That way you can learn what scents might be helpful to you in coming to know yourself and moving in the direction you are trying to go.

Tuning into ourselves at these more subtle levels, whether

in the realm of smell, vision, or the face in general, cultivates an ability to tune into others and our environment on more subtle and nuanced levels. Again, what we are developing is increased awareness that can translate into deeper understanding, greater appreciation, and an ability to make better choices that foster the development of our greatest potential.

We are also seeking to use the many abilities with which Hashem blessed us. Our physical make-up is perfectly designed to support the work of our souls, the real purpose for which we are here. Hashem gave us so many remarkable gifts to use in furthering that purpose. It's up to us to unwrap and appreciate them as best we can.

EXPLORATIONS

FACE

1. Relaxing and Massaging the Face

Bringing your attention to the muscles of your face, feel where there is tension and allow it to melt. Imagine the muscles around the jaws and eyes softening.

Then start to massage your face with your fingertips, beginning with a gentle touch that lets you feel whether a spot is tense or painful. Move from the point of the chin outward along the jawbone, in front of and behind the ears. Then work from the bridge of the nose, outward along the cheekbones toward the temples. From the bridge of the nose, work along the eyebrows, massaging above, below, and directly on the brow. Spend time as well on the area between the eyebrows. Then massage in long firm strokes across the forehead, and gently, with small circular motions, in the temple area. Stroke lightly from the temples up your scalp, imagining that you are drawing tension away from your eyes.

In this massage, pay particular attention to areas which contain sinuses — cheekbones, eyebrows, and bridge of the nose — and notice what you feel.

Tap with the balls of your fingers on your cheeks, across your forehead, around your mouth and over your scalp.

2. Scalp Massage

Put your thumbs on the tips of your ears and, with your middle finger, apply pressure to the point at the top of the head halfway between the ears. Move two finger widths in front of, behind, to the left, and to the right of this point and apply pressure there as well. Then use the balls of your fingers to massage your scalp and help loosen it. Apply as much pressure as is comfortable. Rest your fingers on the back of your head and circle your thumbs along the hairline.

3. Relaxing the Jaw

Open your mouth and slowly stretch your jaws as wide as possible, noticing where you feel restriction in the movement. Repeat several times, gently stretching the jaws a little wider each time. Now letting your jaw hang slack, massage it starting below the ear and moving down and inward toward the chin, above and below the jawbone. Then tap firmly with the fingertips making sure your wrist is loose as you tap.

Move the jaw in a complete circle with the mouth open wide. Do the same motions with the mouth closed, concentrating on the chin. Then open your mouth, stretching your jaws wide again, and let yourself yawn.

4. Sensing Your Face

Lie on your back with legs extended or knees flexed, whichever is most comfortable. Lacing your fingers together, place them over your eyes. Now close your eyes and notice what you see under your eyelids. Keeping your eyes closed, remove your hands and let your eyeballs sink deeper into their sockets.

Now notice the right eyelid, making it high and wide like a big curtain over the eye. Pay attention to the separation of the upper and lower lids and where they touch. Next notice your right eyebrow, following it in your mind from the bridge of your nose to your temple and pulling it toward your temple.

Pay attention to your tongue, letting it get wider in your mouth until it feels like it takes up all the space. Notice your jawbone and follow it from the tip of your chin to your right ear. Pay attention to the inside of the right cheek, to the right side of the upper lip from the middle of the lip to the corner of the mouth, and the same with the right side of your lower lip, letting it come up to meet your upper lip.

Try to feel the air circulating in your right nostril from the base of your nose to the right eyebrow. Imagine that you can breathe between your two eyes and make room between your two eyebrows to breathe in that space.

Lace your fingers together again and cover your eyes. Compare with your first impressions. Now do the other side. Notice any changes in how you feel and the pitch of your voice when you're finished.

5. Face Awareness

As you go about your day, periodically bring your awareness to your face and let go of tension there. Then check in with yourself to find out if, at that moment, you are acting from your outer self or your inner self. Start to notice the difference between the two in terms of how you feel, how you act, and how others respond to you.

EYES

6. Releasing Eye Tension

From Inner Torah: *"The key to working with the eyes is to release tension. If the eyes are open, this can be done by softening the focus and allowing the eyes to move into a receptive posture. To do that, a woman can sense the back of her eyes and let visual stimuli come to her instead of reaching out with her eyes to retrieve them. It also helps to shift from a narrow to a broad focus that includes peripheral vision. Anyone who has ever looked at a beautiful wide vista in nature knows the feeling of relaxation that comes when the eyes are allowed their full range. If the eyes are closed, a woman can gently drop them back in the head, almost as though she were looking down into her body from the inside. For even more release, it can help to use an eye pillow – a small, soft sack, usually filled with flax or other seeds and sometimes fragrantly scented. The slight weight of the pillow gently presses against the eyes and further releases tension. Often the whole face and other parts of the body will relax once the eyes have let go. That opens the way for a deeper sense of connection with the inner world that the body so miraculously contains."*

When you close your eyes in this exploration, imagine them as resting in their sockets, like small stones that you've let slip into a pond. Wait quietly for the ripples to end and notice the sensations throughout your body.

7. Freeing the Eyes

Move both eyes simultaneously in small circles. Touch your forehead above the eyes with your fingertips to make sure those muscles aren't moving. Close your eyes and visualize them moving in circles freely with no effort. Opening your eyes, rotate them again and imagine only the pupils rotating. Close your eyes again and rotate them under closed lids. Touch your eyeballs lightly as you do this to feel the movement, while relaxing the rest of your face. Then open your eyes and again rotate them in small circles, noticing if it's easier now.

8. Changing Focus

Look out a far distance and let your eyes move from point to point along the farthest horizon. Take in detail as though you were scanning the horizon looking for something. Try to see a small area clearly, while maintaining awareness of the whole field. Don't strain to see, rather relax and let your breath through as you look.

Now move the horizon a little closer and again move from point to point, from detail to detail. Continue bringing your point of focus closer until it's as close as possible. Keep noticing the variety and clarity of the details you can see. As you do this exploration, remember to blink constantly and breathe. If your eyes get tired, hold your hands varying distances to the sides of your head and wiggle your fingers to open your peripheral field. You can repeat the same exploration in reverse moving from close to distant focus.

Try this exploration as you're walking down a street, allowing your eyes to sweep out as far as they can see and then to sweep back again, while blinking continually. Our eyes are biologically designed to change from close to distant focus continually yet many people don't use their eyes in a way that allows for this range of motion. Frequent and easy changes of focus loosen the eye muscles.

9. Relaxing Eye Muscles

Close your eyes and draw figure eights in the air with your nose, starting with little ones that relax tiny muscles in the eyes and moving on to bigger ones which relax larger muscles. The figure eights can go in any direction, vertical, horizontal, sideways, it doesn't matter. Just move your head slowly and smoothly. You can also draw arcs and circles.

10. Balancing Your Vision

Imagine that you have an extra eye in the middle of your forehead and imagine a ray of light traveling through that eye straight through your brain to the back of your head. Now imagine that other rays of light are entering your two actual eyes and converging at the same point in the back of your head. Feel the rays meeting in the occipital lobe at the back of the head where vision takes place. Notice whether you feel more balanced in vision and centered in yourself after doing this for a time.

11. Seeing into Your Eyes

Look in a mirror and try to connect with the woman you see there through her eyes. Really try to make contact, to truly see into those eyes. Speak to her aloud and allow yourself to register the response in her eyes. Do this as long as you feel connected and like there is real interaction happening. Don't try to force anything, just stay with what feels genuine.

12. Getting to Know Color

Get a box of crayons, colored pencils, or markers that give you access to a wide array of colors. Then take a sheet of paper, draw a large circle in the center, and divide the circle into as many sections as you like. Color each section a different color. You can make a very large color wheel with many colors or smaller wheels with fewer colors. As you work with the colors, notice how you feel, where in your body the color resonates, and what colors you are most drawn to.

You can also do this with your children, encouraging them to notice which colors they like and exploring with them ways to bring different colors into the home.

13. Color Imaging

One by one, imagine each color of the rainbow filling your body from the inside. See and feel the color growing stronger in you with each breath. After doing this with each color of the rainbow, fill yourself with the color white. Notice how you feel with the different colors and where in your body you're most aware of the impact. Once you get a sense of what is helpful for you, you can use color imaging like you do sound, as a quick balm in moments of stress or discomfort.

NOSE AND SMELL

14. Remembering Smells

Close your eyes and try to remember an important smell from your childhood. Can you remember your mother's scent, any smells in the house or in your classrooms in school? Sense which aromas are linked to good memories. If you're having difficulty remembering a time in your childhood that you'd like to remember, can you associate it with a smell that would help you recollect it?

15. Experimenting with Scent

Using essential oils, scented candles, or perfumes, notice the effect on your feelings when you smell a particular scent. Remember to work with only one scent at a time and not to work longer than fifteen or twenty minutes without taking a break.

Pay attention to which scents help you feel more connected to yourself, calmer, stronger, or more aware. Experiment with bringing the scents you find helpful into your life as additional tools with which to work with yourself. Don't be concerned if this medium doesn't speak to you or you are not interested in using it. It's simply an option to consider as another way of helping yourself.

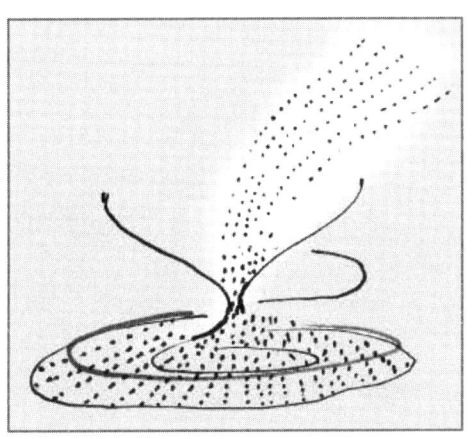

Getting to Know the Energy Body

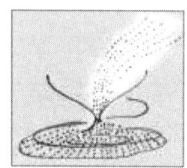

Getting to Know the Energy Body

From *Inner Torah*: *The physical body has an energy body within it. This energy body also extends beyond the physical body. Though we are often unaware of it in daily life, the energy body has as much reality as the physical body. It simply exists on a subtler, less dense plane. Yet it's unmistakable when contacted. It feels like a moving vibration. It flows in a current like water. It holds imprints of life experiences. And it is home to the self's G-dly inner essence...*

The inner energy body is spacious and unbounded, yet contained. It invites stillness, yet provides a gentle current of movement. There is a sense of floating free, yet being solidly supported. Within it events and experiences of a lifetime come into sharper focus, yet fade into the background of a bigger picture. Everything and its opposite, without contradiction, are held in a sea of energy waiting to be explored.

And from *Practical Inner Torah*: *Chazal say that the neshamah fills and sustains the entire body as HaKadesh Baruch Hu fills and sustains the entire world (Berachot 10a). It is understood today that in addition to the solid matter that makes up the physical body, and the electric current of the nervous system... there is also a continuous field of electromagnetic energy that fills the body. This energy field is smaller in amplitude and higher in frequency than the better known frequencies of brain, muscle, and heart. Among other things, it is a repository of our past experiences.*

Inner Torah works with this electromagnetic energy and it is this energy which is accessed in various forms of complementary medicine. The strength, range of vibrations, and coherency of the body's electromagnetic energy are keys to a person's wellbeing. When consciousness or awareness is cut off, the body's flow of energy is disturbed, and blockages, depletion, and stagnation occur...

Every experience brings with it emotions, and emotions affect the energy field as well the flow of energy through the brain. Emotions can be fleeting, passing easily through a field, or they may linger and create a more substantial impact. Repressed emotions typically cause energetic holdings and blockages that over time contribute to habitual emotional patterns. Insight and psychological understanding alone are not enough to shift these patterns. The emotions that created them also need to change so that the field can reorganize in a more coherent way.

We take our old energetic patterns into our present experiences. Our fields are organized at the level of our ability to handle whatever happened to us at the time it happened. That means that whatever our chronological age today, there are aspects of ourselves from earlier times still locked into our energy fields and brains that influence our responses to situations that resonate in a similar way.

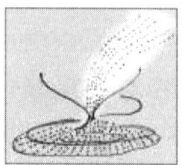

Becoming Energetically Self-Aware

The Inner Torah process focuses primarily on engaging held emotions from a stronger, clearer place in ourselves and thereby releasing blocked or contracted energy. It uses the feelings of energetic and physical discomfort as gates to gain access within. Yet it is also possible to work with the energy itself and thereby invite emotions to shift.

The first step for many is to become aware of the inner energy body and the energy field that emanates from the body. With that awareness, the next step is to learn to recognize what's happening on an energetic level in different situations and at different times. From there, it is possible to deepen connection to one's essential self and expand the amount of energy held while remaining at ease. This, in turn, can increase vitality, patience, flexibility, creativity, joy, and one's sense of well-being.

When we speak of the inner energy body, we're really

speaking of an expression of the soul, the life force, the spark of the Infinite that animates our lives. It is sensed in the space that lies deep inside the physical body. We can access it with attention, actually experiencing the vastness of our beings that transcends anything and everything that is happening in our lives. It is an eternal, timeless part of us, the source of our existence. It always remains the same. In childhood and old age, in health or sickness, in success or failure, it remains unchanged.

This is not an intellectual construct, not something to know with our minds. Indeed, our minds, with their ceaseless focus on circumstances, events, ideas, and a host of other things, often obscure it. Only sensing can open the door to this inner space that is our true home. Anyone can cultivate the ability to sense within in this way. It simply takes awareness and the conscious choice to tap into this deep and rich reservoir that lies within every person. That means taking time throughout the day, whatever you're doing, to bring your attention inside your body — to stop for a minute or a few seconds and concentrate within. The body then becomes a doorway into a deeper sense of aliveness that is always accessible underneath emotions and thoughts. And from this place of heightened awareness, the mind can actually function better.

After a time, it won't even be necessary to stop. You'll be able to sense the vast, infinite world within the borders of your own body at the same time as you're doing whatever you're doing. You'll inhabit your inner world and outer world simultaneously. Hashem breathed the breath of life into us. Life itself is within us; it's only a question of learning to open to it.

As explained in the previous Inner Torah books, the energy field is organized by emotions. Actually, you can think of emotions as aroused energy — a power source. These emotions span a continuum from the most material and basic to the most lofty and refined.

The Breath and Body of Inner Torah

Maybe the simplest way to think about the energy field that emanates from the body is that it is the way in which our inner state manifests outside our physical borders. We all know the feeling of coming into a room and knowing the mood of the person in it before we see or hear anything. Whether the person is angry, sad, happy, anxious, frightened, or anything else, we can sense it in the room.

It's the same when we first see someone we've never met, and before we exchange a word we pick up a sense of whether we feel comfortable with that person, whether we're drawn to get to know her — or the opposite. And it is the same again when we are in the presence of a *tzaddik* or someone deeply immersed in prayer, when we are uplifted just by being in the physical vicinity.

What we are experiencing is the frequency of the vibrations created by the person we are sensing. As a general matter, our grounded physical selves reside in the lower vibrations while our spiritual selves are found in the higher vibrations. Ideally, we want to be able to access the entire spectrum, remaining grounded while at the same time elevating our consciousness to connect more fully with our Divine essence. We want to be able to locate and identify ourselves on all of these levels without contradiction. For, as we've said before, we are both body and soul, and it is our job to integrate the two. The place of integration is one of expanded consciousness that encompasses *gashmiut* (material) and *ruchniut* (spiritual) life simultaneously — exactly what Torah asks of us.

In Inner Torah terms, what this means is being able to work with ourselves on all levels — *pshat, remez, drash,* and *sod.* (See *Inner Torah*, pp. 41–58.) We need to be able to perceive, process, and behave on the higher level of our souls and on the physical, material level. In other words, we need to engage our emotions along the continuum of our consciousness, bringing understanding to both the personality and soul levels of our beings — our lower and higher selves. Ultimately, we want to unify the two into one coherent sense of knowing that encompasses all of us, so that we can act from a place of integration and wholeness.

Our ability to do this depends first and foremost on our level of awareness. The greater our awareness, the more energy can flow and the more we will be able to access our higher plane of knowing — and bring that knowing to bear on the issues and challenges in our lives.

Unfortunately, the ability to sense another person's energy field doesn't always translate into an ability to sense our own. Yet we too are broadcasting our inner states whether we know it or not, and in the process are creating an energetic reality around us that in itself affects how we (and the people near us) feel. For there is reciprocity here — our feelings influence our energy fields and our energy fields influence our feelings.

We all have habitual emotional patterns that define our energy fields. We are emotionally conditioned by childhood experiences as well as whatever experiences our *neshamot* carried into this world from other *gilgulim* (lifetimes). (See *Sha'ar Hagilgulim*, introductions 2, 3, and 4.) The nature, strength, timing, intensity, and persistence of an emotion determine the impact it will have on the energy field, whether it will be an organizing or disorganizing force, how it will restructure the field, and how long it will continue to be an influence.

As children we are essentially captive in situations that demand or allow a certain range of experience, behavior, and response. From that our nervous systems internalize the message that this is the range that life allows — even though it's only the people and events in our lives at that time that are setting those parameters. From that experience, we then build our sense of who we are. In actuality, though, many people growing up are taught to restrict the movement of their energy in ways that are not necessarily consonant with who they really are.

Over time, our experience of reality becomes a function of these unseen and often unknown energetic patterns. They translate into vibrational patterns that cause us to resonate with, and relate to, reality at whatever level is familiar to us from the past. That happens because as adults, we continue to respond as if those circumstances from our past were still current and controlling, when in reality they are long gone and we can give ourselves permission to fully manifest.

The lesson to learn here is that we don't have to be hedged in by old energetic habits and let them limit our perception and experience of life. By developing our awareness and expanding our vibratory range, we can grow in our capacity to realize our true potential and to know G-d.

We can get a glimpse of this possibility when we think about how different experiences and activities can cause temporary shifts in our energy and vibratory level. A good example is in prayer or meditation when we sometimes are able to break through a barrier and access higher vibrational levels. This also can be experienced at times in the creative process. Creativity springs from life force and is heightened when our consciousness is expanded.

The opposite happens when one comes into an impure environment and confronts lower, baser energetic frequencies. For that reason, among others, we ask in our prayers every day to be rescued from "an evil man, an evil companion, an evil neighbor." Just the presence of such forces, in addition to whatever other influence they may exert, can have a negative impact on a person's energy field and pull her down.

In order to shift one's energy field, the emotions that organized it have to shift. That's what we're doing in Inner Torah work when we're helping our younger, vulnerable selves express and release difficult feelings and when we, as adults, are able to give them the love, support, validation, appreciation, encouragement, and guidance they need. In this way, the circumstances and emotions one experienced in the past no longer can control the organization of one's energy field in the present. A new opportunity is created to function from a place of greater ease with an energy field that is organized around loving and supportive input.

We are using the direct relationship between emotions and vibrational patterns in the energy field. Changing the emotions changes the field, allowing us to access higher levels of ourselves, to become more whole. We are helping ourselves to heal and grow, expanding our capacity in the process and enabling ourselves to draw closer to Hashem.

The most powerful source of all emotions resides at the soul level and ultimately needs to be resolved at that level. These soul issues create emotional charge and provoke behavior in everyday life as well. It is important that we remember, even when we are working at personality levels, that our deeper goal is to rectify whatever needs to be rectified in our souls. For we are making the journey through this lifetime for the benefit of our souls; it is our souls which long to manifest G-dliness.

Using Inner Torah, one can engage the part of the self that is having the feelings and by coming into healing relationship with her, shift the emotions and the surrounding energy field. Now, though, we're looking at ways to engage the energy field itself, to change old energetic patterns, and thereby influence our feelings. This can help us feel more whole and more capable of appropriate action even in difficult situations where we might otherwise freeze, explode, blame, or react in other disappointing or damaging ways.

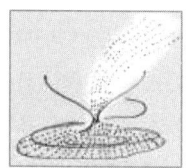

Energetic Boundaries and Movement

One key to the work of strengthening energetically is becoming conscious of what it means to feel separate and connected on an energetic level. Ideally, this is a process that happens gradually during the first few years of life. But often that's not what occurs. Instead, our experiences encourage us to merge with our surroundings and the people we interact with. If a person with whom we need contact is physically present but energetically absent, it's even more debilitating. The sense of where we stop and another person starts is never developed. As a result, we end up tangled in each other's realities in a way that damages relationships and inhibits genuine growth. We become unnecessarily vulnerable to the words and actions of others, a difficulty that can continue for a lifetime if not addressed.

Fortunately, learning to hold boundaries that enable us

Energetic Boundaries and Movement

to feel appropriately separate and appropriately connected is a skill that can be learned once we're aware that we're lacking it. Boundaries come from the inside. They result from knowing and being connected to our genuine selves, the essence of who Hashem created us to be. Our boundaries simply delineate what Hashem brought into existence. To maintain our boundaries, we need to understand how we live inside ourselves and how we interact with the outside world. Everything in this book, and in Inner Torah itself, is aimed at helping us attain that understanding and enabling us to act on it. Becoming familiar with the movements of our own energy is another piece of the puzzle.

All of creation can be thought of as an energy field, within which are found our individual energy fields. The movement of energy in creation is reflected in the movement of our own energy, which ideally moves freely in all directions. In a sense our energy fields are comparable to our breath. Just as the breath is designed to carry us through a wide range of situations and enable us to adapt and respond appropriately, so too our energy fields. And like our breath, the movements of our energy fields are highly sensitive to everything that happens inside and outside of us. Some things can make our energy go flying out while other things can bring our energy scurrying in. So to start, we need simply to notice what's going on with our energy, just like we started the breath work by paying attention to our breath.

The easiest place to begin is with how far our energy extends from our bodies. Torah teaches us that each person is considered to have four cubits, *dalet amot*, around her that are considered her personal space for halachic and other purposes (*Bava Metzia* 10a; *Eruvin* 41b). While opinions vary about the size of a cubit, it is clear that one's boundary extends beyond the physical body itself. It is also known that the two highest levels of the soul hover around the body and are not found within it. (See Ramchal, *The Way of G-d* 3:1:4; *Nefesh HaChaim*, sha'ar 1:15–16).

You can get a sense of your own energetic boundary by sensing how far out from your skin you feel you extend. One way of gauging this is to notice how close to you you're comfortable allowing people or things to be — where you feel your space beyond your body ends. See if this is your usual boundary and how you feel about extending it further out. Also see how you feel pulling it in closer. Pay attention to whether your usual boundary reflects or differs from the norms of your culture in terms of how far people typically extend out and what amount of personal space beyond the body is recognized.

Once you have a sense of where you usually hold your energy boundary, see if you can notice when it changes. When do you become more expansive and feel your energy field bigger? And when do you become more contracted and feel your energy field to be smaller? For most people, expanding and contracting energetically doesn't happen consciously but rather in response to something or someone. Typically, we expand our energy if we like and feel good about what's happening and contract our energy if we don't. It's almost a reflex reaction. Expansion brings us closer and contraction moves us away. In a neutral situation there is a more natural movement between expansion and contraction of which we're probably not even aware.

In a sense, it's another way in which we communicate our feelings about whatever is going on. As with other forms of communication, we want to be able to choose how we respond rather than be trapped in a habitual reaction that may not serve. For example, if something happens that we don't like or find threatening, our automatic response may be to contract away from the person or event and essentially leave energetically. Yet, it may be that we and the situation would be much better served if we stayed present, expanded energetically, and spoke up or otherwise did what was needed.

Usually there are better and healthier ways to object than contracting energetically, which may not only be unproductive but can leave unpleasant negative residue. When our bodies remain and we pull back energetically, an edge of anger and defensiveness can often be felt in our wake. That can be hard to deal with and hurtful to the people on the receiving end of it.

That's not to say that objecting by contracting energetically is never appropriate. Sometimes it may be. But we don't want it to happen every time we're confronted with something we don't like. Being trapped in this way severely limits our ability to be effective, to make an impact, and to manifest our true potential. It leaves us trying to function as adults while our younger, vulnerable selves, who may not have had any alternative to contracting, continue to run our lives. They probably did not have the option of expanding energetically that, as adults, we have. Either the circumstances didn't allow it or they didn't have the skills to do it. From their perspective, contracting energetically may have created a feeling of safety or strength.

As adults today, it is our job to help ourselves develop the ability to say no when we need to, to stand up for ourselves, to object when necessary, and otherwise to take our rightful places. It is up to us to give ourselves permission and the ability to expand. And if we've forgotten or never knew how to expand, it's up to us to learn. If we don't know how on our own, we need to seek out the resources to help us develop these skills. And each time we find ourselves reflexively contracting away from something we don't like, we can invite ourselves to expand and get a glimpse of just what we need to learn to enable us to make that very different choice.

This is important because a small expansion to include an event gives us more freedom of action which, in reality, is the real key to safety and strength. When we contract away from an event — to keep it from touching or influencing us — we limit our choice of response. There is often a closing of the heart as well.

Our ability to expand to include even a difficult event depends as well on breathing. Contraction is usually accompanied by breath holding or shallow breathing. Fear is often at the root. Feeling insecure in our own centers, we instinctively draw a tight, narrow boundary around ourselves. Even if we feel limitless inside that space, we're unable to extend it out, to open ourselves and be free to participate fully in whatever is going on. If we want to expand instead, we need to be willing to breathe into what is happening, to entrust ourselves to our breath and its Divinely designed capacity to modulate our every experience. So energetic awareness and breath awareness go hand in hand; each can facilitate the other.

Habitually expanding energetically and expanding too far are also problematic. They can be elaborate yet unconscious defenses against feeling vulnerable or exposed. Filling the space with our own energy keeps others at bay, essentially acting as an energetic barrier. It's a way to maintain control, to dominate, to avoid encountering other people's realities or being touched by other people's needs. It can appear to be relational but is more of a facade that actually prevents genuine and meaningful engagement.

For the person on the receiving end, it can feel overwhelming, alienating, diminishing, and disempowering. Before they even know what's happening they are overtaken energetically, and unless they are energetically strong themselves, will end up sucked into the expanded person's agenda, likely losing track of their own needs in the process. A person who continually expands or expands too far out also tends to be ungrounded, which presents its own difficulties. (See "Grounding – Standing Solidly on Two Feet.")

Both expansion and contraction are normal and appropriate at different times. The key is not to be stuck in one mode or another, but rather to allow our energy to move freely, choosing whether to expand or contract energetically as needed. From an Inner Torah perspective this means we have to take responsibility for ourselves on an energetic level, as we do on every other level, and not simply react reflexively. The energetic movements themselves produce feelings. For the most part, expanding to a reasonable degree feels better and allows for a more effective response than does contracting. So if we can learn to expand our energy in circumstances that would otherwise have provoked instant contraction, we can feel better and manage better. In other words, by purposely moving our energy, we can influence our feelings and separate them from the event.

The next movement of energy to focus on is up and down, the energy distribution that keeps us balanced. To get a sense of where you fall on this continuum, just notice if you feel your energy more in and around your upper or lower body. You can also notice if the distribution is different depending on whether you're alone or with other people. As a general matter, we do best with our energy distributed in a way that encompasses the whole body. However, there may be occasions when we want to pull our energy up out of the lower body, while in different circumstances we may be much better served by staying closer to the ground. Again, the goal is not to be stuck in one place or the other, but to allow free movement so that we can respond to circumstances appropriately.

The extremes of this movement — a field that is habitually down and a field that is habitually up — have very different characteristics. The habitually dropped field carries a sense of defeat, a feeling of not having the energy to get up. It's prevalent in people who feel like victims, like they can't get what they need. There's a sense of collapse, of wanting to be supported by someone else. It's often accompanied by endless efforts to please, which, it is hoped, might one day cajole someone into providing the longed-for support.

Others may be drawn to or repulsed by such a display of neediness. A fallen field can invite rescue efforts as easily as resentment. It communicates a very different message than a field that someone has consciously let down in order to rest and rejuvenate. One broadcasts helplessness, while the other expresses a deliberate desire to take care of oneself, with no need for intervention or help from someone else. The latter requires grounded energy, something very different than energy that is dropped or lost through a habit of collapse.

The field that is too far up, sometimes even ballooned out of the body, projects just the opposite experience — one of being very energetic, very much in control, very lively, and often very engaging. In the presence of someone with this distribution, one can easily overlook the lack of grounding, of support, for this often very charismatic energy. The unsuspecting recipient of all the attention doesn't realize that underlying it may well be an unconscious need to protect the self by controlling others, similar to what drives those who habitually expand. Keeping energy up and focused on others masks one's own feelings of vulnerability. People who do this find it is easier to make contact with other people from a ballooned place because they feel less exposed.

As I explained in *Inner Torah,* "*The overreaching promotes a sense of merging with the other, while at the same time protecting the deeper, more intimate aspects of a woman's self. For a woman who is habituated to this energy pattern, it can feel very frightening to begin to bring her energy down into her own body. Initially she may feel disconnected from other people and too exposed. Yet what she is working towards is actually a more respectful and honest encounter with others."*

My observation, as described in *Inner Torah*, is that many women have a tendency to live energetically in their upper bodies. It's a pattern that's often present in women who are adept at reading other people's thoughts and feelings, a skill that many developed to survive in their families of origin. As I explained, it is as though they learn to lean out of their own bodies and energy fields into the bodies and energy fields of the people around them. They get busy registering and absorbing everyone else's reality, usually missing the experience of their own. It's also a pattern in women who live in their heads excessively, processing everything through their intellect without making room for emotion.

As with expansion and contraction, we're looking to cultivate the full range of energetic movement without being trapped in one extreme or the other. There will be times when we want our energy more up and times when we want to let it down. Again, our goal is to have the ability to choose the energy distribution that will enable us to realize our potential most fully. That means taking responsibility for getting to know our patterns and being willing to venture into whatever territory we need to explore to bring ourselves into balance.

Rebecca was very outgoing and very involved in her community. In many ways she thrived on all the activity. But she noticed that over time she had grown more and more impatient with her children. And she was concerned. She sensed somehow that she was too excited, too revved up with all her communal work, that it was pulling her further and further out of herself, leaving her less to give at home. In an effort to understand more about what was happening, Rebecca decided to pay attention to what happened to her energy when she got going on a project.

Immediately she noticed that she was ballooning, moving her energy up to generate enthusiasm and motivate the people she was working with. Appreciated as a leader and a hard worker, she got a lot of reinforcement for this posture. But she sensed that it was disconnecting her from some deeper, quieter, more sincere well of feeling inside herself. It was that well from which she needed to draw when she related to her children. But after spending increasingly more time in balloon mode, she found it harder and harder to transition back to this more grounded and patient place in herself.

Yet she was clear that with her children that was where she needed to be. So Rebecca began to work with her energy. Before coming home, she took time to ground and bring her energy field down into her lower torso. As soon as she did so, she felt something inside of her relax and slow down. Then she would just sit for a few minutes and let the excess energy that had built up around her dissipate. She reminded herself as well to come into her exhale, to really let herself settle down inside her inner home before heading to her familial home.

The change was significant. Rebecca described it as her inner gear shift. She was able to tap into the reservoir of patience that she used to have when dealing with her children. At one point in the work, she said that in some ways she would like to live her whole life from this lower and slower gear. But at the same time there was another part of her that enjoyed the hustle bustle. And she knew that her cranked-up level of enthusiasm really did make a difference in motivating others to get things done. So she didn't want to change to that degree, to always live in slower gear. But she was happy now to have the tools to be conscious of what mode she was in and to shift between them as appropriate.

In addition to movement in and out and up and down, our energy fields vary in density. A thick, dense field can block and limit the impact of what's going on around us, while a thin, diffuse field can make us more aware of what's happening. Both have their advantages and disadvantages. A dense field can offer a sense of protection and communicate a feeling of empowerment. If it's too dense and too inflexible, it can dull sensitivity to other people much the same way as overexpansion can. The same armor and insulation that offer a sense of safety operate to block genuine involvement and connection with others. People who are stuck in this energy pattern have a hard time in loving relationships because they feel so separate and unable to merge. Obviously this can be an enormous problem in the context of familial relationships.

A more diffuse field can increase empathy and facilitate feelings of closeness. Diffusing our fields with people we like and trust allows us to merge in a way that is good. It furthers intimacy. But if it's too diffuse or habitually diffuse, it can cause confusion, blurring the line between other people's feelings and one's own. This makes it difficult to know and feel one's own reality and do what needs to be done to take care of it. It also makes people hypersensitive to everything and anything that someone else is doing. That leaves the people with diffused energy susceptible to feeling violated, hurt, and at the mercy of others. And the people interacting with them end up feeling like they're always doing something wrong, that they have to walk on eggshells. This takes a toll on relationships in a different, but equally problematic, way.

As with ballooning, some people diffuse to figure out what other people are feeling. Again, this is a practice which often starts as a survival technique in childhood when other options were not available. As adults, we need to wean ourselves off this habit, realizing that we now have other choices. We also need to realize that we can't ever know for sure that we're accurately reading another person. In fact, very often, assumptions about what's going on with another person are mistakenly self-referenced. People assume that it has to do with them when many times they are not even a factor in the equation. It is sometimes even hard for such people to remember that the person they are so busy trying to figure out actually has a life independent of them, and that whatever that person is doing or feeling could very well be related to any number of things other than them. So diffusing to try to figure someone out is rarely a good idea.

As with the other movements, what is most effective is a natural flow between the two extremes, being able to access varying combinations of denseness and diffusion as needed. To become aware of the density of your field, pay attention to whether you feel the energy around you to be thin or thick. Notice too if it's denser in the front than the back, or denser above your head than under your feet. See how aware you are of what's going on in your environment. Are your antennae always out and probing the world around you? Are you socked in to your own world, oblivious to what's happening outside? Are you able to maintain a balance between experiencing your own reality and that of others simultaneously?

Mira came from a family rife with sibling rivalry. Even in adult life she experienced her siblings as causing problems for her with her mother, inciting her mother against her whenever they got the chance. Wanting to have a good relationship with her mother and to perform wholeheartedly the mitzvah of *kibbud eim* (honoring one's mother), Mira was at a loss as to what to do. Whenever the family got together she would experience her siblings and mother as relating to her with disdain, ignoring

Energetic Boundaries and Movement

her, judging her, and trying to manipulate her. Her reality was dwarfed by theirs. When she got back to her own home, all she could focus on and think about was what everyone else was doing.

When she learned about energy, Mira became interested in looking at how she handled her own energy at these gatherings, hoping that it might be a vehicle for shifting her experience. What she noticed was that she almost evaporated in the presence of her family. Her energy was so diffuse, so stretched out to read the faces, gestures, looks, and comments of her family, that she virtually had no contact with herself. It stunned her. Inside herself she was so busy interpreting and processing all the data that her diffused field was picking up that she only registered the realities of the other people, not her own. Suddenly it was no wonder why she felt so overwhelmed by them.

Her next step was to practice making her field denser. She started in a small den in her house, trying to feel her energy close around her. Then keeping the same level of density, she worked on expanding it to fill the little room. Next she tried to do the same thing while imaging herself at a family gathering. In the beginning, that was almost impossible. But bit by bit she began to strengthen her energetic muscles and was able to hold steady even with her family in mind.

From there she proceeded to a bigger room in her house and did the same thing. Eventually she was ready to start practicing her newfound skill at actual family events. The first few times didn't go well. She flew into a diffused state almost immediately upon walking into the room. But now at least she was aware of what she was doing. And while she couldn't yet manage her energy in that circumstance, she did decide not to process the incoming data, not to busy her mind with what she was picking up. That in and of itself was a relief, but left her feeling empty and strange.

Uncomfortable feelings such as these are common when changing an energetic habit. We have to begin to let go of old ways of dealing before new ways are firmly, or even tentatively, in place. It would be unusual not to feel awkward or even somewhat at a loss in the process. Once she understood this, Mira was reassured and continued with her efforts. With a little more practice, she started to be able to hold her field more densely around her while with her family.

Not only did she pick up less information from the others, but she felt more connected to herself and sensed that she was taking up space differently in the room. That freed her to concentrate on what she wanted to give to her mother without bothering with what anyone else was thinking or doing. It also helped her to trust her own sincerity and worry less about her mother's response. This made the whole exchange less charged and, in turn, freed her mother to do whatever she felt she needed or wanted to do in response to Mira's overtures. By working with her energy, Mira was learning to empower herself – instead of empowering the situation or other people.

Sometimes, rather than energetic movement, we find our fields jammed, not moving in or out or up or down. They're just stuck, usually in a fairly dense and contracted state with a lot of tightly bound energy around the middle of the body. It's the posture of the martyr, the person who is resigned to enduring and maybe even takes some kind of pleasure in being able to bear endless discomfort. She simultaneously communicates her resentment at being trapped and her pride in being capable and able to take it. Underneath, there is usually a lack of self-respect, feelings of shame, guilt, and powerlessness.

While possibly helpful for short stretches that really do demand a head down, nose-to-the-grindstone mode, this is not a stance for the long haul. If prolonged, the absence of

Energetic Boundaries and Movement

energetic movement can be debilitating and deadening for those experiencing it and for those around them. It basically kills joy and resists anything that would feel good or enlivening. This is not what G-d wants of us. The Torah teaches us to be *b'simchah*, to serve G-d *b'simchah*, in joy, as it says, "Serve Hashem with gladness, come before Him with joyous song" (*Tehillim* 100:2). The Vilna Gaon, in his commentary to *Mishlei* 18:14, teaches that happiness sustains a person through infirmity and even heals. We are expected to infuse ourselves, our homes, our communities, and our world with light and joy. And, as we've seen in previous chapters, this requires movement. Our energy fields are no exception.

Free movement of the body's energy is a function of pulsation. Pulsation is actually inherent in the way G-d created the world, referred to in Torah as "run and return." (See Appendix 2.) This is a more subtle movement than the ones we've looked at so far. It's a tiny little back and forth motion that can give life even to the densest field. It brings flexibility to what otherwise would be rigid and unyielding. It creates openness in what otherwise would be closed and impenetrable. It is the release valve that prevents energies from building up to explosive proportions.

With this slight movement, we can access feelings of well-being and reserves of energy within whatever boundary we choose to inhabit. We can let our energy flow even in the most challenging circumstances. We don't need to deaden, numb, or clamp down on ourselves. Instead we can allow a slight feathering, a little shimmer of movement at the edge of our energy field as well as in our inner energy body. That little ripple of movement can be enough to bring us to life. Unfortunately, though, it's often blocked by fear. We equate energetic non-movement with safety. But the sense of control it offers is illusory. We are actually hampered in efforts to respond and take care of ourselves and others when we're frozen and shut down.

Genuine safety and freedom come from being able to stay comfortable in and connected to one's own reality and to Hashem, no matter what is happening. As the *Kuzari* (Reb Yehuda HaLevi) explains, a true *talmid chacham* has such capacity. He can stay centered in his world independent of his environment and the circumstances with which he is confronted. This is one of the great gifts of a life devoted to the study of Torah. The rest of us may have to work harder to do the same, but we too are helped by our dedication to Torah. "It is a tree of life for those who grasp it, and its supporters are praiseworthy. Its ways are ways of pleasantness and all its paths are peace" (*Mishlei* 3:17–18).

We're also helped by remembering that our feelings, no matter how difficult, are only energy in different constellations. Our emotions are an energy source. If we're not afraid to engage them, to move with them, we can access the energy trapped within them and use it for good. That means that we don't want our energy fields to remain motionless for long. We don't want to repress, bury, or ignore what we feel. We don't want to live our lives on automatic pilot, robotically going through our days disconnected from ourselves and all that Hashem has given us.

Hashem created the world to bestow good (*Ramchal, Kelach Pitchei Chochmah* 2–4). It is up to us to make ourselves into vessels that can truly receive that good, no matter what is happening in our lives. When we work with our energy, we can see from yet another vantage point the almost infinite capacity Hashem gave us to become such vessels – and we can be even more grateful.

Reva was a woman who for decades endured what she experienced as a disappointing and difficult life. She shouldered the burdens of her family, feeling that everything was on her; that

Energetic Boundaries and Movement

her husband didn't take care of her in the ways she would have liked; that her children took her for granted; and that nobody really appreciated or even saw her for who she really was.

By the time she came for Inner Torah work, her energetic habits were well-established. Her field was dense, contracted, and devoid of movement. She had donned the mantle of martyrdom long ago and couldn't seem to divest herself of it, though she claimed not to want to go on this way. As she talked about her life, a distinct undertone of resentment came through the weariness that was written all over her.

Listening to her, it was hard to understand why she wasn't taking better care of herself. Her children were older and far more self-sufficient. Several were married. What kept her tethered to her old way of navigating life when at this point she was free to go about things differently? It was a mystery.

Initially she tried to say it was because her husband didn't carry his rightful share of the load, at least not in the way she would have wanted him to. But that still didn't answer the question, because at this point, even if she had to carry the whole load on her own, she still could have done it in a way that was less labored and misery-laden. Then she tried to trace it back to a work ethic in her parents' home that rewarded working oneself to the bone, nothing ever being too much, and never having any free time. Asked if her adult self today subscribed to the same philosophy, it was easy for Reva to say no. She hadn't transferred this impossible standard to her children for the very reason that she didn't agree with it.

So what was it that was getting in the way of her giving herself sufficient rest, nutritious meals, the kind of stimulation and company that would nourish her heart and soul, a schedule that didn't leave her constantly drained — in short, what was getting in the way of her taking good care of herself? There was some very stubborn part of her that seemed not to want to let her do it. All her efforts over the years to try to do things differently had failed.

Ask the stubborn part why, I suggested. When she did, Reva heard that "it's not okay to feel good, not okay to feel pleasure." When she heard those words, Reva understood that while in some ways she had gone beyond the messages she internalized in her parents' home, at least in her parenting, there was still some part of her that believed those messages. That part of herself was putting the same demands on her as an adult that had been put on her as a child. She was doing it to herself! It wasn't her husband and it wasn't her parents' work ethic. It was something in her body that was afraid to feel good.

As Reva was doing this work, her usually dense and contracted field started to lighten and move just a little bit. As this happened, I could see a young girl dancing, happily twirling around. Immediately I understood that dance and movement were a deep part of Reva that had been stifled for a lifetime. We continued with Reva exploring what would happen if she did feel good – would she be less loved, less admired, less respected, less valued? What would she risk losing? The deeper Reva went into herself, the more I saw the image of the dancer. Finally, I suggested she experiment and imagine herself as a young girl dancing. Reva smiled a little dreamily and let herself drift into that image. By now there was real movement in her field.

After a time, I asked Reva to bring her adult self today to meet with that child. When she did, her sense was of feeling aloof. While she was happy that the girl was enjoying herself, she didn't feel connected to her or even feel a desire to talk to her. I suggested she just dance with her, letting the little girl lead her. Tentative at first, the adult slowly let herself be inspired by the girl's exuberance and began to enjoy herself.

By now Reva was smiling broadly and her eyes were lit up. It was as though she was coming back to life. "Did I ever tell you that I always dreamed of dancing?" she said. "No, I told her, but it was all over your energy field." Then she went on tell me about the many resolutions she had made over the years to look into this or that dance class. But she had never done it.

Now, though, she had a bodily experience of the difference it could make for her. She had felt the pleasure and the depth of expression it allowed her. And, for the first time, they felt essential. She didn't want to stay deadened any longer. She wanted to move, to feel alive, to let herself grow, to stop blaming everyone else. She wanted to say "yes" to life, to choose life, as the Torah tells us to do. She could feel that her dutiful yet resentful stance in life had a big "no" embedded in it that she was genuinely sick of. She wanted to involve this dancing part of her in her life decisions now.

No longer motivated solely by a sense of duty, she felt a genuine desire for *simchah* (joy) driving her now. It was the first time in her life that such a thing had been more than an idea. Now she had actually tasted it. She had a bodily experience of the difference in feeling that came from living from a place of *simchah*. And she knew it was up to her, and only her, to allow it to become the way she moved through life.

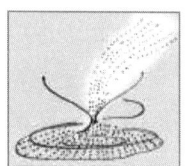

Learning to Work with Energy

Yehudis didn't know anything about energy, not about the inner energy body or the energy field emanating from the body. When the idea was first introduced it made her uncomfortable. She wondered whether it was real, whether it was something that she should get involved with. She wondered too whether it could really help her to make some of the changes she wanted to make. Having encountered this response many times over the years, I wasn't surprised.

Inviting someone to pay attention to herself on a deeper, more subtle level often generates resistance. It is as though a denser, coarser part of our being gets defensive. It doesn't want us to turn our attention away, even momentarily, to focus on a quieter, more internal part of ourselves. Sometimes it's afraid to disrupt lifelong habits, not sure what will come in their wake. Sometimes it is suspicious that maybe forces are being tapped that shouldn't be, and the fear of the unknown sets up a barrier.

Learning to Work with Energy

All of this is normal and need not be a deterrent. Rather, one needs to stay with each of the concerns that arise and speak to them in turn until there is a genuine embrace of the possibilities inherent in energy work. And if there is no such embrace, even after a period of learning and working in this realm, one should let it go. This is not an area for forcing. It is an area for exploring if, and when, one is ready.

With Yehudis, I first assured her that there was nothing other-worldly about the energy work we would be doing. The existence of an energy field within and around the body is well-documented by now. Many medical institutions, including major hospitals, are using healing modalities that work with this energy field. Likewise, various forms of complementary medicine also access and work with it.

Next, using some of the explorations included at the end of this chapter, Yehudis actually experienced what all the words could only allude to. Only through sensing the energy within and around her could she start to feel comfortable working in this realm. As soon as she did, her questions evaporated. She felt herself in connection with a deep place within that offered her instant calm no matter how fierce the storm raging around her.

She quickly took to bringing her attention inside and feeling the life force there when she was busy with her children. When she was bombarded with requests and demands from all directions, she would take just a few seconds to connect with this deeper part of herself. Immediately she would feel more spacious, more relaxed, and more able to flow from one thing to another. Even the continual barrage that previously had made her lose her temper, didn't bother her as much. Hearing it from that place within made it less threatening and less the totality of her reality at that moment. So she had more ability to field it all and stay pleasant.

After gaining some comfort with her inner energy body, Yehudis was ready to start working with the energy field around her. She chose a situation that often happened with her husband when he came home at the end of the day. Deeply absorbed in her own routine, her initial reaction to his coming into the house was to contract, to pull her energy field in to protect herself from what she unconsciously experienced as him intruding on her space. She knew intellectually that it made no sense, that it was his home as much as it was hers. Yet when he came in, bringing all the tension and frustration from his day, she instinctively pulled away. She knew her husband felt her distance and wished she could be more welcoming.

Her first step toward changing this pattern was to become aware of how it felt to contract and expand her energy field. She realized that when she contracted her field she closed down inside, putting a shield around her heart. She felt less relaxed, less open, less friendly than she did when she expanded her field. So first she practiced expanding and contracting her energy field intentionally. She wanted to see how the mechanism worked inside of her now that she was conscious of what she was doing.

Next she practiced envisioning her husband coming home and not contracting, staying in the more expanded place she was in before he entered. That was harder to do. She had to pay attention to the feelings that came up inside her when she tried and to talk to the parts of herself that were reluctant to open up under that circumstance.

Slowly she got better at staying expanded while visualizing her husband coming home. She learned how to use her breath and grounding to help her do it. Then, without saying anything to her husband, she started to practice in the actual circumstance. This too took time. She allowed herself to develop a little at a time, staying slightly more open with him each time she tried.

Learning to Work with Energy

She didn't want to fake or force this. It was too important to her marriage.

At first, she didn't notice anything different in her husband's response. He was so used to coming in and encountering her in a contracted place that he didn't notice anything changing. Yehudis actually didn't mind, since she felt she needed time to get this one. It was easier for her initially to just work with her own reaction without yet having to field anything different in her husband's response.

In time, as Yehudis's energetic muscles got stronger, she found she was able not only to avoid contracting when her husband came home, but she actually was able to begin to expand her field in a way that felt to him more like an embrace than a rejection. And that he noticed. He started to soften and relate to her more warmly. He didn't know what had changed, he just knew that he felt more welcome, more loved, when he came home.

Yehudis was thrilled. She no longer felt like she was a prisoner to some force inside herself that made her behave in ways that she really didn't want to. It was never a matter of not loving her husband as far as she had been concerned. It was just this thing that happened when he came home at the end of the day that she had thought she was powerless to control. Once she saw that she wasn't, a whole new world opened up for her that allowed her also to discover the root of her old impulse to contract. Not only had she overcome the difficulty with her husband, she had gotten to know herself better in the process.

Despite her initial reservations, Yehudis was someone who was more drawn to working first with her energy and her body, and then moving from there into relationship with the younger, vulnerable parts of herself that were driving her habitual responses. Someone else might prefer to work from the other direction, first using the Inner Torah process and then supplementing that with energy and/or bodywork. Much depends on the individual. There is no right or wrong way here. What is being developed is an ability to tune into the self and decide how best to go about something. It's another aspect of taking responsibility and treating oneself in a respectful, caring way.

Hindi could never fully relax as long as anyone else was around. She felt some part of her attention focused on, or at least aware of, the other person at all times. We went inside to discover the root of this feeling, and here's what happened.

Hindi saw herself as a young girl on long, hot Shabbat afternoons looking alone, forlorn, and miserable. Although she was one of many siblings, she only saw this younger self alone. When the adult Hindi today went to spend time with that little girl, she felt resistance. She didn't have the patience or the energy to deal with her, she said. I suggested she not try to do anything but rather just put herself in the same physical space as the little girl.

When she did that, Hindi saw herself sitting in a chair outdoors and the little girl standing off to the side near some trees. The little girl wasn't doing anything, just standing there. Still adult Hindi felt tense and couldn't relax. Somehow the girl's presence bothered her.

I asked Hindi to notice if there were any energetic cords, lines of energy, running from her to the girl. Having learned to become aware of her energy, Hindi took a minute to pay attention and realized that there were. To her surprise, she was the one who was attaching herself to the girl, not the other way around. I asked her to try to sense what would happen if she pulled those energy lines in, if she let the girl go. Immediately adult Hindi said she wouldn't be needed, she would be all alone. The feeling of being all alone was one she had recognized in the little girl wandering about on those long, hot Shabbat afternoons. Yet now it was the adult

Learning to Work with Energy

echoing those same feelings. For a minute she was confused.

Then she started to understand. She recalled as a little girl feeling judged, misunderstood, not tolerated, scorned, envied, and generally rejected by her siblings. She would feel these things most strongly on those long Shabbat afternoons, when there wasn't much to do and she had time to herself. She saw now that at some point in her development she had responded to these outcast feelings by making herself helpful to the others. Feeling needed became the mask behind which she forged her connections, not only with her siblings but with others as well. Beneath the mask, however, lurked all the difficult feelings the little girl felt before. Her adult had become as dependent on the mask as the child had been.

Once again exploring how she would feel if she pulled in those energy cords she had attached to the girl, Hindi realized her adult self was afraid that the little girl would go away, wouldn't be interested in her, wouldn't like her. Hindi was amazed to see how off her initial perception of the situation was.

When we began and the adult first encountered the child, her immediate posture was defensive. The child would want more from her than she had the patience or energy to give. Now she saw that the demand wasn't coming from the child. It was her adult self's need to be needed that created the hook with the child that felt non-negotiable. The child, as it turned out, was actually okay just standing there on her own with adult Hindi nearby. It had been the adult who felt uncomfortable and couldn't relax in that scenario.

Now Hindi had two pieces of work to do. One was with her energy, and the other involved having a talk with the part of herself that was hooked on being needed in order to feel her existence and her connection to others. Starting with her energy, Hindi again pulled in the cords she felt running to the little girl. This time she brought them inside herself, allowing them to become part of her inner energy body.

Deep within her she envisioned a flame, an eternal light, and she surrounded it with the form of her body. She allowed herself to feel the perimeter of her physical self as the container in which her light could shine. She imagined her body as a beacon with light emanating from it. With all this, she was able to establish a sense of her self, separate and independent from the little girl. It was a huge step.

Next she talked to the part of herself that so badly needed to be needed. She explained to her that when she was a child and her siblings shunned her, she couldn't hold onto a sense of herself or of her relationship to others. At that time in her life, her family circle was her world. It was the mirror in which she saw herself reflected. She had nothing and no one else to hold on to. "That was then," she said to her, "and you did what you needed to do to survive. You made yourself helpful to others which in turn made you more visible to yourself and connected, at least in that way, to them. At the time, it seemed like your very existence depended on this, and maybe it did.

"But now, I'm an adult," Hindi said. "I'm part of a world that is much bigger than the world of my family of origin. I have a husband and many children of my own, as well as friends, colleagues, neighbors, students, and a host of other people in my life. I have a wealth of experience from a wide range of life challenges. I have a way to know myself today that I didn't have then. I no longer have to carve out a place for myself that is dependent solely on others needing me. I know now that I exist and have value as a person, regardless of whether I am fulfilling someone else's need.

"Of course, it's wonderful when I can be helpful to another person," she continued. "I will always want to do that. It's something that never needs to change. What you need

Learning to Work with Energy

to understand, though, is that the reality that is you and the relationships you forge with others are not a function of your ability to fulfill needs. It's a function of who you are. So that today you can relax and just be in the presence of another person without feeling like you have to be constantly vigilant, constantly on-guard, constantly alert to a possible need.

"In the beginning it might make you uncomfortable," she went on. "You might feel nervous or awkward or scared. That makes sense. We're talking here about forging relationships with others out of completely different soil. We're talking about allowing both you and the other person to just be yourselves, occupying the same physical space, and allowing whatever interaction is going to happen between you to grow up naturally from there.

"Think about it," she said, "if you are able to relax in this way around other people, they won't immediately feel like such a potential burden to you. Your first reaction won't have to be that you don't have patience or energy to deal with them. You've been feeling that way because you've been projecting your need to be needed onto them and translated it as neediness on their part that you don't want to have to deal with."

All that was left for Hindi now was to practice. Fortunately, she was scheduled to go to a family *simchah* in another town the next day, where she would be with family members and friends. It was the perfect opportunity in real time to watch whether and how she hooked herself into these people. Did she run energetic cords out to them? Did she hold on with thoughts? Did she grab onto energy or words from others directed at her that might not have been meant to hook her but rather to allow her to engage in whatever way she felt comfortable, including not at all? Was she free to even experience an overture from someone else like that, or was it immediately thrown into the "need bin" and responded to automatically from there?

Once she became aware, she could practice pulling those energetic cords and thoughts back inside her own container. She could keep coming back inside her body and envisioning herself from the inside — a full and light-filled presence. And she could keep reminding herself that the other person is also a separate being in her own right, whom there is no need to fear nor to control.

The prospect of being able to genuinely relax and feel at home in the presence of another person was unbelievably exciting to Hindi. This difficulty had plagued her for more than forty years. In many ways it had dictated the rhythm of her life which had alternated between intense involvement with other people and periods of virtual seclusion.

It also had caused her enormous confusion. She knew that helping others was a good quality, a *middah* that she wanted to have. And yet she knew that her impulse to help could turn to resentment and provoke resistance in her more often than she cared to think about. And her feelings then were anything but admirable and desirable. It had all been a big mishmash, and she had basically careened through life desperately trying to achieve some kind of balance that, for reasons she didn't understand, had always eluded her.

Now, for the first time, she felt like she had real insight into what was going on. She actually experienced herself as the true source of her dilemma. That was perhaps the biggest gift of all, because now she could do something about it. It was just a question of time, she told herself. She had no doubt that with Hashem's help she could leave these old habits behind and come into a new and much freer, happier place with herself and others. And that's exactly what happened. "I'm not the same person," she told me months later after returning from a visit with her family. "I'm relaxed, comfortable, and really able to be myself. It's been a remarkable transformation."

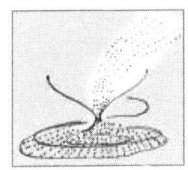

EXPLORATIONS

INNER ENERGY BODY

1. Sensing Energy

Rub your hands together, including fingers and thumbs, and then hold them at whatever distance from each other allows you to feel a slight pressure or sense of something palpable between your hands. Don't worry about how far apart your hands are. Just allow yourself to feel the energy ball in your hands, whatever size it may be. Then move your hands in and out a short distance to get a feel for bouncing and pulsating energy.

2. Sensing Your Body

Bring your attention into your body. Notice which parts you can feel, which you can't feel, and which you vaguely feel? Can you be in your head and aware of the other parts of your body at the same time, or do you cut off at the neck? The goal is to inhabit your whole body with awareness.

3. Sensing Your Inner Energy Body

Bring your attention inside the borders of your body, letting your eyes drop back in your head as though you were looking down into your body from inside your skull. Notice what you feel inside you. Are you numb? Is there any sense of movement, tingling, heat, sensation of any sort. Notice what happens as you keep your awareness within. Can you feel the subtle energy in your body? Can you experience it from within as a field of energy?

4. Inner Energy Body Awareness in Daily Life

As you go about your day, remind yourself to bring awareness inside your body even as you do other things. Waiting in line, sitting in traffic, and other times when you have nothing else to do — and would normally go into your head and get busy with a thousand thoughts — are good opportunities to practice connecting with your inner energy body! Then do whatever you have to do from there — from your whole body, connected to your inner energy field.

You can also try bringing your awareness within and focusing on your inner energy body when confronted with a difficult situation. Doing this for just a few seconds will help you respond from a clearer and deeper place in yourself than you otherwise would.

ENERGETIC BOUNDARIES AND MOVEMENTS

5. Energy Field Awareness

Check how far out your field extends, whether it is more up or down, and how thick or thin it is. Think of being in an elevator alone and then with other people coming in. Notice how it affects your field. Can you feel your field expand and contract? Picture yourself in different situations and circumstances in your life and see how far you extend or how deep inside you retract beneath your skin.

6. Childhood Recollections

Take a few minutes to think about the messages you internalized as a child that shape your energetic habits. What range of experience, response, and behavior were deemed appropriate in your childhood environment? How comfortable was that range for you then? In what ways are you still operating within that range? How comfortable is it for you now?

7. Feeling Separate and Connected

Imagine yourself talking to different people in your life who are of varying degrees of closeness to you. Notice how well you are able to experience yourself as a separate person and how well you are able to feel connected to the other person. Do you maintain a sense of separateness while in connection? Do you merge and lose a sense of yourself? What happens when you try to hold the sense of separateness and connectedness simultaneously?

8. Expanding Your Energy

Notice how far your energy extends from your body. Try moving it out further, filling the space in whatever room you find yourself in. Notice any feelings that expanding your energy in this way brings up inside of you. Try to just stay with the feelings and breathe without trying to figure anything out. Does your comfort level change?

9. Objecting Without Contracting

Think of a situation you don't like and practice relaxing instead of contracting. Notice the parts of your body that tighten when you think of the situation and consciously relax the tightness. Allow your body to soften while still thinking of the situation. Feel the feelings without muscular or energetic contraction. Then try expanding your energy to include the event within yourself. Notice what you feel when you do this.

If you're able to, try this practice while you're actually dealing with a situation that you don't like or feel comfortable in.

10. Moving Energy Up and Down

Using a room as your boundary, fill it with your energy only from the waist up. Notice how you feel. Then try it only from the shoulders up, from the neck up, and finally from the eyes up. Each time notice what you sense and feel.

Using the same room, this time fill it with your energy only from the waist down. Notice how you feel. Then try it only from the hips down, the knees down, and finally let your energy drain into the ground. Each time notice what you sense and feel.

As you go about your day, when you notice your energy moving too far up, see if you can bring it down. And if you notice your energy too far down, see if you can bring it up.

11. Maintaining Balance

Try to fill the space in a room with your energy coming from your whole body. Let your energy go into the ground, up into the air and out to the sides simultaneously. Pay attention to how that feels. Allow the energy to move freely. Imagine yourself in different situations in your life maintaining this more balanced energy distribution and see what happens. Continue to work with the images until you feel a greater sense of comfort and ease.

12. Recognizing Diffusion

Find a space that you can fill with your energy to the point where you feel your energy become thin enough to start to merge with your surroundings. If no indoor space is big enough, you can do this outside.

Pay attention to whether your field diffuses when you are with other people, whether you are merging with them or maintaining your own boundary. If you have a tendency to merge, try envisioning yourself in a spacesuit as you're interacting with them. Notice if this helps you to stay inside yourself and relate from there.

13. Building a Denser Field

Stand near the center of a room and fill it with your energy. When you've filled it, bring your energy in around you to a distance of three or four feet. Notice how it gets denser as you bring it in. Then let your energy go back out and fill the room. Then bring it back in. Notice that it's denser than the last time. Continue exploring in this way to give yourself a sense of what a denser field feels like. Try the same thing in different spaces.

14. Practicing Pulsation

Hold the denser field established in exploration 13 and, without expanding or contracting, try bouncing the edges. The movement is something like the slight bouncing movement you made with your hands to feel the ball of energy between them in exploration 1. This time though you're bouncing the edges of your energy field, allowing a slight back and forth motion.

Whenever you experience your energy as jammed or stuck, try this slight pulsing motion to reinvigorate yourself.

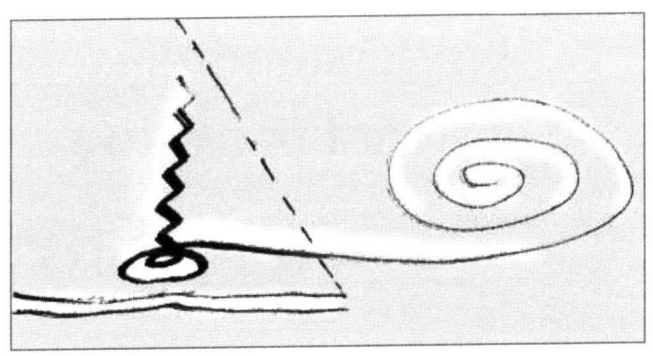

Understanding Sensory Processing

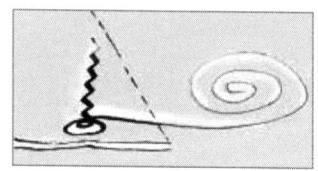

Understanding Sensory Processing

Taking responsibility for oneself in the realms of breath, body, and energy as part of coming to know one's Inner Torah means many things. On the most superficial level, it means devoting the necessary time and attention to maintain the health of one's physical body and to attempt to heal any illness that arises. On a deeper level, it can mean looking beyond physical symptoms, once physical causes have been ruled out, for underlying emotional or spiritual issues that may be causing pain or other types of physical discomfort. And on a still deeper level, it can mean working with the breath, body, and energy to know and come into relationship with more of one's true essence.

It can also mean recognizing when the root of a difficulty is not emotional and not physical in the sense of a particular ailment, but rather a problem in the processing function of the system as a whole. In other words, bodily experiences that generate uncomfortable feelings can be misconstrued and attributed emotional significance that they don't deserve. Something else may be at work and it is our job, as custodians with Hashem of our well-being, to be interested and open to finding out what that is.

Hadassah had three children under the age of six. When she related to them one on one, she was fine. But as soon as she had them all together, she felt herself frayed, disoriented, impatient, and irritated. She described a typical scenario, where she was playing with her five-year-old son. Her three-year-old constantly interrupted them, climbing on her, disrupting whatever they were doing, and basically driving her to distraction. If her youngest, the fourteen-month-old, would start crying or need something at the same time, she was finished. All she wanted to do at that moment was to crawl in a hole and cry. It was so overwhelming for her.

Hadassah tried to deal with the problem by taking parenting courses, setting goals for herself, and working hard to control what she saw as her negative and inappropriate reactions to her children. She felt terrible about herself, felt she was a terrible mother, and worried about what would be with her children.

Focusing on her *middot* and her emotions, Hadassah had overlooked the role of her body in the dilemma she was facing. Bringing her awareness to her physical body, Hadassah began to notice what happened as her attention was diverted from whatever she was doing with one child by the antics or cries of another. First she noticed that she started to disassociate, to feel herself remote from her body and the room. Then she noticed that she was trying to manage the various stimuli with her head; she was no longer present with her full self, who might have had more capacity. Her goal was survival — to bring down the level of stimulation to something more manageable for her. She really wasn't able to tune into any of her children and their needs, she was so desperately, and unconsciously, trying to manage her own.

There was something going on here that was beyond her conscious control. Unbeknownst to her, Hadassah was dealing with a condition known as sensory defensiveness. Her nervous system was overly sensitive to stimulation and sensation; sensory input that for others was bearable, or even enjoyable, was a nightmare for her. When she had all of her children together, Hadassah went into sensory overload. Feeling overwhelmed, her nervous system drove her to defend against over-stimulation and preserve herself. The difficulty originated in her brain and its limited ability to process sensory input. What was driving her response was not an emotional issue but rather a deficiency in her sensory processing system.

The brain screens, sorts, and responds to sensory information to organize feelings, thoughts, perceptions, and actions. The sensory information it processes comes both from outside and inside the body. This process of the brain, called sensory integration, is unconscious. Through it we are able to give meaning to what we experience and respond in an appropriate way.

In the case of dysfunction, the brain is not processing or organizing the flow of sensory impulses in a way that gives a person the right information about herself or her world. Perception is distorted, there is disorganization instead of organization, and a desperate need to balance out the nervous system is created.

For someone like Hadassah, just the realization that this

Understanding Sensory Processing

was what was happening to her, that she wasn't a bad person or otherwise disturbed, was enormously liberating. She immediately started to look into what could be done to help her nervous system become less vulnerable to the barrage of sensation that she experienced with her children and, when she thought more about it, elsewhere as well. She read everything she could find on sensory integration problems, both as they affect children and adults. And she found an occupational therapist who could work with her in the very specific ways that have been devised to help adults with sensory processing issues.

Slowly but surely Hadassah learned how to take care of herself in the sensory realm and to make the lifestyle changes she needed. With her newfound insight, she was also able to spot behaviors in two of her children that suggested that they too might have some sensory integration problems. Having learned that treatment is even more effective in children than in adults, Hadassah was happy to be able to give them occupational therapy as well and, hopefully, help them avoid a lot of the suffering she had endured without ever realizing the source.

By paying attention to what was happening in her body, Hadassah had discovered an important piece of her life puzzle. She was then able to locate the right resources to provide the help she needed. In Inner Torah terms, Hadassah had been willing to be the meaningful adult in her life, the adult who really paid attention and tried to understand the distress she was experiencing, the adult who could research the issue and find help. By taking responsibility in this way, she opened new doors both for herself and her children.

Other clients I have worked with have done the same with attention deficit disorder issues that were not diagnosed in childhood. After struggling for years with behaviors that could not be changed by inner work, *middot* work, or other forms of intentional conscious intervention, these women traced their difficulties to ADD. They then did what they needed to do to educate themselves about the condition and find a treatment approach that was right for them.

Inner Torah helped them to take charge of themselves and their lives in a new way. Instead of judging and berating themselves for their perceived deficiencies — in the way that many of them had experienced in childhood — they began to look at themselves with a loving eye and to slowly unravel the mystery that was at the root of their seemingly intractable problems.

The transformation in one's life that can come with this kind of acceptance and taking care of oneself is enormous. It is amazing to witness the shift in someone who for a lifetime has been blaming and judging herself — and then she finds out that her difficulties stem from something she didn't know was happening in her brain and which she could not influence or control without very specific interventions.

That is not to say that the going is easy. Often, there is great upset to be worked through as a woman takes in her sometimes very real limitations and contemplates what they might mean. The life she had envisioned, when she believed everything was in her control and surmountable, may no longer be a possibility for her. She made need to amend her aspirations. So while there is a certain relief at what amounts to an accurate diagnosis and a treatment plan, there is also disappointment and a sense of loss of the self that one envisioned herself to be.

The process of working through such feelings is itself an opening to new dimensions, allowing a woman to come into relationship with herself in a more real and realistic way. Often there's also a strengthening of *emunah*, as a woman ultimately comes to appreciate that this situation too is from Hashem, and that if it is a part of her life story, she can trust that it is something that her soul needs to experience in this lifetime. She recognizes that the ways the newly discovered limitations will ask her to grow are invariably just what she needs, in order to be who G-d created her to be. And she is humbled and uplifted at the same time.

Embodied Life – Wholeness and Holiness

Embodied Life – Wholeness and Holiness

Many clients tell me that every time they do anything that helps them inhabit their bodies and live from there, they are enlivened and encouraged. I feel the same way. Our holy souls descended into physical bodies to enable them to act in the physical world. Through the body we are able to express the soul's higher reality in this lower plane of existence.

It seems like one of the biggest maladies of our time is that we are living outside of our bodies, outside of this miraculous gift Hashem gave us to house our souls. Things can happen when we live disembodied lives that wouldn't happen if we were really inside ourselves – things that are hurtful to ourselves and other people, things that distance us from Hashem. From inside ourselves, we naturally seem to take more care.

Breath, movement, sound, speech, song, and touch can all

function to bring us inside ourselves. The deeper we can reach within, the further we can reach without. The more fully we can participate with ourselves, the more fully we can participate with others and Hashem. Everything starts with the power of our connection to ourselves.

To experience oneself as an embodied, flesh-and-blood human being who is a creation of G-d may be the most profound experience possible. Doing so brings us face to face with G-d's most magnificent and miraculous creation, the human body, and at the same time humbles us as we contemplate the reality that a spark of the Infinite — something so precious and holy — is contained in such a finite and, in many ways, vulnerable, vessel.

There is something both stunning and comforting about meeting life from inside one's body. What's stunning is how vital and alive every experience is, how real we are to ourselves and others are to us. There is actual sensation of a dimension beyond the physical that animates our existence. It is no longer a theoretical or theological construct. It's reality. The comfort comes from the simplicity of being with what is without embellishing or creating elaborate stories. It also becomes easier to take care of oneself, to do what is needed to sustain oneself, without the drama that comes from self-neglect and foisting off responsibility onto others.

What we're talking about really is the intersection of body, consciousness, and holiness — the capacity to hold all three, to hear and integrate the wisdom of these varied G-d-given mediums. Efforts to develop such capacity are geared toward bringing us into wholeness, into the entirety of our beings on all levels. In doing the work to reveal our essence, we are furthering G-d's ultimate will in Creation to reveal to the world His essence.

The explorations included in this book are not intended to

The Breath and Body of Inner Torah

be a "practice" that is separate from life. Rather they are intended to be invitations to come into awareness in a way that informs and enhances life. The notion that our bodies, minds, and spirits are separate entities to be tended to distinct from one another is misguided. Our awareness needs to be expanded to encompass all three simultaneously so that we live from the entirety of ourselves, whatever we are doing or called upon to deal with.

From this comes an integration of inner and outer, a purity of being unmarred by hidden agendas and disguised needs. Our true essence begins to permeate everything we do, propelling us toward wholeness by uniting the hidden, inner part of us with our outer selves. That really is a mark of holiness — when the inside is the same as the outside, when our thoughts, words, and deeds are truly motivated by a desire to know and serve Hashem from the unique place He assigned each of us.

Perhaps the clearest indication Hashem gave us that He wants from us what is specifically ours is that He made every body different. "Just as each individual's face is unlike another's, so is each individual's *da'at* unlike another's," teach Chazal (*Yerushalmi, Ketubot*, chap. 9).

The particular manifestation of Hashem that each person embodies is found nowhere else. That tiny piece of the universal puzzle belongs solely to that person. It is his or her responsibility to cull it from the dross of life and contribute it to the bigger picture asked for from the *klal*. Ironically, the more we are able to individuate in this way, the more we are able to know ourselves as, and to be part of the *klal*, part of the breath and body of the Jewish people.

Our mission as a people is to be a vessel for Hashem's light in this world. That light is a light of understanding and awareness, of consciousness that G-d's light is the essence of all things. Our days on this earth are meant to be dedicated to the joy of penetrating within, of sensing purpose, of uncovering meaning, of finding connection to G-d and His light in every corner of ourselves and our lives. And it is that Light that is meant to shine out from each and every one of us into the world.

As Moshe Rabbeinu reminded us, the goal of knowing and fulfilling the Torah, of knowing and fulfilling G-d's word, is not hidden from us and is not distant. It is right here, inside our very own selves. "It is not in heaven, [for you] to say, 'Who can ascend to the heaven for us and take it for us so that we can listen to it and perform it?' Nor is it across the sea, [for you] to say, 'Who can cross to the other side of the sea for us and take it for us, so that we can listen to it and perform it?' Rather, the matter is very near to you – in your mouth and your heart – to perform it" (*Devarim* 30: 11–14).

Appendices

APPENDIX 1

The Relationship of Body and Soul[*]

When delving deeply into the workings of the body, it's important to understand its place in Creation and, most importantly, its relationship to the soul. For the body does not exist in a vacuum. It is an integral part of Hashem's plan and must always be remembered as such when we give it attention.

Without this consciousness, our efforts to enlist our bodies to help us realize our G-d-given potential can backfire and, *chas v'shalom*, take us in the opposite direction. The key is to remember that the body is here to serve the soul. Everything we do to enhance our connection to the body is done in order to help the soul achieve its purpose in this lifetime. The body in and of itself, independent of its relationship to the soul, is not our focus.

Rabbi Moshe Chayim Luzzatto, also known as the Ramchal,

---

[*] This appendix presents the insights of Rabbi Moshe Chayim Luzzatto, the Ramchal, from his classic works *Derech Hashem* (*The Way of G-d*), translated by Aryeh Kaplan, Feldheim Publishers, 4th revised ed., 1983, and *Da'at Tevunot* (*The Knowing Heart*), translated by Shraga Silverstein, Feldheim Publishers, 1982.

in his books, *Derech Hashem* (*The Way of G-d*) and *Da'at Tevunot* (The Knowing Heart), offers a remarkable glimpse into the intricate workings of this most miraculous relationship between body and soul. Reading and understanding his writings ensures that our foray into the world of the body will be part of, and not antithetical to, our *avodat Hashem*.

The following paragraphs are a compilation of passages from these two powerful works. The words are those of the Ramchal, as translated by Rabbi Aryeh Kaplan, *zt"l*, and Rabbi Shraga Silverstein.

> G-d created man consisting of two opposites – his pure spiritual soul and his unenlightened physical body. The soul derives from the radiance of G-d's countenance, from the revealed splendor of G-d's glory. It is eternally enduring and pure in essence. In contrast, the body is the product of the concealment of G-d's countenance, His not revealing the splendor of His Glory. It must undergo a process of purification and refinement that ultimately includes death, destruction, and rectification.
>
> Concealment of G-d's countenance and the shining of His countenance are the foundations and the root of G-d's conduct with all of His creatures. And it is upon these foundations that the fusion of body and soul is based – the body and all of its operations proceeding from concealment of countenance, and the soul and all of its operations from its luminescence.
>
> G-d created man as body and soul together, to take upon themselves [i.e., the body and the soul] all of the holy service – the Torah and the mitzvot which were given to them – and to receive together the eternal reward. In addition to providing us with life and the ability to think, the soul also has the function of purifying the physical matter of the body. The soul has the power to elevate the body step by step, until even the body can derive pleasure from drawing close to G-d, which is the ultimate

Appendix 1 • The Relationship of Body and Soul

purpose of man's creation and referred to as "perfection."

Both body and soul are drawn toward their respective natures, the body toward the material and the soul toward the spiritual. G-d gave man the power to give ascendancy to one or the other — to the material or to the spiritual in himself. If he follows the material promptings of his eyes and his heart, then his soul, instead of fulfilling its intended function of helping the body by refining it, will, to the contrary, suffer great loss and deterioration, sinking into darkness. If, on the other hand, man walks in the ways of Torah and mitzvot, the soul will gain ascendancy over the body.

G-d created man in this way for man's good alone, so that he merit reward through his deeds by perfecting himself and completing his creation. G-d made the body of coarse, dark matter, unfit to shine in the light of His holiness. And in contrast to this, He made the pure soul, hewn from under the Throne of Glory, and brought down and infused into this body, to purify and sanctify it.

The end intent of the infusion of the soul into the body is not that it animate it for this brief lifetime; but its central purpose is to refine it completely, to elevate it from the depths of the dark earthy abyss to the highest station — to the rank of the ministering angels. This indeed is what occurred with Moshe, of blessed memory, who so refined and enhanced his earthiness that he actually attained to the level of an angel, so that all of Israel saw that the skin of Moshe's face shone. And Chanoch and Elijah actually ascended to heaven in their bodies after they had greatly refined their earthiness.

The soul is able to purify the body through the performance of mitzvot and the observance of the Torah; for a mitzvah is a candle and the Torah is light. And the more Torah and mitzvot the soul acquires, the more refinement it achieves for the body and the more merit for itself in fulfilling the will of its Creator. But because of the sin of Adam HaRishon, the soul cannot fully purify the body until the body dies and deteriorates and a new structure is composed that the soul can enter and purify. It was therefore decreed that man should die and then be brought back to life. This is the concept of Resurrection of the Dead (*Techiyat HaMeitim*).

So, while refinement of the body is the prime activity of the soul in this world, it cannot fully effect this refinement before death. At death the body returns to the earth from which it came and is completely purged of impurity. Then when it will be reconstituted, the soul will descend into it, illuminating it with a great light which will purify it and heal it completely.

This receives expression in *Midrash HaNe'elam, Vayeira*: "Our sages have stated: 'The soul, while in Eden, is nourished by the Heavenly light and clothes itself in it; and when, in time to come, it re-enters the body, it is with that light itself that it re-enters.'" And, "The Holy One, Blessed be He, stores this body in the ground until it decays and is purged of all its foulness."

The entire world must similarly be destroyed and then renewed. This is the meaning of what our sages taught, "Six thousand years will the world exist, and for one thousand it will be desolate. At the end of this thousand years, G-d will again renew the world." The true time and place of reward will therefore be after the resurrection in the renewed world. Man will then enjoy his reward with both body and soul. The body will be purified by the soul, and will therefore also be in a proper state to enjoy that good.

Since it has been decreed that man must die, body and soul must remain separated until the time comes for them to be recombined. During this period of separation, an appropriate place must exist for each of the two separate parts. The body thus returns to its element, decomposing and losing its form. Since the body originated from the dust, it must return to it,

Appendix 1 • The Relationship of Body and Soul

and this is what G-d told Adam: "You are dust, and to dust you must return" (*Bereishit* 3:19). The body must undergo decay and decomposition, remain in the earth for an appropriate time, and finally be reconstructed anew so that the soul can re-enter it.

During this intermediate time, however, the soul also needs a place. It is for this reason that G-d prepared a Soul World. When a soul leaves its body, it enters this Soul World and remains there in a state of rest while the body undergoes what it must. During this period, the soul experiences sublime delight, very much like that which will be bestowed on the individual later in the period of genuine reward. After the resurrection, body and soul will again combine.

In this lifetime, the soul cannot shine with radiance appropriate to the excellence that it actually attains, but it all remains concealed in the soul's essence until the time comes for it to be revealed. The soul, however, bears no blame whatsoever for this. It is only the nature of the body that prevents its full expression. The body, however, also suffers a great loss because of this, since during man's physical lifetime it cannot be appropriately purified by the soul. During man's physical lifetime, the soul is imprisoned and cannot spread its radiance. It furthermore cannot perform its proper task, which is the purification of the body.

When the soul leaves the body and enters the Soul World, however, it can then radiate freely with a brightness that befits it as a result of its good deeds while associated with the body. Through both this and what it can attain in the Soul World, the soul is able to regain the power that it lost while associated with the body. This in turn makes it more qualified for its ultimate function after the resurrection, namely, the purification of the body.

Even before a soul enters the body and attains perfection through its deeds, it already has a high degree of intrinsic perfection. This intrinsic perfection and brilliance is so great that it should be able to purify man's physical being to such an extent that he would no longer be considered a mortal human being. The soul, however, is held back by G-d's decree. Its power is obstructed and its brilliance reduced, so that it cannot do anything at all to accomplish this. The soul thus remains imprisoned and restrained to the degree required by G-d's plan, and it can only act upon the body to the extent that G-d's wisdom allows.

As the soul continues to participate in good deeds, it should likewise be able to spread out and radiate, thus purifying the body. The same decree, however, holds it back and prevents it from functioning freely until it reaches the Soul World. When the soul is recombined with the body after the resurrection, however, it will no longer be bound or restricted, and will enter the body with all its brilliance and strength. The body will then experience a great enlightenment and will not have to develop gradually as a child now does. The soul will immediately shine forth and purify it to a very great degree.

This does not mean, however, that the resurrected man will not be able to continue to elevate himself. The instant that the soul re-enters the body, the individual is raised to a high spiritual level, and the body experiences its initial enlightenment. At this point, the body will immediately be on a higher level than it could ever possibly attain in its first life. This level, however, is not permanent, and the complete man, both body and soul, will still be able to elevate himself in relation to the initial level upon which he is placed.

A single soul can be reincarnated a number of times in different bodies, and in this manner, it can rectify the damage done in previous incarnations. Similarly, it can also achieve perfection that was not attained in its previous incarnations. The soul is then ultimately judged at the end of all these incarnations. Its judgment will depend on everything that took place in all its

Appendix 1 • The Relationship of Body and Soul

incarnations, as well as its status as an individual in each one.

The crucial point, however, is the fact that all is truly fair and just, as the Torah states, "The Creator's work is perfect, all His ways are justice" (*Devarim* 32:7). No created thing can encompass G-d's thoughts or the profound depth of His plan. We only know that, like all other such concepts, the principle of reincarnation as one of man's experiences also follows the rule of fair judgment, as decreed by G-d to perfect mankind in general.

Even if the body realized its greatest potential of refinement, it will still be distinguished from the soul, in that the soul is a noble luminous entity emanating from the radiance of the Blessed One's countenance, whereas the body is an entity resulting from the concealment of the Blessed One's countenance. It is susceptible of refinement, however, to the extent of its nature – to that extreme degree where very little difference is perceivable between it and the soul. But in spite of this, the soul will remain soul, insusceptible of defect, and the body, to the contrary, a thing defective by nature, but attaining the refinement afforded it [by the soul].

We find, then, that man's Divine service and His receiving reward center around two periods, which make up his entire existence. For now, in this world, the body is coarse and dark and the soul must charge it with light and sanctity to refine and illuminate it. And the completion of this process – after death and resurrection – ushers in the period of receiving reward, when they will both present themselves for eternal, goodly reward.

The soul, in its essence and source, is exalted in greatness; but, so that it enter this body, the Holy One, Blesssed be He, diminishes its light and potency, leaving it only as much as is appropriate for the body in this world. It can be compared at that time to the moon, to which it was said, "Go and diminish **yourself**" (***Chullin*** **60b**) – whereas in respect to the time to come it is stated: "And the light of the moon will be as the light of the sun" (*Yeshayahu* 30:26). It is in the power of the soul, according to the perfection of its deeds, to make ascent after ascent until it reaches its supreme height. But, because of the lesser magnitude assigned it in this world, it remains cabined and confined within the body all the days allotted to it on earth, to be tried and proven through the trials of the *yetzer hara*, evil inclination.

Indeed, it was for this purpose that the *yetzer hara* was invested in man, as our sages have stated: "The evil inclination was created solely for the purpose of trying man" (*Zohar* I 106b). And in accordance with the quality of its deeds, the soul merits for itself the ennoblement of ascending level after level. So that in the time of reward all souls carry their deeds with them and rise in station in accordance with them. And it is on this plane that they return and refine their bodies at the time of the resurrection – after which they will rejoice in a superabundance of perfection eternally. In other words, whereas in the beginning, in order to enter the body, the soul had to diminish its light, in the second entry, on the contrary, it must come with all of its light, so that the refinement is effected completely.

And there is a benefit to the soul itself by virtue of its perfecting the body – to rise higher and higher, to add strength to strength and glory to glory. What is more, even when it is in this world, within the body, it achieves ascent and ennoblement in accordance with its deeds. For there is no comparison between the soul of a man who has occupied himself with the study of Torah and with mitzvot, and achieved knowledge of the glory of his Creator, and a soul devoid of all these. But its ascent does not reach the point of enabling it to change the body to the extent that its refinement is apparent, except in the case of a select few, the rare chosen ones of the Lord, such as Moses, our teacher, of blessed memory, Chanoch, and Elijah. As far as others are

Appendix 1 • The Relationship of Body and Soul

concerned, however, though it will be ennobled through its acts, this ennoblement will not proceed so far as to be evident in the body. But "good will not be withheld from its proprietors" in time to come — each according to his deeds.

To further distinguish between body and soul, the Ramchal goes on to explain:

> It is written: "Let us make a man in our image, according to our likeness." For, in relation to all of the exalted qualities which we distinguish in the Blessed One in His acting on the level of His creatures, we find corresponding qualities in the figure of man. For example: The eye of man corresponds to the eye of His providence, which exercises surveillance over all the dwellers of the earth to judge all of their deeds, as it is written, " 'Let me go down now and see . . .' (*Bereishit* 18:21); this teaches us that a judge must abide entirely by the evidence of his eyes" (*Sanhedrin* 6b). The ears of man correspond to G-d's listening to the prayers of men and to all of their praises, as it is written, "And the Lord heard their wailing" (*Shemot* 2:24). And our sages haves said: "Know what is above you — a seeing eye and a listening ear" (*Avot* 2:1). The mouth of man corresponds to G-d's speaking in a vision to His prophets, and causing the glory of His voice to be heard by His angels, mighty in strength, executors of His word. And similarly, all of the other components of the body can be well understood as paralleling in their form and function the qualities to which He resorted in the making of His creations.
>
> And the general structure of man's body — right and left, with a doubling of parts on either side: two eyes, two ears, two hands, two feet — this corresponds to the two-fold nature of the Blessed One's qualities, whether for loving-kindness or for punishment, for turning to the right, to merit; or to the left, to culpability.
>
> The body consists of specific parts and organs, each assigned

specific, limited functions. The soul, in itself, however, is one, entirely removed from all of the aspects of the body, all of its ways being different ways, absolutely dissimilar to those of the body, even insofar as sensations are concerned. But because it performs all of the actions of the body while in it — it is the soul which hears through the ears of the body, the soul which sees through the eyes of the body, and the like — it is therefore referred to as seeing, hearing, etc.

[The soul] is not to be understood, however, as intrinsically invested with such attributes. For though it is the soul alone which sees (and not the body, which is inanimate), so that it is the agency through which men, in fact, see things as they do, it is not to be understood because of this that this is its natural manner of seeing. For its way is entirely different from all of the ways by which the body functions, and it is entirely unfathomable to a man as long as he exists in a body. But because it adopts the way of the eye, to see through its mechanism, it is therefore referred to as "seeing," and so with all the other functions.

In sum, the soul is a single creation, entirely divorced in essence from all the ways of the body, but created in such a way as to perform all that is implanted in the organs of the body according to their nature. And because it adopts these mechanisms and performs all these actions in the body, they are all attributed to it.

As explained earlier, G-d employs two modes — concealment of countenance and illumination of countenance, which are root and cause of body and soul, respectively. These two modes operate jointly and there are various consequences as either concealment or illumination gains ascendancy. G-d desired to make manifest the orders and modes of His creation. Along these lines, the two modes which govern man's conduct, and in accordance with which he was created, are reflected in man himself, in the two

Appendix 1 • The Relationship of Body and Soul

parts of which he is composed and constructed – body and soul. The soul is conjoined to the body and permeates all its parts so that every act results from their joint operation.

All the greatness to which the soul has access is concealed behind this earthly layer of skin and flesh. It is the bodily layer that is visible. Only the soul can comprehend all that is involved in the ascent toward holiness or in its opposite, the descent away from holiness. As King David said, "I will thank You, for I have been singled out for wonders. Your deeds are wondrous, and my soul knows it well" (*Tehillim* 139:14). For the body cannot conceive these things as the soul can; for they are perceptible not through earthiness, but only through spirituality.

Aside from the figure of the body, and aside from the form of the soul within, there is something which results from the union of both – radiance of countenance. It is this which distinguishes the living from the dead. And not this alone, for even a change in the disposition of the soul within the body is reflected in the face. Witness the ashen countenance of the ill. And, what is more, even the musings of the heart are reflected in the face. A smiling countenance, an angry countenance, a cordial countenance – all are witnesses of the thoughts hidden in the recesses of the heart. And this expression inheres neither in the soul alone (for it is manifested by the body), nor in the body alone (for the body has no expression without the soul), but it is born of the union of the body and soul.

The body after it is purified will be as it was before Adam's sin – a vestment of light, a rarefied almost spiritual body, not something coarse and gross as it is at present. Likewise, deterioration occurs only to this lowly, earthly form and not to any form higher than it. When a man dies, his soul leaves him and his body returns to the earth from which it came. Man is made of the darkness of earthiness (resulting from concealment of G-d's countenance) and of spirituality that animates and refines him (resulting from the illumination of G-d's countenance).

Man lives in this world as long as the Creator shines his countenance on him. As soon as the Creator stops shining His countenance on him so that only the darkness in his nature remains, the soul will leave the body, which will be as dead as a lifeless stone. It will also be subject to dissolution and decay. As it is written, "You hide Your face; they are confounded. You take their spirit; they perish and return to their dust" (*Tehillim* 104:29).

But because the Creator will not completely conceal the countenance of His goodness forever — for some spark of His light will illuminate the darkness of the concealment of His countenance for the continuance of the universe — this body, too, will not undergo complete dissolution, and the soul will not leave it completely, but there will occur what our holy teachers have received through tradition. There is found among the bones in the grave a life-giving element termed "osseous vapor," which sustains the dead for purposes of resurrection, so that those who are resurrected are not new creations but the very ones who have died, as it is written, "And He will sate your spirit with purity and will invigorate your bones" (*Yeshayahu* 58:11).

The end of all of man's ascension is that which had been anticipated at the outset. For, considering the soul's noble extraction, it follows that in its nature there must be that which provides for the attainment of the greatest possible perfection in the end. It is just that it is charged from above: "Go and diminish yourself!" until it returns to its original status by elevating itself through its deeds.

But it is not to be understood that it is of minor stature in its creation and attains greatness subsequently, for there is nothing new under the sun. The opposite is the case. It is noble in the

Appendix 1 • The Relationship of Body and Soul

greatness of its origin and subsequently diminished, pending a return to its pristine strength. In any event, the end of the process is what is first contemplated. Accordingly, it is the perfection of man which is projected first, after which ensues his diminution, to be followed by an ascent of the stages by which he descended, to return to the perfection established for him in the beginning.

The perfection of man, then, is what is first envisioned. This is the state and time in which the soul alone holds sway, the body exercising no form of dominance whatsoever, as if it did not exist. For it will be entirely subservient and subject to the reign of the soul in its purity, so that it will not even go by name, but will simply possess existence without dominance. And this goes without saying, for the dominance of the body is but darkness and blackness to the soul, corporeality being nothing other than concealment of countenance, even a modicum of which exercises a deterring influence.

For it is impossible for even the slightest bodily dominance not to result in a corresponding diminution of light and power in the soul. Therefore, the time when the soul will reign in all its strength, when it will lack nothing of its bounty of perfection — that is the time when the body will exercise no dominance whatsoever. It is not to be thought, however, that the body at that time will have no existence (for we have already explained that both body and soul must receive reward); but it will have no dominance, being entirely bound up with the soul and inseparable from it. It will do nothing of its own accord and will desire nothing that the soul does not desire, so that it will be almost indistinguishable as an entity in itself, but will be assimilated among the pure powers of the soul.

At the other end of the spectrum is the situation in this world where the body exercises dominance in all of its aspects. This stage is divided into two parts, but is still one stage. This is because the aspects of the body, even as body, can manifest themselves in two ways: in a mundane manner, the manner of beasts, or in the manner of holiness and Divine service: "In all your ways, know Him" (*Mishlei* 3:6), all of one's acts proceeding from correct intent, as will be the case in the time to come, of which it is stated, "And I will give you a heart of flesh" (*Yechezkiel* 36:26) – as would have been the case with Adam had he not sinned. But, in any event, they are both aspects of corporeality, for eating is necessary, drinking is necessary; they cannot be dispensed with. Whether it be mundane eating and drinking or holy eating and drinking – both are aspects of corporeality.

In the world as it is now, we see the body in a state of complete dominance, as a man who is lord of his home, this being its place and no other. In the seven-thousandth year, however, the righteous rise from the earth and the body remains outside its natural sphere, as a man wandering from home, or as a guest lodging for the night. For this reason it will manifest no dominance, but will correspond in status to that of Moses our teacher, of blessed memory, in his ascent of Mount Sinai. Once he rose above the earth, he no longer followed the ways of the earth dwellers.

It is in this respect that our sages referred to the seven-thousandth year as "A day which is all Sabbath, eternal rest" (*Sanhedrin* 97a), the body resting from all corporeal functions, which are represented by the days of the week. At this stage, however, the body has not yet abrogated its nature, for the creation has not yet been renewed. But from this renewal onward, a period referred to as "tomorrow to receive their reward" (*Eruvin* 22a), there is no further need for the dominance of the body (such dominance being necessary only for the performance of Divine service in its time), but its essence will be subsumed in that of the soul, so that it will rejoice eternally in the Heavenly good.

Appendix 1 • The Relationship of Body and Soul

From the words of the Ramchal it should be clear that the partnership of body and soul is deep and enduring. The body derives its life from the soul. Anything we do to come more fully into our bodies is for the purpose of allowing the soul greater access to do its holy work of refinement. The more we are able to experience ourselves as embodied, the more we can appreciate that it is the soul that enlivens us and to which we owe our allegiance.

APPENDIX 2

A Torah Perspective on Body and Breath

The Wisdom and Wonder of the Body

The body is Hashem's most magnificent creation in the physical world, truly wondrous in its workings. The *Zohar* tells us that Hashem created man with wisdom. The great kabbalist Rabbi Moshe Cordovero, *zt"l*, explains that this refers to the human body, which Hashem created with unfathomable wisdom.

Yet, remarkably, most of us take the body for granted, often ignoring it and sometimes abusing it. Even if we treat it well, we are often oblivious to its messages and ignorant of its workings. By paying attention and becoming aware of how perfectly our bodies support the work of our souls in this world, we can draw closer to Hashem and more fully realize the purpose for which we were created.

Moreover, the body is not merely an ingenious creation able to perform in incredible ways. It is actually a physical replica of a person's holy soul, which is identical to the Torah itself. Physical and spiritual realms are always intertwined with one another. Every aspect of physicality has a corresponding level of spirituality. The human body, though formed from the four material elements (earth, air, fire, and water) reflects the soul and the Torah. Its 248 limbs correspond to the 248 positive mitzvot, and its 365 connecting sinews and vessels (ligaments, arteries, veins, etc.) correspond to the 365 negative mitzvot — all of which parallel the spiritual limbs of the person's soul. (See *Sha'arei Kedushah* 1:1.)

The *Zohar* (III 29b) says that a person is Torah. When the Torah says that Hashem wanted to create man in His image (*tzelem*) and likeness (*d'mut*), *tzelem* is a reference to the written Torah and *d'mut* is a reference to the Oral Law (ibid. 35b).

Since the human body is designed to correspond to the Torah, it reflects the inner structure of the worlds, the ten *sefirot*. Each part of the body corresponds to a different *sefirah*. For example, the right and left arms represent *chesed* and *gevurah*, the trunk of the body represents *tiferet*, the right and left legs represent *netzach* and *hod*. Every movement a person makes causes ripples in the spiritual worlds above. Many sources also describe the human body as corresponding to the *Beit HaMikdash*. For example, the Vilna Gaon writes that the head represents the holy of holies; the upper torso, the *heichal*; the lower torso, the *azarah*; the lower extremities, the *Har HaBayit* (*Yahel Ohr* on *Zohar, Parashat Terumah*).

With these correspondences in mind, the process of coming into awareness of the body, understanding its workings, and learning how to use it more effectively to become who we were created to be, is elevated beyond the physical to the spiritual. Any activity that involves learning about or working with the body needs to be approached in this way. The body is a testament to G-d's greatness, to the infinite dimension of His handiwork. To know and to access this dimension of ourselves only increases our awe of Hashem. As King David said in *Tehillim*, "Every part of my physical being shall declare, 'G-d, Who is like You'" (*The Hirsch* Psalms 35:10).

Appendix 2 • A Torah Perspective on Body and Breath

Our appreciation for the great gift of our bodies is reflected in the prayer we say, often multiple times a day, after eliminating waste, *Asher Yatzar*:

> *Blessed are You, Hashem, our G-d, King of the universe, Who fashioned man with wisdom and created within him many openings and many cavities. It is obvious and known before Your Throne of Glory that if but one of them were to be ruptured or but one of them were to be blocked it would be impossible to survive and to stand before You for even one hour. Blessed are You, Hashem, Who heals all flesh and acts wondrously.*

There are *gedolim* who say that one who recites this blessing with proper *kavanah*, carefully pronouncing each word, will remain healthy and free from illness.

Within the workings of the body, it is the breath that represents the most direct connection to Hashem. It is written, "And Hashem, G-d, formed man of dust from the ground, and He blew into his nostrils the soul of life; and man became a living being" (*Bereishit* 2:7). Rashi explains that G-d created man of both lower (earthly) and upper (heavenly) matter; his body was from the dust of the earth and his soul was from the spirit.

The *Zohar* says that "one who blows, blows from within himself," indicating that man's soul is part of G-d's essence. Of course, G-d's essence is inconceivable to anyone but G-d Himself. At this level we refer to G-d as *Ein Sof* — Limitless — transcending all name, description, or concept. Rav Chaim Volozhiner describes at length how the holy four-letter ineffable Name — *Shem Havayah* (ה/ו/ה/י) — is the Name that refers to the level at which the Ein Sof connects to the conceivable creation (see *Nefesh HaChaim*, *sha'ar* 1). It is the level of connection of the Supreme Creator of all and His creation.

The connection of two such different levels — Creator and created

309

— is in itself a wondrous dimension of G-d's handiwork. Man is called an *olam katan*, a small world. Man contains within him every ingredient and every force that exists in the entire creation. The connection between the soul, which is the essence of Hashem, as it were, and the physical body, is a miniature model that correlates closely to the great and wondrous connection between *Ein Sof* and His creation. Just as that great connection trickles down to every particle of the entire creation which could not and would not exist without it, so, too, the connection of soul and body reaches every cell of the human being. The life of every cell in the body is dependent on this wondrous connection. It is that fusion of soul and body that is highlighted in the seal of the *Asher Yatzar* prayer, when we say, "Blessed are You, Hashem, Who heals all flesh and acts wondrously" (*Rema, Orach Chaim* 6:1).

Speech and Silence

As mentioned before, the connection of body and soul was accomplished when G-d blew into the nostrils of man. The Torah writes that when Hashem blew into his nostrils the soul of life, "man became a living being" (*Bereishit* 2:7). Targum Onkelos explains this means that man became a "being of speech." This is why speech requires breath; there can be no speech without using breath to create the sound. Intelligent speech is the natural by-product of breath that connects the spiritual with the physical. Since speech directly links us to Hashem, we have an enormous obligation to use it authentically and properly.

In the *berachah* of *Asher Yatzar* the word ומפליא (*u'mafli*), "wondrous," comes from the root word פלא (*pele*), "wonder." Rabbi Akiva, in *Otiyot D'Rabbi Akiva*, explains that the first letter of the alphabet, אלף, stands for אפתח לשון פה ("I will open the mouth to speech") and in reverse it stands for פה לשון אפתח ("The mouth of speech I will open"), the first letters of which spell the word פלא,

Appendix 2 • A Torah Perspective on Body and Breath

wonder, which is the word used in *Asher Yatzar*. Rabbi Akiva ascribed the word פלא to "the mouth of speech being opened." The wonder of speech derives from the wondrous connection between the spiritual and the physical inherent in breath.

This connection between spiritual and physical was created with the *middah* (character trait) of *chochmah*, wisdom. This is why *Asher Yatzar* begins: "*Asher yatzar es ha'adam be'chochmah* — Who created man with wisdom..." It is written, "And wisdom gives life to its owner..." (*Kohelet* 7:12).

Rabbi Shimon ben Gamliel said, "My entire life I have grown up among the *chachamim*, the wise men, and I have found nothing better for the body than silence" (*Avot* 1:17). The wisdom with which G-d created man, connecting man's physical body to a living soul, is the great *chochmah* that continually brings life to its owner. It is a function of the breath that Hashem blew into man. Rabbi Shimon ben Gamliel had grown up among the holders of life-giving wisdom, but found nothing better for the body than the silent primary connection of spirit and body, which we recognize as breath.

It is written, "They [words of Torah] are life for those who utter them" (*Mishlei* 4). The Gemara (*Eruvin* 54a) says that they are life for those who utter them with their mouths, rather than learn them silently. Yet silence is the best thing for the body. Chazal said: "A word is worth one *selah* [coin] and silence is worth two." They also said, "*Seyag l'chochmah shetikah* — The fence (protection) for wisdom is silence." Speaking words of Torah is the essence of life itself, and is most valuable. Otherwise, silence is more valuable than speech.

With regard to prayer, speech is a requirement. In order to fulfill the mitzvah of praying one must utter the words of the davening. However, there is an even higher level of connecting to Hashem without the use of speech as we know it. At the splitting of the Sea of Reeds, Hashem said to Moshe, "Why are you crying out to me? Tell the Children of Israel, and they should travel... and you should be silent." This led to

The Breath and Body of Inner Torah

their saying *shirah* — a level essentially beyond human speech where the *Shechinah* spoke, as it were, through their throats.

We normally see such a high level of prophesy only in Moshe Rabbeinu. Prophesy reflects great balance and connection of one's body and soul. The root of the word *nevuah*, prophesy, is *niv*, speech. Chazal compared the level of a *chacham* (a wise one) and a *navi* (a prophet) and concluded that since *chochmah* is the level that provides life to its owner, and life is the very connection between one's spiritual soul and physical body, *chacham adif m'navi* — the level of a wise one is greater than that of a prophet (*Horios* 13a). Wisdom employs silence, which is superior and more beneficial to the body than any other trait, including speech.

Chazal said that with the closing of the era of prophesy, the era of Torah erudition opened up with increased intensity. The post-prophetic era is referred to by Chazal as the era of *shetikah*, silence, when G-d does not speak to the people through prophets. Chazal said that the "delicacies" that the Jewish people bring to Hashem during the era of silence are greater than those in the era of prophesy.

Hashem's "silence" alludes to *hester panim*, the concealment of His countenance, as it were. It is therefore a time when we have difficulty appreciating His constant *hashgachah*, His constant involvement in the world and in our lives. Paradoxically, it is the time of our greatest connection to Him, similar to the primal connection of spirit and body brought about by breath. It is the time of *chacham adif m'navi*, where silence prevails over speech.

The turning point from the era of prophecy (speech) to the era of *chochmah* (silence) occurred at the time of the destruction of the first *Beit HaMikdash*. At that time, Hashem showed His people that He was still very close to them, even though His silence would make it difficult for them to realize it. The way He showed them was through the *keruvim*, which, along with the holy ark, were taken out of the *kodesh hakodashim*, the holy of holies, and were seen by the people

Appendix 2 • A Torah Perspective on Body and Breath

to be embracing. The embrace of the *keruvim* was always a sign of Hashem's closeness to His people.

The Spiritual Process of Breathing

When G-d created the human body, He placed the breathing apparatus, which constantly maintains the connection between body and soul, in the chest. Although it is the lungs that inflate with air, the act of breathing is mostly carried out by the diaphragm, which is often called the spiritual muscle.

The diaphragm is a large dome-shaped muscle that spreads across the body underneath the heart and the lungs. The process of inhaling and exhaling involves shifting of the diaphragm's position. On inhale, the dome of the diaphragm flattens and the low pressure inside the lungs causes air from the outside to be drawn in, inflating the lungs. On exhale, the dome of the diaphragm rises, pushing the air out of the lungs.

Chazal refer to the diaphragm as the *parsa*, the wall that separates between the upper, more spiritual part of the body, and the lower, more physical part of the body. Since breath is the vehicle through which the wondrous connection between the spiritual soul and the physical body is sustained, it makes sense that the diaphragm, the primary breathing muscle, is located between these two parts of the body.

Upon inhaling, the diaphragm constricts the lower section of the body and increases the volume of the lungs in the upper, more spiritual section. When exhaling, the diaphragm rises, increasing the space of the body's lower, more physical section and decreasing the volume of its upper, more spiritual section. In that sense, inhaling represents a process of increased spiritual dominance – taking in from the outside – and exhaling represents a process of increased physical dominance or presence – coming deeper into the physical body.

In both instances, it is the spiritual realm that sustains the life of the physical realm. When the upper part of the body expands and constricts the lower part on inhale, it allows oxygen to enter the system and be transported by the blood to every cell in the body, providing it with life. When exhaling, the lower, more physical realm expands and the upper, more spiritual realm contracts. During this stage, the body is rooting itself, expelling waste, and preparing to receive the next inhale, the next infusion of new spiritual life and light into the more physical realm. It is through the exhale that the body makes itself into a *kli*, a vessel, for Hashem's light.

The body without connection to the soul is like a clod of earth. Its incredibly great potential is realized only when it is inhabited by the soul. When connected, body and soul compete for dominance. Our job is to see to it that the soul prevails and makes the body holy as well.

In order to live, our bodies need nourishment from food and air. Food is primarily a physical form of nourishment; it directly addresses needs of the body that are a result of its physicality. Given its secondary importance to the spiritual realm, food is not necessary on a constant basis. A person can live for days without food. Eating can also diminish one's spiritual awareness, allowing the body to dominate the soul, unless one focuses intently on the spiritual nourishment that is hidden deep within the food.

Air, on the other hand, is a more spiritual form of nourishment, and given its primary importance, is necessary on a constant basis. One cannot live more than several minutes without oxygen. When inhaling, we take in life-giving oxygenated air and bring it into every cell of our physical body. When exhaling, we assimilate this non-physical intake into our bodies, thereby raising the body's spiritual level. This is the significance of the expansion of our body's lower, more physical section into its upper, more spiritual section, upon exhaling. This motion creates the dome of the *parsa*, whose apex reaches the bottom of the heart.

Appendix 2 • A Torah Perspective on Body and Breath

The process of contraction and expansion is the way in which G-d created the world, including the Heavenly hosts and angels. It is written, והחיות רצוא ושוב, "and the *chayot* run toward and return" (*Yechezkiel* 1:14). The *chayot* and all other Heavenly beings are in a constant process of drawing near to and distancing themselves from G-d. Their spiritual level pulsates, as does the life blood in our bodies, and the breath in the process of inhaling and exhaling.

When inhaling, we draw near to Hashem by increasing our spiritual intake. When exhaling, we digest that spiritual intake and prepare the body for a further drawing near with the next inhale. Both inhaling and exhaling, drawing near and distancing, are essential to our spiritual development. Both are ways in which we express the glory of the Creator.

This is essentially what King David wrote as the closing verse of *Tehillim*: כל הנשמה תהלל י-ה הללוי-ה, "Let all souls [every breath] praise G-d, *Hallelukah*." Chazal expound that the *neshamah* alludes to the word *neshimah*, breath. Each breath should be praise to G-d. The name י-ה represents the holy pure intellect of G-d, as it were. Each breath should be a victory of the spiritual soul over the physical dust that is man.

It is written, כי בי-ה ה' צור עולמים, "For the Lord our G-d is an eternal Rock" (*Yeshayahu* 26:4). The first of the two holy names in this verse is י-ה. Chazal taught that the word עולמים, "eternal," also means "worlds." They explain that Hashem created *olam haba* (the next world) with the letter *yud*, and *olam hazeh* (this world) with the letter *heh*. These two letters together make up the holy name י-ה. This name, representing both *olam haba* and *olam hazeh* and their connection, likewise represents the connection between physical and spiritual, body and soul, that is reflected in the breath. This explains why it is the name that King David used in *Tehillim* when he wrote, "Let all souls praise G-d (י-ה)." It also helps us better understand why Chazal interpret the verse as a reference to breath.

Whispered Prayer

The *Amidah*, the standing prayer, is called *Shemoneh Esrei*. Another name for it is *tefillah b'lachash*, prayer in a whisper. We are required to whisper the *Shemoneh Esrei* rather than daven it aloud. The Gemara (*Ta'anit*) connects the answering of one's prayers with his ability to pray in a whisper. Nobody else should hear, and one should barely and almost imperceptibly hear himself. The Gemara debates if thinking the words of prayer is sufficient. The halachah is that thinking is not sufficient, and we are obliged to articulate the words, davening in an almost inaudible whisper. This slight whisper places the prayer almost at the level of breathing, the level of silence, a level that can be even more eloquent than speech.

It is at this level, referred to as *kol demamah dakah*, a still small voice – a whisper – that the Heavenly angels perceive Hashem's glory. (See the prayer of *Unetaneh Tokef* on Rosh Hashanah and Yom Kippur.) The word *kol* means "sound" or "voice," and the word *demamah* means "stillness" or "silence." *Kol demamah* is a form of speech that can be described as the sound or voice of silence. It is a combination of silence and speech that addresses G-d's presence and His concealment.

When we daven, we express our knowledge and firm belief that Hashem is the only true existence, and everything else is nothing more than an expression of His will. The Gemara refers to prayer as *devarim ha'omdim be'rumo shel olam*, "words that stand at the height of the world." The word *olam*, "world," also means "concealment." The world is a form of concealment of Hashem's Oneness, and words of *tefillah* stand at its height, which is the connecting point of the Creator and the creation – the epitome of the wondrous connection of the spiritual and the physical. That level is called פלא, "wonder," and is known as כתר, "the Crown."

Before reciting *Shemoneh Esrei*, in the morning and evening we precede it with the Shema, whereby we accept upon ourselves the yoke

Appendix 2 • A Torah Perspective on Body and Breath

of G-d's Heavenly Kingship. In the first verse of Shema we proclaim that Hashem is One. This proclamation says that whatever exists in any and every direction throughout the entire universe is nothing but His will, and nothing else exists. This was also the central message of *ma'amad Har Sinai*, the giving of the Torah on Mount Sinai, as it is written: "You have been shown to know that Hashem, He is the G-d. There is none beside Him" (*Devarim* 4:35).

In Shema, when saying the word *echad*, one must have in mind to proclaim that Hashem is the only force and existence in all four corners of the world and everything above and below. One must emphasize the last letter of that word *echad*, the letter *dalet*, and lengthen its utterance, being careful that it should not sound like there is a vowel under it, such as "*echaduh.*" This is difficult to do. So if one is unable to do it properly, it is better not to lengthen the sound of the letter *dalet* than to say it with a vowel under it, which has substantial halachic implications.

The technique for proper lengthening consists of letting your tongue remain against the palate while continuing to allow air to flow toward your mouth from your windpipe, activating your vocal cords. You should not actually allow the air to enter your mouth, but rather allow room for it in the back of the throat by a slight forward movement of the lower jaw, while the tongue remains tight on the palate and the sound is still continuing. This cannot be done for very long, but it is the proper way to lengthen the *dalet*.

The sound of this lengthening will be only slightly perceptible in comparison to regular speech. In uttering the *dalet*, our breath overrides our speech. This is the moment of proclamation that nothing exists but Hashem, all that we see and perceive is our perception of His will, and nothing is truly real on its own. In this, both our connection represented by speech, and our seeming disconnection which is actually our deeper connection, represented by silence, act in harmony together to extol the Oneness of Hashem. It is His Oneness that makes it possible.

The Breath and Body of Inner Torah

The connection of the spiritual and physical realms is also reflected in the posture of *tefillah*. The standing position of *Shemoneh Esrei* represents the strength and sovereignty of the body — the physical realm. We learn to stand in *tefillah* from the *tefillah* of Avraham Avinu, as it is written, ". . . in the place where he had stood before Hashem" (*Bereishit* 19:27). Avraham was in control of his physical body, as Chazal say that when Hashem changed his name to אברהם, he ruled over all 248 limbs of his body. This is implied by the *gematria* of the name אברהם, which is also 248.

Avraham submitted his entire physical being and existence to the will of G-d. This submission was expressed in his standing in *tefillah*. The first *berachah* of *Shemoneh Esrei* is the *berachah* of *Magen Avraham*, the Shield of Avraham. We are required to bow both at the beginning and end of this *berachah*, which represents the essence of our prayer. Just as Avraham submitted his whole physical body to Hashem, so too we bow to Hashem and submit our physical beings to Him. In that way, our *tefillah* acknowledges the importance of man in his physical form and his total submission to the will of Hashem.

Since every breath we take is a form of connecting with Hashem, Who blew the breath of life into man, it's important for us to develop our breathing capacity. Rabbi Akiva said that Torah is to *klal Yisrael* what air is to human life. Just as a person cannot exist even for a short time without air, so too *klal Yisrael* cannot exist without Torah. Torah is the life of *klal Yisrael*. And just as Torah heals every part of the body, breathing can also bring us to greater healing and wholeness.

The more we can appreciate the wonder of the body, the wonder of the connection between body and soul inherent in breath, and the wonder of our ability to influence the workings of the body with our awareness, the more we can grow in our awe and love of Hashem. And that, in the end, is the true purpose of our existence.

APPENDIX 3

A Look at Color

The colors and the order of the colors in the rainbow are related to the days of Creation.

Violet and indigo, the innermost colors, are connected to the first day of Creation, when Hashem created light. The Torah tells us that G-d said, " 'Let there be light' and there was light. G-d saw the light was good, and G-d separated between the light and the darkness" (*Bereishit* 1:3–4). Rashi cites the Gemara which says that on the first day, the light that Hashem created was mixed together with darkness, and then Hashem separated the light from the darkness.

Violet is at the end of light's visible spectrum. It represents the *Kisei HaKavod*, G-d's Throne of Glory. Beyond it is ultraviolet. The innermost color of the rainbow representing G-d's Throne of Glory is as far as we can see — we cannot visualize beyond it. The next color outward is indigo, a dark color, which symbolizes light and darkness together. Indigo is almost indiscernible to the average human eye — a feature that makes it most appropriate for a color connected to the first day of Creation. As Chazal said, that was the day G-d created light that was mixed with darkness. Rashi also quotes Chazal as saying that Hashem created a special kind of light on the first day that He hid for the righteous to use in the next world.

The light of the first day included qualities that caused it to be hidden and difficult to see. Both violet and indigo are included as the lights of the first day of Creation. Violet, representing the Throne of Glory, is connected more closely to the Creator, and indigo represents the process of creating light that is at the level of human perception. This visible spectrum of light is but a short segment of the full spectrum of light G-d created.

The color violet affects the skeletal and nervous systems of the body. It balances and purifies physical and spiritual energies. It stimulates inspiration. And it helps the body assimilate nutrients and minerals. The color indigo is known to integrate, purify, strengthen the immune and lymph systems, and balance the hemispheres of the brain. Like violet, it too heals on both the physical and spiritual levels.

The next color of the rainbow is blue. This represents the second day of Creation, when G-d created the firmament and called it heaven. It is what we perceive as the color of the sky. We see the sky as blue because blue is the frequency of light that is most easily scattered and dispersed when it travels through the atmosphere.

The color blue is known to quiet our energies, strengthen the respiratory system, awaken intuition and creativity, and be cooling to the body. It is a color of devotion, peace, and tranquility. The Torah commands us to have *techeilet*, a certain shade of blue, in tzitzit. Gazing at these blue threads on the corner of the tallit is supposed to remind us of all the mitzvot that we are commanded in the Torah. Chazal explain that we are reminded by association. The blue threads are reminiscent of the color of the ocean, which is reminiscent of the color of the sky, which is reminiscent of the *Kisei HaKavod*, G-d's Throne of Glory.

The fourth color of the rainbow is green. This color corresponds to the third day of Creation, when Hashem created the vegetation that grows in this world. The color green is known to balance our energies,

Appendix 3 • A Look at Color

soothe the nervous system, calm inflammations, and to be restful.

The fifth color of the rainbow is yellow. This corresponds to the fourth day of Creation when G-d created the luminaries in the firmament of the heaven. The sun, the source of our natural light, looks yellow. The color yellow is known to stimulate our mental faculties, promote digestion, stimulate the liver, and strengthen the ebb and flow of the glandular and nervous system.

The sixth color of the spectrum is orange. Orange corresponds to the fifth day of Creation, when G-d created the fowl and the fish and every living being that creeps. The blood of many of these creatures is not really red, but more like orange. The color orange is known to influence emotional health, stimulating social inclinations and joy. It also strengthens the muscular and eliminative systems and helps to revitalize the physical body.

The seventh color of the spectrum is red. The color red corresponds to the sixth day of Creation, which is the day of the creation of Man. It is written, "For the blood, it is the life" (*Devarim* 12:23). The life of a human being is in his blood; even the name אדם, "man," contains the word דם (*dam*), which means "blood." The name also implies redness. The color red is called אדום, (*adom*). (An animal's life soul is also in his blood, as it is written: "But flesh with its soul, its blood you shall not eat" [*Bereishit* 9:4].) The importance of human life is referred to as the redness of blood. The halachah is that if one is given the option of being killed or taking the life of another person, he is forbidden to save himself by taking the other man's life. The Gemara explains this by saying: "Why would you think that your blood is redder than his?"

Red is the last color on the spectrum, before the light again becomes invisible to the naked eye and is called infrared. Red is also the color that represents *din*, judgment; the sixth day of Creation, on which man was created, is Rosh Hashanah, the Day of Judgment. The color red is a stimulating and warm color. It's known to awaken

The Breath and Body of Inner Torah

physical life force, strengthen physical energy, and aid the circulatory system.

Red, at one end of the visible spectrum, is the closest to the physical realm. Esav was red because he represented the physical world. Red refracts at a more gradual angle than the other colors because the physical realm does not deflect it as much. Violet, at the other end of the visible spectrum, is the most spiritual color. It refracts at a sharper angle than the other colors because it is further from the physical realm and deflected much more.

So far we've seen that the colors of the spectrum, which are the colors of the rainbow, correspond to the six days of Creation, but we have not mentioned Shabbat. Shabbat is the day that is more connected with the World to Come, where the physical realm will no longer shatter the spiritual realm. The seventh day, Shabbat is represented by white light, which is whole and has not been refracted into many components. Shabbat is a day when we are united with everyone around us, like the white light which is the result of the unification of all the colors in the visible spectrum. White is the color of purification. It works on all systems of the body. It's strengthening, cleansing, and stabilizing.

Right before Shabbat enters, we light Shabbat candles. Shabbat candles represent the whole white light – a spiritual level, untouched by the lower physical realm. On Shabbat we are to rise above the six days of the week and live on a different plane. Chazal say that we light Shabbat candles for *shalom bayit*, for peace in the home. While the simple meaning is, as the *Rishonim* explain, in order not to bump into things in the dark, the words of Chazal always have a deeper meaning as well. *Shalom*, peace, is from the word *shalem*, wholeness and completeness. The light of the Shabbat candles represents the wholeness and completeness of the *bayit*, the house, the world in which our souls live. Shabbat is the day of whole light, untouched by earthly yearnings and distractions.

Appendix 3 • A Look at Color

With the exit of Shabbat we make *Havdalah*. We light another candle, this time one with more than one wick, and we recite a blessing: "Blessed are You, Hashem, our G-d, King of the universe, Who creates the illuminations of the fire." We use the plural form – illuminations – to distinguish the many lights of the visible spectrum from the single illumination of white light. Whereas Shabbat represents the single whole illumination of white light, when we make *Havdalah* and enter the weekdays, we bless Hashem for the refracted spectrum of light which pertains to the level of the six days of Creation.

Glossary

Aharon – Aaron, the brother of Moses and the first High Priest

Adam HaRishon – Adam, the first man

Akeidah – the binding of Isaac on the altar, one of the ten trials of his father, Abraham

Amidah – lit. "standing"; the central prayer of Judaism recited three times a day while standing

Amoraim – the collective authors of the Gemara

Am Yisrael – the Jewish people

Ari – Rabbi Yitzchak Luria, a sixteenth-century mystic from Safed, also known as the Arizal

Avodah – lit. "work"; service; prayer

Avodat Hashem – service of G-d

Avraham Avinu – the patriarch Abraham

Azarah – the part of the *Beis HaMikdash* that all Jews were permitted to enter, located before the *heichal*

Ba'al Shem Tov – lit. "Master of the Good Name"; Rabbi Yisrael ben Eliezer, an eighteenth-century mystic from Eastern Europe/Ukraine, the founder of Chassidut

Ba'al teshuvah – lit. "one who returns"; returnee to Torah observance; a Jew from a non-observant background who accepts the yoke of Torah observance

Bayit – house

Glossary

Bein adam l'chaveiro – lit. "between man and his friend"; a category of laws concerning one's relationship with his fellow human beings

Beit HaMikdash – Holy Temple in Jerusalem

Bilam – Balaam, a non-Jewish prophet described in *Bamidbar* 22-24

Binah – understanding; the third of the ten *sefirot*

Bitachon – trust, specifically trust in G-d

Bnei Yisrael – children of Israel

Berachah, berachot – blessing(s)

Chassidic, Chassidut – the movement within Judaism founded by Rabbi Yisrael Ba'al Shem Tov (1648-1760) that emphasizes inner and mystical aspects of the Torah

Chava – Eve, the first woman

Chayot – a category of angels

Chazal – acronym for *Chachamim zichronam livrachah*, i.e., our Sages, of blessed memory, referring to the Talmudic Sages

Chein – grace; charm

Chesed – the attribute of loving-kindness; the fourth of the ten *sefirot*; an act of kindness or giving

Davening --- praying

Eitz hada'at – lit. "the tree of knowledge"; the tree of knowledge of good and evil in the Garden of Eden, the fruits of which Adam and Eve were forbidden to eat

Emet – truth

Emunah – faith

Gadlut – maturity, greatness; used in *Kabbalah* to refer to a high level of spiritual development

Gashmiut – physicality; materialism

Glossary

Gemara – the vast work of the Amoraic Sages (third through sixth century) that explains the Mishnah; the Gemara serves as the foundation of Jewish laws and customs

Gevurah – strength; the fifth of the ten *sefirot*

Gilgul, gilgulim – transmigration of souls; reincarnation

Halachah – Jewish law

Hashem – G-d

Hamotzi – lit. "the One Who brings forth"; the blessing said before eating bread

Havdalah – blessings said at the conclusion of Shabbat and festivals

HaKadosh Baruch Hu – The Holy One, Blessed Is He; G-d

Har HaBayit – the Temple Mount of the *Beit HaMikdash*

Heichal – the holy chamber in the *Beit HaMikdash* before the holy of holies

Hitbodedut – lit. "self-seclusion"; a form of prayer and meditation with the goal of forging a close, personal relationship with G-d

Hod – splendor; the eighth of the ten *sefirot*

Holy of holies – holiest innermost chamber of the *Beit HaMikdash* in which the holy ark was located

Ikveta d'Meshicha – lit. "the footsteps of Messiah"; the period of time preceding the coming of Mashiach

Kabbalah, Kabbalistic – lit. "tradition"; Jewish mysticism

Katnut – smallness; a term used in Kabbalah to refer to a less developed spiritual level

Kedushah – holiness

Keruvim – cherubs; winged, golden angels on top of the holy ark

Kriyat Shema – the recitation of Shema

Klal – community

Glossary

Kohen, kohanim — member(s) of the priestly cast, who officiated in the Holy Temple when it stood

Lashon Hakodesh — lit. "holy tongue"; Hebrew

Lashon hara — evil speech; slander

Lesheim Yichud — a specific, short Kabbalistic prayer recited by some before doing a mitzvah

Ma'aseh — an act or action

Mashiach — Messiah

Matan Torah — the giving of the Torah on Mount Sinai

Matzliach — successful

Mezuzah — a piece of parchment, inscribed with the verses of the Shema, affixed to the doorposts of Jewish homes

Middah, middot — character trait(s)

Midrash — the homiletic teaching of the Sages

Mishnah — halachic and other teachings of the Tannaim (early Sages) compiled by R' Yehuda HaNasi.

Mitzvah, mitzvot — commandments(s); also used to refer generally to a good deed

Modim — the blessing of gratitude to G-d said in the *Amidah* prayer

Moshe, Moshe Rabbeinu — Moses our teacher

Mussar — Torah ethics

Neshimah — breath

Neshamah, neshamot — soul(s)

Netzach — eternity; victory; the seventh of the ten *sefirot*

Niggun — Chassidic song or melody

Nishmat Kol Chai — prayer praising G-d, said Shabbat and festival mornings

Glossary

Noach – Noah

Olam haba – the world to come

Olam hazeh – this world

Panim – faces; facets

Parashah – Torah portion

Pasuk – biblical verse

Pesukei d'zimrah – lit. "verses of praise"; a collection of blessings, psalms, and verses that are recited daily during morning prayers

Penimiut – inside; inwardness

Rabbi Moshe Chayim Luzzatto (the Ramchal) --- eighteenth-century kabbalist and Torah scholar who authored many important works, including *The Path of the Just*, *The Way of G-d*, and *The Knowing Heart*

Rabbi Moshe Cordovero – also known as the Ramak, a sixteenth-century mystical scholar from Safed and elder contemporary of the Arizal

Rabbi Schneur Zalman of Liadi (the Baal HaTanya) --- eighteenth-century Chassidic master, founder of Chabad Chassidut

Rashi --- acronym for Rabbi Shlomo Yitzchaki, an eleventh-century sage and Torah scholar, author of the most learned commentaries on Chumash and Gemara

Ratzon – will

Rav Chaim Volozhiner --- foremost disciple of the great Torah luminary the Vilna Gaon; author of *Nefesh HaChaim* and other works; founder of the yeshivah movement

Rebbe Nachman --- an eighteenth-century Chassidic master, founder of Breslov Chassidism; great-grandson of the Baal Shem Tov

Rishonim – lit. "early ones"; the Sages of the eleventh to fifteenth centuries

Glossary

Rosh Hashanah — Jewish New Year

Ruach hakodesh — divine inspiration

Ruach ra — spiritual impurity

Ruchniut — spirituality

Satan — term of reference for evil, the evil inclination, and the angel of death

Sefer Torah — Torah scroll

Sefer Yetzirah — a book of Jewish mysticism attributed to the patriarch Abraham

Sefirah, sefirot — divine "vessels" or "emanations," the ten attributes through which G-d manifests

Shabbat — the Sabbath

Shalom — peace

Shalom bayit — marital harmony

Shechinah — Divine presence

Sheker — falsehood

Shema — the fundamental declaration that G-d is One

Shemoneh Esrei — the *Amidah*

Shofar — ram's horn blown for religious purposes

Simchah — joy; happiness

Tallit — prayer shawl

Talmid chacham — Torah scholar

Talmud — Hebrew word for Gemara

Tanya — Chassidic work written by Rabbi Shneur Zalman of Liadi, the founder of Chabad

Targum Yonatan — Aramaic interpretive translation of the Bible

Techeilet — blue; the blue threads in tzitzit

Glossary

Techiyat hameitim — resurrection of the dead

Tefillah — prayer

Tefillin — phylacteries; black leather boxes containing parchment inscribed with biblical verses, worn by Jewish men especially during prayer

Tehillim — Psalms

Teshuvah — lit. "return"; return to the service of G-d; repentence

Tiferet — beauty, the sixth of the ten *sefirot*

Tzaddik — righteous man

Tzitzit — fringes worn on four-cornered garments by Jewish males, as reminders of the commandments

Yaakov Avinu — the patriarch Jacob

Yesod — foundation; the ninth of the ten *sefirot*

Yitzchak Avinu — the patriarch Isaac

Zohar — a mystical commentary on the Torah and one of the earliest and most authoritative Kabbalistic texts; the complete body of Zoharic works includes the *Zohar* itself, *Tikunei Zohar,* and the *Zohar Chadash*

MIRIAM MILLHAUSER CASTLE is a healer, teacher, conflict resolution specialist, and lawyer. She developed the Inner Torah process and is the author of *Inner Torah: Where Consciousness and Kedushah Meet*, *Practical Inner Torah: A Guide to Going Within*, and *Walking Mom Home: Sharing the Blessings of This Life's Final Journey*.

Working in person and on the telephone, she helps women around the world come into more authentic relationship with themselves and G-d through the Inner Torah process. The fruits of her experiences and client work are shared through soulful books that guide and inspire. She also teaches classes, conducts workshops, and provides training in Inner Torah.

The author lives in Jerusalem with her husband, Rabbi Dovid Castle. Her website address is www.innertorah.com; her email address is info@innertorah.com.

RABBI DOVID CASTLE received his rabbinical ordination from Telshe Yeshiva and was a student of Rav Yitzchok Hutner in Kollel Gur Aryeh, both in the United States and Israel. He has served as *rom* and *menahel ruchani* in Yeshiva Gedolah Itri, *rosh yeshivah* of Beis Midrash LeTorah, and head of various other Torah institutions. He has also founded and directed other educational institutions in Israel, including the seminary Bnos Yaakov Yerushalayim (BYY). Rabbi Castle's published works include *To Live Among Friends: Laws and Ethics of Everyday Interactions* (two vols.), *Living With the Sages*, and *Darkei Dovid* (two vols.). His email address is dcastle@netvision.net.il.